COMMERCIAL VEHICLE LAW

A GUIDE FOR ADVOCATES
AND OPERATORS

AUSTRALIA
LBC Information Services
Sydney

CANADA and USA
Carswell
Toronto

NEW ZEALAND
Brooker's
Auckland

SINGAPORE and MALAYSIA
Thomson Information (S.E. Asia)
Singapore

COMMERCIAL VEHICLE LAW

A GUIDE FOR ADVOCATES
AND OPERATORS

**JONATHAN LAWTON
AND
MIKE JEWELL**

FIRST EDITION

**LONDON
SWEET & MAXWELL
1998**

First Edition 1998

Published in 1998 by
Sweet & Maxwell Limited of
100 Avenue Road, Swiss Cottage, London NW3 3PF
(http://www.smlawpub.co.uk)
Typeset by Dataword Services Limited of Chilcompton
Printed and bound in Great Britain by
MPG Books, Bodmin, Cornwall

A C.I.P. catalogue
record for this book
is available from
the British Library

ISBN 0–421–583908

ACKNOWLEDGEMENTS

The authors would like to thank leading transport consultant Colin Ward, of Ward International, for his invaluable assistance over engineering technicalities and the well known and respected Scottish lawyer David Ritchie for his equally invaluable assistance with the differences between Scottish law and its English and Welsh counterpart.

CONTENTS

	Page
Acknowledgements	v
Table of Cases	xi
Table of Statutes	xiii
Table of European Legislation	xiv
Table of International Codes and Agreements	xv
Table of Statutory Instruments	xvii
Table of Abbreviations	xxiii

| 1. INTRODUCTION | 1–01 |

2. BRAKES	2–01
Prosecution	2–05
Prosecution Evidence	2–10
Vehicle Inspector	2–10
Police	2–13
Leaks on the system	2–14
Adjustment	2–16
Defence	2–17
Leaks	2–21
Mitigation	2–30
Consultant Engineer's Comments	2–39

3. DANGEROUS/INSECURE LOADS	3–01
Prosecution	3–08
Construction and Use Regulations, reg. 100	3–09
Prosecution Evidence	3–12
Defence	3–16
Mitigation	3–27
Road Traffic Act, s.40(A)	3–30
Prosecution Evidence	3–31
Defence	3–32
Mitigation	3–35
Consultant Engineer's Comments	3–36

4. ABNORMAL LOADS	4–01
Prosecution	4–06
Prosecution Evidence	4–10
Vehicle Inspector/Trading Standards Officer	4–10
Police Evidence	4–11

CONTENTS

Defence   4–13
    Weight   4–13
    Axle Weights   4–15
    Dimensions   4–16
    Notice of Movement   4–17
    Assistants   4–18
Mitigation   4–19

5. PERISHABLE FOODS   5–01
   Prosecution   5–08
   Prosecution Evidence   5–11
   Defences   5–14
   Mitigation   5–21

6. OVERLOADING   6–01
   Prosecution   6–08
   Prosecution Evidence   6–11
   Defences   6–20
   Mitigation   6–33
   Consultant Engineer's Comments   6–40

7. DANGEROUS SUBSTANCES   7–01
   Prosecution   7–09
   Prosecution Evidence   7–11
       Prosecution Witnesses   7–12
   Defences   7–14
   Mitigation   7–19
   Consultant Engineer's Comments   7–24

8. DANGEROUS VEHICLES   8–01
   Prosecution   8–02
   Prosecution Evidence   8–03
   Defences   8–04
   Mitigation   8–09
   Consultant Engineer's Comments   8–12

9. LENGTH AND WIDTH   9–01
   Prosecution   9–03
   Prosecution Evidence   9–08
   Defences   9–11
   Mitigation   9–19

10. WHEELS   10–01
    Prosecution   10–04
    Prosecution Evidence   10–05
        Vehicle Inspector   10–05
        Police   10–06

CONTENTS

Defences		10–09
Mitigation		10–10
Consultant Engineer's Comments		10–18

11. Tyres — 11–01
Prosecution — 11–11
Prosecution Evidence — 11–13
    Vehicle Inspectors — 11–13
    Police Evidence — 11–15
Defences — 11–17
Mitigation — 11–26
Consultant Engineer's Comments — 11–29

12. GOODS AND PASSENGERS CARRYING VEHICLE OPERATORS LICENSING SYSTEM — 12–01
Public Inquiries before Traffic Commissioners and Licensing Authorities — 12–01
Disciplinary cases — 12–10
Cases involving the Environmental Provisions — 12–15
The Transport Tribunal — 12–26
Offences — 12–30
Mitigation — 12–31

13. DRIVERS' HOURS AND TACHOGRAPHS — 13–01
Definitions — 13–08
Exemptions — 13–09
Explanation of Terms — 13–10
    Daily Driving Limit — 13–10
    Continuous Driving — 13–11
    Fortnightly Driving Limit — 13–13
    Daily Rest Period — 13–14
    Weekly Rest Period — 13–18
    Journeys by Ferry Boat or Train — 13–20
Emergency Provisions — 13–22
Prosecution — 13–25
    Summary offences involving the use of tachographs — 13–25
    Offences committed by drivers — 13–26
    Offences committed by employers — 13–27
    Either way offences — 13–30
Prosecution Evidence — 13–37
Defences — 13–38
Mitigation — 13–46
Drivers' Hours — Domestic Rules — 13–49
    Defences — 13–69
    Mitigation — 13–70

CONTENTS

14. VEHICLE EXCISE DUTY   14–01
    Prosecution   14–02
    Prosecution Evidence   14–04
        General   14–04
        Vehicle Excise and Registration Act 1994, s.29 14–06
        Vehicle Excise and Registration Act 1994, s.37 14–10
        Vehicle Excise and Registration Act 1994, s.44 14–11
    Defence   14–12
        Vehicle Excise and Registration Act 1994, s.29 14–12
        Vehicle Excise and Registration Act 1994, s.37 14–18
            Recovery vehicles   14–27
            Vehicles used for exceptional loads   14–30
            Locomotives   14–32
            Showmens' vehicles   14–35
            Works trucks   14–36
    Mitigation   14–50

15. MITIGATION   15–01

16. THE POSITION IN SCOTLAND   16–01

APPENDIX 1: "PG9", Testers Manual, Categorisation of Defects A1–01
APPENDIX 2: Jurisdiction   A2–01
APPENDIX 3: Code of Practice: Safety of Loads on Vehicles   A3–01
APPENDIX 4: Code of Practice for Dynamic Axle Weighers   A4–01
APPENDIX 5: Code of Practice for the Weighing of Goods
            Vehicles on Conventional Weighbridges, etc. A5–01
APPENDIX 6: Diagrams   A6–01
APPENDIX 7: Glossary   A7–01

Index   221

TABLE OF CASES

All references in the right-hand column are to paragraph numbers

Alan Geoffrey Bird Case C–235/94 13–23
Alston v. O'Brien [1992] S.C.C.R. 238; [1992] S.L.T. 856......... 15–05

Baron Meats Ltd v. Lockhart [1991] S.C.C.R. 537.............. 16–03

Coggins (P. W.) v. The Licensing Authority for Goods Vehicles in
    the Metropolitan Traffic Area, *The Times*, 28 February 1985 13–43
Cornish v. Ferry Masters Ltd [1975] R.T.R. 292 3–19
Crown Prosecution Service v. Charlton (December 15, 1993) (Sixth
    Chamber) Case C–116/92; [1994] 2 C.M.L.R. 600 13–11

DPP v. Cargo Handling [1992] R.T. 318; (1992) 156 J.P. 486 13–40
DPP v. David Anderson t/a Spotmix CO/372/96........... 14–42, 14–48

Forgan v. Hamilton [1995] S.C.C.R. 733...................... 16–03

Grays Haulage Ltd v. Arnold [1966] 1 W.L.R. 534; 130 J.P. 196;
    [1966] 1 All E.R. 896 13–44

Hart v. Bex [1957] Crim.L.R. 622, DC. . 4–22; 10–17; 11–28; 15–08, 15–09
Hill & Sons (Botley & Denmead) Ltd v. Hampshire Chief Con-
    stable [1972] R.T.R. 29; (1971) 115 S.J. 675, DC........... 13–44
Hillman (Ross) Ltd v. Bond [1974] Q.B. 435; [1974] 2 W.L.R. 436;
    [1974] R.T.R. 279 13–44

James & Son Ltd v. Smee [1955] 1 Q.B. 78; [1954] 3 W.L.R. 631;
    [1954] 3 All E.R. 273 13–44

Kelly v. Shulman [1989] 1 All E.R. 106; [1989[R.T.R. 84, DC,
    1988, DC.. 13–17
Knowles Transport v. Russell [1975] R.T.R. 87; [1974] Crim.L.R.
    717... 13–43

Leathley v. Robsons Border Transport [1976] R.T.R. 503 3–26

Martin v. Boulton and Paul (Steel Construction) Ltd [1988] I.C.R.
   366.. 7–16
Michielsen and Geybels Transport Service NV (June 9, 1994)
   (Sixth Chamber) Case C–394/92; [1994] I E.C.R. 2497...... 13–08

NFC Forwarding Ltd v. DPP [1989] R.T.R. 239; [1989] Crim.L.R.
   377, DC... 2–18; 3–31
Nicholls v. Carmichael [1993] S.C.C.R. 991 16–03

Osman, Mills and Chalker, December 9, 1993 (92/6361–2–3/Z4) .. 13–36

R. v. Abergavenny Justices, ex p. Barratt [1994] R.T.R. 98; (1994)
   158 J.P. 259, DC........................ A2–05, A2–06, A2–09
R. v. Blandford [1955] 1 W.L.R. 331; 99 S.J. 223; [1995] 1 All E.R.
   681, CCA A2–06
Redhead Freight v. Shulman, *The Times*, May 12, 1988, DC...... 13–42
Rodger v. Normand [1994] S.C.C.R. 861...................... 16–05
Ross v. Hillman Ltd v. Bond. *See* Hillman (Ross) Ltd v. Bond.... 13–44

Simmons v. Fowler (1950) 48 L.G.R. 623; 115 J.P.J. 322,
   DC....................................... 2–17; 3–16, 3–31
Smith of Maddiston Ltd v. Macnab [1975] J.C. 48; [1975] S.L.T. 86   16–03

Thomson v. McPhail [1992] S.C.C.R. 466..................... 16–05
Turf Publishers Ltd v. Davies [1927] W.N. 190, DC A2–06

Valentine v. MacBrayne Haulage Ltd [1986] S.C.C.R. 692 16–04
Van Swieten B.V. (June 2, 1994) (Sixth Chamber) Case C–313/92;
   [1994] E.C.R. I–2177............................. 13–08, 13–15

Walker-Trowbridge Ltd v. DPP [1992] R.T.R. 182.......... 3–19, 3–33

TABLE OF STATUTES

All references in the right-hand column are to paragraph numbers. Paragraph numbers printed in **bold** type indicate where the statute is set out in part or in full.

1920 Money Football Betting Act (c. 52) A2–06

1925 Criminal Justice Act (c.86)—
s.3(1) A2–06

1952 Magistrates' Courts Act (c.55)
s.1(2)(b) A2–06

1968 Transport Act (c.73) 12–02, A2–06
Pt VI 13–02
s.96 13–02
(11A) **A2–06**
s.97 .... A2–06
(1)(a) A2–06
s.97A **A2–06**
(1)(a) **A2–06**
(2) **A2–06**
s.103 .... A2–06
(7) ... A2–03, **A2–06**

1972 Road Traffic Act 1972 (c.20). A5–01
European Communities Act (c.68)—
s.4 .... A2–06
Sched. 4 .... A2–06

1974 Health and Safety at Work etc. Act (c.37). A3–01
s.15(1) 7–09
s.33(c) 7–09
s.36 7–18
s.40 7–16

1976 Road Traffic (Drivers' Ages and Hours of Work) Act (c.3)—
s.2(1) A2–06
s.3 ...... **A2–03**, A2–06
(a)–(c) **A2–03**
International Carriage of Perishable Foodstuffs Act (c.58). 5–02
s.7 5–09
(1)(a), (b) **5-08**
(c) **5-08**, 5–10
ss.8–11 5–08

1980 Magistrates' Courts Act 1980 (c.43)—
s.1 ...... A2–04; **A2–06**
(1) **A2–06**
(2) **A2–06**
(a) **A2–06**
(b) .. A2–04, **A2–06**, A2–07
s.2 .... **A2–06**
(1) A2–06
s.123 .... A2–06

1981 Public Passenger Vehicles Act 1981 (c.14). 12–03
Animal Health Act (c.22). A5–01
Forgery and Counterfeiting Act (c.45)—
s.3 13–35

1988 Road Traffic Act
    (c.52) 2–05, 2–06; 6–12
    s.34 2–12
    s.39 2–12
    s.40 . . A2–05, 2–19; 3–10,
      3–30,   3–32,   3–33,
      3-35; 4–09; 8–02; 10.4;
      11–12
    (a) 8–02
    (d) 3–08, **3–30**
    s.41 . . . 4–07, 4–09; 11–11
    (2)(a) 9–03
    s.41A 2–05, 2–17
    s.41B 6–08
    (2)(a) 6–29
    s.42 . . . 2–17; 9–03; 10–04
    ss.96–99 13–01
1994 Vehicle Excise and
    Registration Act
    1994 (c.22). 14–01
    s.29 . . . . 14–06, 14–12
    (1) 14–02
    s.30 14–03
    s.37 . . . . 14–10, 14–18
    (1) 14–02
    s.38 14–03
    s.44 . . . . 14–03, 14–11
    s.46 14–08
    s.52 . . . . 14–04, 14–07
    (2) 14–04
    Sched. 1 . . . 14–01, 14–26
    Pt IV 14-24, 14–36

1994 Vehicle Excise and
    Registration Act
    1994—*cont.*
    Pt IV para. 4(6) . . . 14–36
    Pt V 14–24, 14–27
    Pt VI 14–24, 14–30
    para. 6(1)(b)
    14–23
    para. 6(3) . . 14–10,
      14–30
    Pt VII 14–24
    Pt VIII, para. 14 . . 14–24,
      14–25, 14–38
    para. 16(1)(b)
    14–10
    Sched. 2 . . . 14–41, 14–44
1995 Finance Act (c.4). . . . 14–01;
    16–07
    Sched. 4 . . . 14–01, 14–24
    Pt. III 14–09
    Pt. IV, para. 26 . . . 14–01
    Pt. IVA, para. 5(2),
    (3) 14–28
    para. 11 . . . 14–27
    para. 12 . . . 14–30
    para. 14 . . . **14-38**
    (5) 14–35
    (16) 14–38
    Goods   Vehicles
    (Licensing   of
    Operators) Act
    (c.23). 1–01; 12–03

TABLE OF EUROPEAN LEGISLATION

Reg. 3820/85 (O.J. L370). . . 13–01
    Art. 7 (1) A2–06
    Art. 8 (1) 13–08

    Art. 13 13–09
Reg. 3821/85 (O.J. L376). . . 13–01
Reg. 3314/90 (O.J. L318). . . 13–01

TABLE OF INTERNATIONAL CODES AND AGREEMENTS

Agreement on the International Carriage of Perishable Foodstuffs and on the Special Equipment to be Used for Such Carriage (ATP)................. 5–02
    Annex 1
    paras. 1–5 5–03
Code of Practice for the Carriage of Radioactive Materials by Road (1982 Impression).......... A3–01
Department of Transport Code of Practice for the Weighing of Goods Vehicles on Dynamic Axle Weighers........ A4–01
Department of Transport Code of Practice for the Weighing of Goods Vehicles to check whether they are overloaded using Conventional Weighbridges or Axle Weighing Devices Designed to weigh Stationary Vehicles........ A5–01

Department of Transport Supplement to the Code of Practice for the Weighing of Goods Vehicles on Conventional Weighbridges etc................... A5–01
Department of Transport Code of Practice – Safety of Loads on Vehicles............. A3–01
European Agreement concerning the work of crews of vehicles engaged in International Road Transport) (AETR).............. 13–06
European Agreement for the International Carriage of Dangerous Goods by Road 1968 (ADR)...... 7–02, 7–05, 7–06, A3–01
    Annex A 7–04

TABLE OF STATUTORY INSTRUMENTS

All references in the right-hand column are to paragraph numbers. Paragraph numbers printed in **bold** type indicate where the regulation is set out in part or in full.

1919 Conveyance of Live Poultry Order 1919 (S.R. & O. 1919 No. 933). . A3–01

1924 Order of Secretary of State (No. 11) making byelaws as to the conveyance of explosives on roads and in certain special cases 1924 (S.R. & O. 1924 No. 1129). A3–01

1931 Gas Cylinders (Conveyance) Regulations 1931 (S.R. & O. 1931 No. 679). A3–01

1940 Compressed Gas Cylinders (Fuel for Motor Vehicles) Conveyance Regulations 1940 (S.R. & O. 1940 No. 2009). A3–01

1947 Petroleum (Inflammable Liquids and other Dangerous Substances) Order 1947 (S.I. 1947 No. 1443) A3–01

1951 Conveyance of Explosives Byelaws 1951 (S.I. 1951 No. 869). A3–01

1957 Petroleum Spirit (Conveyance by Road) Regulations 1957 (S.I. 1957 No. 191). . A3–01

1958 Conveyance of Explosives Byelaws 1958 (S.I. 1958 No. 230). A3–01

Petroleum (Carbon Disulphide) Order 1958 (S.I. 1958 No. 257). . A3–01

Carbon Disulphide (Conveyance by Road) Regulations 1958 (S.I. 1958 No. 313). . A3–01

Petroleum Spirit (Conveyance by Road) Regulations 1958 (S.I. 1958 No. 962). . A3–01

1959 Gas Cylinders (Conveyance) Regulations 1959 (S.I. 1959 No. 1919) A3–01

1962 Carbon Disulphide (Conveyance by Road) Regulations 1962 (S.I. 1962 No. 2527) A3–01

1966 Petroleum Spirit (Conveyance by Road) (Amendment) Regulations 1966 (S.I. 1966 No. 1190) A3–01

1968 Petroleum (Carbon Disulphide) Order 1968 (S.I. 1968 No. 571... A3–01

1970 Drivers' Hours (Goods Vehicles) (Modifications) Order 1970 (S.I. 1970 No. 257)... 13–02

Poison Rules 1970 (S.I. 1970 No. 798)........... A3–01

Radioactive Substances (Road Transport Workers) (Great Britain) Regulations 1970 (S.I. 1970 No. 1827) A3–01

Petroleum (Corrosive Substances) Order 1970 (S.I. 1970 No. 1945) A3–01

1971 Corrosive Substances (Conveyance by Road) Regulations 1971 (S.I. 1971 No. 618).. A3–01

Drivers' Hours (Passenger and Goods Vehicles) (Modifications) Order 1971 (S.I. 1971 No. 818)... 13–02

Petroleum (Inflammable Liquids) Order 1971 (S.I. 1971 No. 1040) A3–01

Inflammable Liquids (Conveyance by Road) Regulations 1971 (S.I. 1971 No. 1061) A3–01

1971 Inflammable Substances (Conveyance by Road) (Labelling) Regulations 1971 (S.I. 1971 No. 1062).......... A3–01

1973 Petroleum (Organic Peroxides) Order 1973 (S.I. 1973 No. 1897)...... A3–01

Organic Peroxides (Conveyance by Road) Regulations 1973 (S.I. 1973 No. 2221) A3–01

1974 Radioactive Substances (Carriage by Road) (Great Britain) Regulations 1974 (S.I. 1974 No. 1735) A3–01

1975 Transit of Animals (Road and Rail) Order 1975 (S.I. 1975 No. 1024) A5–01

Radioactive Substances (Road Transport Workers) (Great Britain) (Amendment) Regulations 1975 (S.I. 1975 No. 1522) A3–01

International Carriage of Dangerous Goods (Rear Marking of Motor Vehicles) Regulations 1975 (S.I. 1975 No. 2111).......... 7–02

1977 Conveyance by Road of Military Explosives Regulations 1977 (S.I. 1977 No. 888).. A3–01

1978 Motor Vehicles (Construction and Use) Regulations 1978 (S.I. 1978 No. 1017)...... A3–01

s.74A A3–01

s.97 .... A3–01

(1)–(3) A3–01

s.80A A3–01

s.140 .... A3–01

Weighing of Motor Vehicles (Use of Dynamic Axle Weighing Machines) Regulations 1978 (S.I. 1978 No. 1180) A4–01

Motor Vehicle (Construction and Use) (Amendment) (No. 5) Regulation 1978 (S.I. 1978 No. 1317).......... A3–01

1979 Transit of Animals (Road and Rail) (Amendment) Order 1979 (S.I. 1979 No. 1013) A3–01

Motor Vehicles (Authorisation of Special Types) General Order 1979 (S.I. 1979 No. 1198).. 4–02; 9–01; 14–31; A3–01

Passenger and Goods Vehicles (Recording Equipment) Regulations 1979 (S.I. 1979 No. 1746).......... A2.06

1981 Magistrates' Courts Rules 1981 (S.I. 1981 No. 552).. A2–06

1981 Dangerous Substances (Conveyance by Road in Tankers and Tank Containers) Regulations 1981 (S.I. 1981 No. 1059) A3–01

1983 Radioactive substances (Carriage by Road) Regulations (Northern Ireland) 1983 (S.R. 1983 No. 344).......... A3–01

Motor Vehicle (Construction and Use) (Amendment) (No. 2) Regulations 1983 (S.I. 1983 No. 1983 No. 471).. A3–01

1984 Road Vehicles Lighting Regulations 1984 (S.I. 1984 No. 812)....... A3–01

1985 International Carriage of Perishable Foodstuffs Regulations (S.I. 1985 No. 1071)... 5–03, 5–10

reg. 16 5–10

1986 Road Vehicles (Construction and Use) Regulations (S.I. 1986 No. 1078) 4–01, 4–02; 9–01

reg. 3 .... 2–09; 9–12; A1–13

(2) 9–15

(h) 9–13

reg. 7 ... 4–07; 9–04, 9–11

(1) 9–04

reg. 8 ... 4–07; 9–05, 9–11

(1) 9–05

reg. 18 .. 2–07, 2–17, 2–21

(1) 2–07

1986   Road Vehicles (Construction   and
Use) Regulations
—*cont.*
  reg. 27 .... 11–10; 11–11,
                 11–12, 11–13
    (1)(a) **11–11,**
                 11–16
     (b) **11–11,**
                 11–15
     (c) **11–11,**
              11–15, 11–19
     (d) **11–11,**
              11–15, 11–27
     (e) **11–11,**
                 11–15
     (f) **11–11,**
              11–15, 11–22
     (g) 11–15,
             11–19, 11–23
       (i), (ii) 11–10,
                 11–11
     (h) 11–11
    (2) **11–11**
    (3) **11–11**
    (4)(a)(i)–(iv) **11–11**
     (b)(i), (ii) **11–11**
     (c), (d) .. **11–11**
     (e)(i)–(iii) **11–11**
     (f) **11–11**
    (5)(a), (b) .. **11–11**
    (6)(a) 11–22
     (i)–(iii) **11–11**
     (b), (c) .. **11–11**
  reg. 77 .... 6–08, 6–10
  reg. 78 .... 6–08, 6–10
  reg. 80 .. 4–07; 6–08, 6–09
    (1)(a), (b) ... 6–09
  reg. 81 ...... 4–16; 9–06,
              9–08, 9–12
     (b) 9–13
     (e) 9–14
     (h), (I) 9–15
  reg. 82   4–08; 9–06, 9–08,
               9–12
     (7) 9–09
  reg. 100 3–09

1986   Road Vehicles (Con-
struction   and
Use) Regulations
—*cont.*
  reg. 181(1) ... 2–05, 2–08;
        3–09, 3–16, 3–25,
          3–26; 10–04
    (2) 3–08, **3–09,**
         3–10, 3–16, 3–20,
         3–26, 3–31, 3–33,
             3–35
    (3) **3–09**; 4–09;
          6–08; 8–02
  Sched. 12 .... 4–08, 4–11;
        9–06, 9–07, 9–08,
          9–09, 9–21
  Pt 1 para. 1(a) 9–17
    para. 2 9–16
    paras. 3, 4 9–18
Community   Drivers'
  Hours   and   Re-
  cording   Equip-
  ment (Exemptions
  and Supple- men-
  tary   Provisions)
  Regulations 1986
  (S.I.   1986   No.
  1456)..... 13–01, 13–09
Community   Drivers'
  Hours   and   Re-
  cording   Equip-
  ment Regulation
  1986 (S.I. 1986
  No. 1457)...... 13–01;
                A2–06
Drivers' Hours (Har-
  monisation with
  Community
  Rules)   Regu-
  lations 1986 (S.I.
  1986 No. 1458).. 13–01,
              13–02
Drivers'   Hours
  (Goods Vehicles)
  (Modifications)
  Order 1986 (S.I.
  1986 No. 1459).. 13–02

1986 Drivers' Hours (Goods Vehicles) (Exemptions) Regulations 1986 (S.I. 1986 No. 1492)......... 13–02

1987 Community Drivers' Hours and Recording Equipment (Exemptions and Supplementary Provisions) (Amendment) Regulations 1987 (S.I. 1987 No. 805).......... 13–01

Drivers' Hours (Goods Vehicles) (Keeping of Records) Regulations 1987 (S.I. 1987 No. 1421).. 13–02, 13–56

1988 Goods Vehicles (Plating and Testing) Regulations 1988 (S.I. 1988 No. 1478)......... 14–47
Sched. 2(4) 14–47

1991 Passenger and Goods Vehicles (Recording Equipment) Regulations 1991 (S.I. 1991 No. 381)... 13–01

1992 Road Traffic (Carriage of Dangerous Substances in Packages etc) Regulations 1992 (S.I. 1992 No. 742).... 7–02
reg. 7(1) **7–10**
reg. 10(1) **7–10**

1992 Road Traffic (Carriage of Dangerous Substances in Road Tankers and Tank Containers) Regulations 1992 (S.I. 1992 No. 743)........... 7–02
reg. 16(1) **7–10**
reg. 19(1), (2) **7–10**

1992 Road Traffic (Training of Drivers of Vehicles Carrying Dangerous Goods) Regulations 1992 (S.I. 1992 No. 744).... 7–02
reg. 4 .... **7–10**
reg. 10(1) **7–10**, 7–13

1993 Transit of Animals (General) Order 1973 (S.I. 1973 No. 1377)...... A3–01

1994 Carriage of Dangerous Goods by Road and Rail (Classification, Packaging and Labelling) Regulations 1994 (S.I. 1994 No. 669)—
reg. 2 7–07
Sched. 1 7–07

Chemicals (Hazard Information and Packaging for Supply) Regulations 1994 (S.I. No. 3247)........ 7–04

1997 Chemicals (Hazard Information and Packaging for Supply) (Amendment) Regulations 1997 (S.I. 1997 No. 1460)... 7–04

ABBREVIATIONS

CHIP2 – Chemicals (Hazard Information and Packaging for Supply) Regulations 1994.

C.U. – Construction & Use Regulations [Road Vehicles (Construction and Use) Regulations 1986].

F.A. – Finance Act 1995.

GVW – Gross vehicle weight.

LGVs – Large goods vehicles (previously known as heavy goods vehicles).

PCVs – Passenger carrying vehicles (previously known as public service vehicles).

PG9s – The prohibition notice imposed by V.I. inspectors and police officers when a vehicle is found to be defective.

RTA – Road Traffic Act 1988.

STGO – The Motor Vehicle (Authorisation of Special Types) General Order 1979.

T.M. – Tester's Manual published by the Vehicle Inspectorate Agency.

VEA – Vehicle Excise Act 1994.

V.I. – The Vehicle Inspectorate – an agency of the Department of Transport.

VSO – Vehicle Special Order.

CHAPTER 1

INTRODUCTION

Whilst the ability of enforcement authorities to check the condition of **1–01**
commercial vehicles, whether passenger or goods, has existed for many
years it is clear that, following the introduction of the Goods Vehicles
(Licensing of Operators) Act 1995 and the associated regulations, enforcement has become a priority. It is also clear that courts are prepared to look
at the maximum available penalties rather than at the bottom end of the
scale.

The majority of the offences that are considered in this book are offences **1–02**
which, in the event of a conviction, are required to be notified to the Traffic
Commissioner for the area in which the vehicle is licensed. It is already
clear that Traffic Commissioners are going to respond swiftly to maintenance related convictions, and any single conviction could, if of sufficient
gravity, result in the loss, or suspension, of the licence. Reports of decisions
by Traffic Commissioners to revoke licences appear with alarming fre-
quency in the trade press. It should, therefore, be seen as a matter of
importance that those who operate commercial vehicles are adequately
represented.

This book is intended to assist those advocates who, whilst frequently **1–03**
appearing in court, are asked less frequently to act for clients who drive or
operate commercial vhicles, and who may, therefore, welcome some
assistance in recognising the nature of those offences, in the event of a
client seeking representation. This book does not deal with day to day road
traffic matters such as driving without due care or driving with excess
alcohol. It is assumed that those who use the book will have in their library
the text of those Acts and Regulations that are fundamental to road traffic
advocacy and, for that reason, only section references have been given.
However, legislation has been quoted where it seemed to be particularly
helpful.

It has to be remembered that we cannot expect magistrates to have **1–04**
technical knowledge about commercial vehicles, although there are some
that do, and we have to accept that the public are largely prejudiced against
those who drive and operate large vehicles or coaches. It is, for these
reasons, particularly important that those who appear in court to represent
these drivers and operators have at least sufficient knowledge to assist the
court to understand the problems.

The position is exacerbated because it would appear that there are **1–05**
performance pressures on those who have the responsibility for enforcing
the law in so far as it relates to commercial vehicles. Many of the defects

1

considered in this book, which result in cases being brought before the courts, are based upon the subjective opinion of the examining police officer, trading standards officer, or vehicle inspector. The courts see those officers as having specific skills to carry out that role and it is, therefore, particularly difficult to disturb those opinions. The task is made no easier if those of us who appear to represent these defendants, seem to the court to have no adequate knowledge of the issues.

1–06   Consideration should always be given to using an independent engineer to support the defence. That may be true even when it can only be by way of mitigation. We will see, looking at the problem of lost wheels, how critical that independent evidence can be.

1–07   Somewhat improbably it is an area in which the ability to argue the law continues to be of substantial importance. It is our hope that this book will encourage those advocates, who find themselves required to act in this type of case, to become as fascinated by the opportunity to argue law in the context of commercial vehicle operation as are its authors.

CHAPTER 2

BRAKES

Generally, all braking systems work in the same way. Pressure on a foot **2–01**
pedal causes hydraulic fluid or air to operate a mechanism which applies
pressure between a lined brake shoe or pad on to a disc or drum. Small
commercial vehicles will have hydraulic systems, larger vehicles will have air
operated systems.

All vehicles have at least two braking systems. One being the service **2–02**
break used whilst the vehicle is in motion. The other being the parking
brake. On large commercial vehicles there will normally be three systems,
the third being a fail-safe device that causes the brakes to be applied if
there is a dramatic loss of air from the service system.

The driver of a large vehicle will have warning devices in the cab to draw **2–03**
attention to any loss of air pressure. These will be a gauge, a buzzer, or a
light, or any combination of the three.

The most common faults are: **2–04**

    (a) leaks on the air line or brake actuators (this happens less often on
        a hydraulic pipe),
    (b) mechanism out of adjustment,
    (c) brake linings worn,
    (d) loss of hydraulic fluid,
    (e) the parking brake on articulated trailers being inoperable,
    (f) brake components out of adjustment,
    (g) incompatibility of connections,
    (h) oval brake drums,
    (i) parking brake inoperable.

PROSECUTION

Defects in a braking system will be prosecuted under the Road Traffic Act **2–05**
1988 (RTA 1988). These are two sections available to the prosecutor:

    (i) section 40A,
    (ii) section 41A, which authorises prosecution where there has been
       a failure to comply with either regulation 18(1), or, less com-
       monly, regulation 100(1) of the Road Vehicles (Construction
       and Use) Regulations 1986 (C.U. Regs.).

Section 40A is a comparatively new section which stands on its own for **2–06**
the purpose of prosecution. It creates an offence where the condition of the
part is such that its use involves danger to others. It is arguably the most

3

successful route for the prosecution because not only can it reflect the subjective view of the Vehicle Inspectorate or police officer, but it may attract a subjective response from the court which can be difficult to disturb.

2–07   Regulation 18 is a complex regulation which incorporates a table of minimum braking standards expressed as a percentage effort. Regulation 18(1) makes no direct reference to that table and only requires that the brakes shall be in good and efficient working order.

2–08   Regulation 100(1) again requires that all parts and accessories shall be maintained in good and efficient working order.

2–09   "Braking Efficiency" is defined in regulation 3 of the C.U. Regs. and, as a definition, is critically important to the analysis of most cases in which it is alleged that the brakes are defective.

Prosecution Evidence

Vehicle Inspector

2–10   The vehicle will either be examined at the roadside, at a Testing Station, or sometimes, when a vehicle has been involved in an accident, at suitable commercial premises. The quality of the evidence is likely to be affected by the site with the better evidence resulting from a formal examination at a fully equipped testing station or garage.

2–11   Vehicle Inspectors work to a guide known as the Testers Manual (T.M.) although the formal title is the *Heavy Goods Vehicle Inspectors Manual*. This looseleaf publication can be obtained from the HMSO (ISBN 0 11 551063 X) and it details every part of a goods vehicle that is required to be inspected, with a guide as to how that inspection should be carried out.

2–12   Braking Systems are dealt with between section 34 and section 39 and, taking Service Brakes as an example, the guide looks like this:

38	Service Brake Operation
Method of Inspection	Reason for Rejection
1. For systems using pressure or vaccum, with the reservoir at maximum pressure or vacuum, note the reading on the gauge and fully depress the pedal. Keep the pedal pressed and observe the gauge reading.	1. Pressure or vacuum gauge reading drops while the pedal is kept depressed indicating a leak in the brake system.

Note: This inspection cannot be carried out on vehicles fitted with pressure or vacuum brakes and no gauge. In such cases, the system must be examined for leaks during the under-vehicle examination.

4

2. For hydraulic systems, fully depress the pedal and keep it depressed under steady pressure. Check if the pedal tends to creep down.

2. For a hydraulic system the pedal tends to creep down while depressed.

Note: For some brake systems a small amount of creep may be due to elasticity in the brake components.

3. For hydraulic systems, depress the pedal and observe if there is sponginess.

3. For a hydraulic system sponginess when the pedal is depressed.

4. On some lighter vehicles brake action is assisted by vacuum from the engine. Check if this is operating satisfactorily by partly depressing the pedal, starting the engine and checking whether the pedal can be felt to dip.

4. No dip can be felt when the engine is started indicating vacuum assistance is not working satisfactorily.

5. If the vehicle or trailer is fitted with a brake anti-lock system check the warning lamp for the correct sequence of operation.

5. Brake anti-lock warning lamp does not follow its correct sequence of operation.

Note: Design sequence varies with the type of system. See manufacturers technical data for correct sequence.

6. If a vehicle is fitted with full power hydraulic brakes, check that pressures are maintained when all brakes are off and the engine is switched off.

6. Pressure not maintained in a full power hydraulic system with brakes off and the engine switched off.

Note: About 10 minutes should be allowed to elapse during which the inspection of other test items should continue. Loss of pressure will be indicated by the operation of the low pressure device, *i.e.* a warning light or appearance of semaphore flag device.

Police

2–13 A police officer will examine the vehicle at the roadside or, usually following an accident, at commercial premises. In the latter case the inspection may be carried out by a civilian engineer employed by the police for that purpose.

Leaks in the system

2–14 Where the system is hydraulic the evidence will be to the effect that either fluid was found on parts of the vehicle adjacent to the hydraulic pipes or that, whilst the vehicle was standing, drops of fluid appeared on the ground. The fluid level in the reservoir may also be lower than the minimum indicated on the reservoir.

2–15 An air leak will be described as being audible either continuously or when the brakes are applied. In serious cases it may be said that the loss of air was apparent from the gauges in the cab.

Adjustment

2–16 The purpose of the mechanisms allowing brakes to be adjusted is to ensure that optimum pressure can be applied by the brake shoe to the drum. The evidence will be:

    (i) The length of the stroke on the adjuster exceeds that prescribed in the Testers Manual.

    (ii) Visual inspection of the drum demonstrates that the gap between the shoe and the drum is excessive.

    (iii) That the wheel can be turned manually – possibly with a bar – when the brakes are applied.

    (iv) That the brake drum was cold when all the others were hot, indicating that there had been no friction between the drum and the shoe.

    (v) That the brake cable on the trailer of an articulated trailer was broken or slack, or that the handbrake lever on the trailer was inoperative.

    (vi) That the percentage braking effort recorded on a rolling road brake tester was less than that required by law.

    (vii) That the brake shoe linings were worn to excess.

    (viii) That the brake shoe linings were contaminated by oil.

In all these cases the prosecution may also allege that there has been inadequate maintenance.

DEFENCE

2–17 There is scope for error in the wording of the summons. The normal section of the RTA 1988 used to support C.U. Regs. prosecutions is section 42. Where brakes are concerned the appropriate section is 41A. Where regulation 18 is used it is always worth comparing the wording, and "subsection", of the summons with the regulation itself. Since the decision in *Simmons v. Fowler* (1950) 48 L.G.R. 623, DC, it is clear that the prosecution must identify the part about which the complaint is made with reasonable certainty.

Where an articulated vehicle is involved the prosecution must correctly **2–18** identify the wheel or wheels about which complaint is made and, in particular, direct the summons to either the tractor or the trailer: *NFC Forwarding Ltd v. DPP* [1989] R.T.R 239.

Section 40A of the RTA 1988 is independent of the C.U. Regs. but the **2–19** summons must, nonetheless, correctly identify the target.

Where a vehicle is operating under a hire agreement, or under a sub- **2–20** contract the "user" may not have been correctly identified.

Leaks

It can be argued that ultimately the only criteria against which the efficiency **2–21** of a brake can be tested is the relevant legal requirement. Regulation 18 of the C.U. Regs. sets out in clear terms the percentage which will be considered to be the minimum standard.

In many cases an air, or hydraulic, leak will have no real effect on the **2–22** ability of the brake to achieve the required standard. The only satisfactory test is to put the vehicle on a rolling road. An operator against whom a complaint is made should, if at all possible, have the vehicle checked on such a road before any adjustment is made following the enforcement check.

A rolling road test should always take place when the vehicle is under **2–23** load.

Key points to consider are, in the case of air brakes, the rate of loss **2–24** against the capacity of the vehicle's own compressor, and the circumstances in which the leak could be heard. In the case of a hydraulic system the level in the fluid reservoir at the time of the check. In the event that the minimum level is exceeded it may well not be possible to maintain that the brakes were not efficient. It is, additionally, always worth confirming with the manufacturer whether the level includes a "safety margin". In other words whether the brakes might be expected to operate efficiently with less than the "minimum" amount of fluid in the reservoir.

Where the stroke of the brake adjuster is alleged to have been excessive **2–25** it may be worth asking the witness whether any record of the measurement has been retained and, in any event, confirming the standard set out in the T.M. It has to be remembered that the distance required in the T.M. can never be an absolute standard; some variation must be possible without adversely affecting the efficiency of the brakes.

Where a vehicle is inspected following an accident it is worth considering **2–26** whether the defect could result from accident damage or from interference by those recovering the vehicle. It is common practice to release ["back off"] the brakes to facilitate recovery. Equally both air pipes and hydraulic pipes are susceptible to impact damage or stress.

Where contamination of the brake lining by oil or other fluid is alleged it **2–27** is important to confirm how the inspection was carried out. A look through the examination port in the brake plate may be less than satisfactory.

Where an allegation of contamination is made the operator should strip down the drum as soon as possible after the check, ideally using an independent garage or engineer for that purpose. Again it should be remembered that accident damage may well cause contamination of the linings particularly if the vehicle has been on its side or at a marked angle.

2–28   Where there is either doubt about the circumstances in which the prosecution is brought, or about the efficiency of the brakes, consideration should be given to seeking assistance from an independent engineer. Whenever checks are carried out at the roadside the view of the enforcement office may well be a subjective view, which is, on examination, unsupported.

2–29   The problem is that the offence is, in effect, absolute, and it may well be difficult to attack the prosecution evidence, however subjective it may be.

MITIGATION

2–30   The majority of the defects in the braking system that have been considered can arise over a short period of time. A leak in an airline can appear at any moment and, unless there is a sufficiently sharp loss of air to cause one of the in-cab warning devices to operate, the driver may well have no knowledge of the problem.

2–31   The "adjusters" are designed to allow the gap between the brake lining and the drum to be altered to accommodate the normal wear on the lining that occurs in the course of a vehicle's use. When a check is carried out just before a routine safety check by the operator the length of the stroke may be longer than that contemplated in the T.M.

2–32   The driver may be able to say that nothing had occurred in the course of the journey to give her/him any cause for concern. S/he may also be able to say that there was no visible problem at the start of the day's work when the vehicle was checked.

2–33   The driver may also be able to rely on the fact that a recent safety check was carried out by the company or its engineers, and that it was appropriate to rely on that fact as an assurance that there was no problem of which s/he should have been aware.

2–34   The drivers position may be less good where the prosecution allege that the fault was such that any competent driver was bound to realise that the brakes were not as they should be.

2–35   The employer's position is, of course, one removed from that of the driver. The employer can only respond to a defect that occurs whilst the vehicle is in use if the driver reports it. Examination of the tachograph may suggest that the brakes were working normally, equally the chart may disclose aggressive use of the brakes by the driver during the course of the day which could affect the adjustment.

2–36   The employer may be able to say that the driver was instructed to, and had the opportunity to, report any apparent defect arising in the course of the journey and that, in the absence of such report, the employer could not not have been aware of the fault. This will be particularly persuasive where the employer uses a system of written defect reporting.

The employer should also be able to produce maintenance records to **2–37** demonstrate, not only the regularity of the necessary checks, but also that the brakes had been examined and either found to be free from fault, or to have needed work which was done.

Depending on the gravity of the case it may be useful to call an engineer **2–38** to support the mitigation. This is particularly true if it is to be urged that the defect could have arisen during the course of the journey.

CONSULTANT ENGINEER'S COMMENTS

Whilst the Commercial Vehicle industry is constantly seeking to improve **2–39** the technology of every aspect of the vehicles it produces, it is probably true to say that braking systems are improving at a faster rate than any other element of a vehicle. Water cooled disc brakes, for instance, not only give improved braking performance but also create new challenges for mechanics and new opportunities for systems failure. The ability of an operator to establish that there are adequate maintenance systems in place, and that the staff are properly qualified to implement those systems is critical.

It should also be remembered that some parts, such as brake linings, **2–40** have a limited working life which may depend on the nature of the work that the vehicle is doing. There is a massive difference between wear on a vehicle used for site tipping work and one used for long distance haulage.

Defective braking systems form the basis of the majority of the Defect **2–41** Notices (P.G.9) issued by enforcement officers and are frequently seen as having been caused by a significant failure of the maintenance system. In those cases where the enforcement officer takes the view that the maintenance system is at fault the Defect Notice will be marked with an "S" and this will have an immediate and adverse effect on the Operators Licence.

It should be remembered that the view of the enforcement officer is, **2–42** more often than not, a subjective view rather than one based on measurement, and a subjective view is always open to challenge.

Finally, it should be remembered that the vehicle will have been designed **2–43** to operate at weights which are greater than those permitted by law in this country and that, therefore, the capability of the braking system will be greater than might at first appear.

CHAPTER 3

DANGEROUS/INSECURE LOADS

3–01 Prosecutions for dangerous or insecure loads arise not only when some part of the load has either come off the vehicle or moved from its original position, but also when, in the view of a police officer or vehicle inspector, the method by which the load is secured is inadequate.

3–02 There is a guide to load security, the *Code of Practice Safety of Loads on Vehicles* which was reprinted in 1995 and is available from HMSO. It is also printed as Appendix 3 to this book. This small book is invaluable in understanding the problems of load security but it is only a guide. It takes "sample" loads and discusses the way in which those loads should be secured. It also deals in some detail with the equipment that is available by way of load restraint.

3–03 Specifically the load can (a) come off the vehicle or out of a container on the vehicle, (b) move from the position in which it was originally placed or, (c) in the case of a liquid load, leak. It may also be said that the method by which the load is secured on the vehicle is so inadequate as to constitute a danger.

3–04 The cause of these problems may be (i) incompetent fastening, (ii) a failure of the fastening equipment or, (iii) collapse of some part of the load itself. Additionally the manner in which the vehicle was driven may have put stresses on the load and its fastenings that could not have been anticipated.

3–05 It follows from this that, when faced with a summons alleging a dangerous or insecure load, it is important to have a clear understanding of the load, the fastenings that were applied, and the circumstances in which the load failed. This exercise is particularly difficult in those cases in which a complaint is made about a load that has not moved but which is, in the view of the reporting officer, inadequately fastened. Frequently you will be told that the method that has been adopted is one that has been used over many years without incident. That may not assist if the method is disapproved by the Code of Practice. (This book was not widely published and there are still many operators who are unaware of its existence.)

3–06 Prosecutions often follow a complaint that small items have fallen from the load, for example, gravel from a tipping lorry, rubbish from a skip, or even sand blown from the top of a load of sand. It should be remembered, however, that a vehicle passing over a small item on the road surface may throw it up giving the impression that the piece has fallen off the vehicle.

These cases are always serious as the perception of public danger is very **3–07** high and the court needs to be persuaded to understand the circumstances in which the incident occurred.

PROSECUTION

There are two possible approaches for the prosecution.   **3–08**
  (a) Regulation 100(2) of the C.U. Regs.
  (b) Section 40A(d) of the RTA 1988.

CONSTRUCTION AND USE REGULATIONS 1986, REG. 100

100.—(1) A motor vehicle. Every trailer drawn thereby and all parts and **3–09** accessories of such vehicles and trailer shall at all times be in such condition, and the number of passengers carried by such vehicle or trailer, the manner in which any passengers are carried in or on such vehicles or trailer, and the weight, distribution, packing and adjustment of the load of such vehicle or trailer shall at all times be such, that no danger is caused or is likely to be caused to any person in or on the vehicle or trailer or on a road.

Provided that the provisions of this regulation with regard to the number of passengers carried shall not apply to a vehicle to which the Public Service Vehicles (Carrying Capacity) Regulations 1984 apply.

(2) The load carried by a motor vehicle or trailer shall at all times be so secured, if necessary by physical restraint other than its own weight, and be in such a position, that neither danger nor nuisance is likely to be caused to any person or property by reason of the load or any part thereof falling or being blown from the vehicles or by reason of any other movement of the load or any part thereof in relation to the vehicle.

(3) No motor vehicle or trailer shall be used for any purpose for which it is so unsuitable as to cause or be likely to cause danger or nuisance to any person in or on the vehicle or trailer or on a road.

The traditional tool for the prosecution is regulation 100(2), but that sub- **3–10** section allows a defence on the issue of the foreseeability of the likelihood of danger. Section 40A creates an absolute offence where there is a danger of injury to any person, and is increasingly preferred by the prosecution.

The prosecution will be brought normally by the police.   **3–11**

Prosecution Evidence

Where a load has fallen off a vehicle the court will simply hear evidence **3–12** about the load and its position after the incident. There may be a sketch plan and it is increasingly likely that there will be photographs. This type of case gives the prosecution a substantial opportunity to highlight the potential for injury, indeed one must recognise that these cases can, and do, involve fatalities. It may well be appropriate to challenge the way in which the case is presented if there is too much emphasis on the potential danger, particularly if the facts make it clear that the incident was the result of an unforeseeable occurrence. Where chains, straps, or ropes, have failed there may be forsenic evidence about the condition of the equipment although it is still common for officers to give a subjective view on the suitability of the restraints.

3–13 Where loads have simply moved, the evidence will deal with the position after the movement or slip has occurred and, particularly in these cases, there will be evidence about the method of security that was used. Sometimes there will be a video of the load moving. One of the problems faced by the prosecution in these cases in that a load can move without any loss of tension in the straps, ropes, or chains.

3–14 Where it is alleged that a piece of, say, timber gravel or sand has fallen from a vehicle, or it is alleged that some potentially dangerous substance, such as diesel oil from a bulk tanker, has fallen off a vehicle, the evidence will nearly always be based on witness statements only. The very nature of the occurrence making it unlikely that the prosecution will be able to produce the offending item.

3–15 The temptation is for the prosecution to rely on the simple fact of the lost load to establish the offence and, on occasions, the prosecution evidence will be very short.

Defence

3–16 Under regulation 100(2) there must be a defect in the security of the load itself. Where the defect is in the vehicle or the trailer then this offence is not made out. Equally the defect must be in the security of the load. When the loss arises from a defect in the "weight, distribution, packing and adjustment" of the load then the appropriate regulation is 100(1). Where the wrong sub-section is used then the prosecution must fail: *Simmons v. Fowler* (1950) 48 L.G.R. 623. (In fact *Simmons v. Fowler* is an important case in all construction and use cases). The prosecution must identify the complaint with sufficient clarity to enable the recipient of the summons to understand what is being alleged but it can be very difficult to distinguish factually between "loss" and inadequate packing or adjustment.

3–17 Where the load is lost as a result of a defect in the vehicle or the manner in which the vehicle was driven then that is not an offence under this regulation. The most common situation in which this argument may be relevant is when the vehicle falls over. This usually happens when the vehicle is negotiating a bend. The point being that, if the load is well secured, it will go with the vehicle even if, on impact, some of the fastenings may be broken. This is normally apparent from evidence at the scene, but, in practice, police officers often appear to be determined to establish that the load was "lost" prior to the accident. Articulated vehicles are, from time to time, subject to a condition known as the "slow roll phenomenon". When an articulated vehicle is negotiating a tight bend, as on a round-a-bout, a combination of the radius of turn, the speed of the vehicle, and the camber of the road, can cause the vehicle to roll over. The speed will always be slow, and the tachograph should be examined to look at the vehicles performance prior to the accident.

In a case in which the argument is that the vehicle "went first" the **3–18** condition of the fastenings may be critical. Police officers and Vehicle Inspectors may refer to old, dirty ropes, or rusted chains, or dirty, worn, security straps. It needs to be remembered that all this equipment is designed to be used and will get worn in appearance, dirty, and sometimes rusty. A 10mm split-film polypropyline rope is effectively impervious to rain, oil, and dirt but, to an inexperienced eye, may well appear to be inadequate if it has been in use for some time. Where there is a potential dispute on the capability of the fastenings the obtaining of expert evidence should always be considered. The manufacturers will have published the technical specifications of the ropes or other equipment and it should be easy to obtain copies for the court.

The issue of "foreseeability" may afford a defence. In the old case of **3–19** *Cornish v. Ferry Masters Ltd* [1975] R.T.R. 292, a pallet collapsed in the course of the journey. It was agreed that neither the company nor the driver could possibly have been aware of the latent defect, but they were convicted because the court held that the case must turn on the factual circumstances as they were, and not on the knowledge of the defendants. This decision confirmed the absolute nature of the offence. More recently, however, the courts have opened the door to the argument that the occurrence was unforeseeable. In the case of *Walker-Trowbridge Ltd v. DPP* [1992] R.T.R. 182, the court indicated that it would consider the manner in which the load was secured against the journey that was to be undertaken in deciding whether the load was "insecure". In other words, if the load was adequately secured for the journey that was contemplated, having regard to the nature of the route and the weather, they would be prepared to listen to an argument that the loss of the load was unforeseeable. They convicted in the particular case because, although the load was "secure" in the practical sense, the route included a low bridge, and the risk that the load might be knocked from the vehicle was foreseeable. In an unreported Crown Court decision in 1987 the court at Knutsford declined to convict following the loss of a metal plate weighing some 1.5 tonnes on the grounds that no one could have foreseen that it would "lift" in the course of the journey with the result that it struck a bridge and was knocked from the vehicle.

As we have seen, police officers do prosecute under regulation 100(2) **3–20** even though there has been no loss or movement of the load. They simply assert that, as the result of their "professional" observation, they were satisfied that the load was inadequately secured.

These cases are difficult because of the clear challenge that must be **3–21** made to the officer's evidence. Courts tend to support the officer particularly because of the public perception of the danger that can result from load loss. In practice, however, the police frequently display a substantial lack of knowledge about load security. The first matters that should be tested by the defence are the allegations that are being made about the fastening systems. The expression "dirty old rope" is frequently used by officers but, as has been noted, modern ropes may look both old and dirty, but may have strength that, depending on the number of ropes that are used, is far in excess of the restraining criteria referred to in the Code of

Practice. Equally the strength of the hooks set along the platform of the vehicle or trailer for use with the ropes, and sometimes referred to as "roping hooks", is frequently under-estimated. Chains all have a pre-determined load range which can be obtained from the manufacturer. Good operators will regularly check chains for weakness.

3–22   The other problem that can arise results from the question of the amount of friction between the load and the surface of the loading area of the vehicle. The regulation contemplates the fact that the weight of the load may be sufficient in itself to make the load secure. The Code of Practice, however, views the existence of friction between the load and the vehicle as a security "bonus" (section 6.1). It has to be remembered that those who load the vehicle may have to balance the weight distribution on the vehicle because of the problems of axle overloads, against the absolute security of the load.

3–23   Frequently, however improbably, in these cases of police observation, the load is allowed to proceed without any adjustment being made to the security of the load. It can then be argued that the decision of the officer to allow the load to proceed in an unaltered condition to its destination is a pragmatic test of the security and, if the load arrives in one piece, the court should be satisfied that the load was safe.

3–24   In all these cases it may be helpful to use a consultant either in relation to the strength of the fastening systems or in relation to the method of load restraint that was used.

3–25   Finally there is the defence that, if there was an offence, it was an offence under regulation 100(1) of the C.U. Regs. Modern packaging techniques using metal or nylon bands to secure a number of boxes to a pallet, or to shrink wrap items on to a pallet or in to a unit that can be more easily handled, are part and parcel of day-to-day life in the haulage industry. It is properly arguable that the "load" is made up of a number of these banded or shrink-wrapped units, and these units are then secured on to the vehicle. Liquids are, of course, carried in plastic or metal drums and containers which, again, are in turn secured on to the vehicle.

3–26   Where a band snaps, a vacuum wrap is torn, or a container cracks or leaks, then the offence is regulation 100(1) and not regulation 100(2). The argument can be difficult and, in *Leathley v. Robsons Border Transport* [1976] R.T.R. 503, the court observed that a "common sense approach should be adopted".

Mitigation

3–27 In those cases in which the load loss is caused by a latent defect, of whatever sort, the court should be asked to give an absolute discharge to the driver and, if there are two defendants, the operator. Where the loss results from the failure of the ropes or other securing system, the driver will be expected to have examined them with reasonable care, and the operator will be expected to have provided suitable equipment but, subject to that, a discharge would be appropriate. Where the loss results from the failure of some part of the load, or vehicle, then it is difficult to see how the driver or operator could be blamed in any way unless, of course, the failure of the vehicle can be laid at the operators door. It should not be forgotten that the court may need "persuading" however clear the circumstances may seem to the advocate. Consideration should always be given to producing technical literature about the restraints that were used to try to prevent the court making a subjective judgment.

The operator may be able to lay the blame entirely on the driver. An **3–28** examination of the tachograph in conjunction with a look at the road where the incident occurred may show that the driver was the author of his/her own misfortune by driving in a manner that was entirely inappropriate. The operator may also be able to show that the driver ignored advice that has been given either in the course of training or otherwise.

Sometimes the load is lost as the result of an emergency created by some **3–29** other person. There is a fine line between an emergency that might be anticipated in the ordinary course of driving, and one that is really so extraordinary as to be outside the band of foreseeability without amounting to a defence. In such a case, again, an absolute discharge should be sought.

ROAD TRAFFIC ACT 1988, s.40A

Section 40A(d) allows prosecution where: **3–30**
> "the weight, position, or distribution of its load, or the manner in which it is secured, is such that the use of the motor vehicle or trailer involves a danger of injury to any person."

Prosecution Evidence

Although this section avoids the defence of "foreseeability" all the other **3–31** matters considered in relation to regulation 100(2) apply. Perhaps the most important point is that the section clearly separates the offence between a "motor vehicle" and a "trailer". It would seem to be arguable that, where the load is lost from a trailer, a summons alleging an offence in relation to a vehicle will be fatally flowed. Certainly that would be the position if *Simmons v. Fowler* is followed. Additionally there is the case of *NFC Forwarding Ltd v. DPP* [1988] R.T.R. 239, which underlines the need for the prosecution to specify either the motor vehicle or the trailer when the legislation contemplates separate offences.

Defence

The prosecution have to identify the vehicle or trailer precisely, as we **3–32** have seen. Additionally they must identify the alleged cause of the loss of the load. Section 40A contemplates four separate possible causes of the offence, each of which raises different issues in relation to the defence. It may be, therefore, that the case may be challenged on the basis that the evidence adduced by the prosecution does not support the allegation.

There may be, under this section, no opportunity to argue on the issue of **3–33** "foreseeability". The case of *Walker-Trowbridge Ltd v. DPP* was prosecuted under regulation 100(2), the test under section 40A is, of course, whether the incident involved the "danger of injury etc. . . .". Where there is the danger of injury, which is almost inevitable when there is the loss of a load, or part of a load, it seems that the necessary ingredient of an offence under section 40A is established.

3-34　The position is different if there is loss of, say, sand blown from a vehicle that is inadequately sheeted. It must be arguable that, viewing the matter subjectively, it would be difficult, if not impossible, to hypothecate a situation in which the presence of small quantities of a substance, such as sand or small gravel chips, might be said to involve the danger of injury.

Mitigation

3-35　The mitigation under section 40A is identical to that suggested for regulation 100(2).

Consultant Engineer's Comments

3-36　This is one of the few situations in which there is no "grey area". The load either "is" or "is not" dangerous; it either "is" or "is not" secure. Security of a load is not simply a question of tying the proper knot, but a comparatively complex issue turning on an understanding of modern security systems involving not only chains, straps and ropes, but also pallets, vacuum packing and liquid and gas tight hatches. Many insecure load cases depend upon establishing whether the abnormal movement of the vehicle caused the load to move or whether the load moved on the vehicle. This is particularly true in cases where the vehicle has overturned.

Chapter 4

ABNORMAL LOADS

Every commercial vehicle on the roads of the U.K. is required to operate **4–01** within the requirements of the C.U. Regs. which, in particular, limit the weight, width, and length of vehicles.

It is clear, however, that vehicles do move along the roads which are **4–02** heavier than the maximum weight of 38,000 kg, wider than 2.58 m (refrigerated vehicles), and longer than 18 m without necessarily breaking the law. In the majority of cases these vehicles will be moving in accordance with the provisions of the Motor Vehicles (Authorisation of Special Types) General Order 1979, known commonly as the STGO. It is critically important to understand that these regulations achieve their effect by exempting the vehicle in question from the normal restrictions imposed by the C.U. Regs. No offence is created by the STGO. The STGO is directed to vehicles carrying an "abnormal indivisible load" which is defined as:

"(a) a load which cannot, owing to cost or risk of damage, be carried by a heavy motor car or trailer or a combination of such vehicles complying in all respects with the requirements of the C.U. Regs., or

(b) owing to its weight cannot be carried by a heavy motor car or trailer or a combination of such vehicles having a total laden weight of not more than 38,000 kg and complying in all respects with the requirements of the C.U. Regs."

Under the STGO the maximum length is 27.4 m, and the maximum **4–03** width is 6.1 m. There are three categories of weight:

Category 1. up to 46,000 kg.
Category 2. up to 80,000 kg.
Category 3. up to 150,000 kg.

(Vehicles can move above these limits under an authority issued by the Department of Transport. The permit will be journey specific and is known as a VSO.)

The most important requirement of the STGO is that notice of any **4–04** intended movement shall be given to the relevant Highways and Bridges Authority and, in certain circumstances, to the police. This means that where a journey takes the vehicle through the areas of a number of county and police authorities the operator should have copies of the various notices which will normally have been faxed. Whilst the STGO sets out the form of the notice and the relevant periods of notice, the fact is that there is a very wide discretion. There is a degree of pragmatism, and, in certain cases, it is not unknown for a notice to be accepted by telephone on the morning of the intended movement.

4–05   The purpose of these notices is to allow the Highways and Bridges Authority to confirm a route that will accept the axle and train weights that have been notified, and to allow the police to determine whether an escort is required and whether, for other reasons, such as likely traffic congestion, time limits should be imposed. The notice to the Highways and Bridges Authority will include an indemnity against any damage that might result from the passage of a heavy vehicle over the Authorities roads and bridges. The majority of routes are, by now, well established, and an experienced operator should be able to propose a route that will be acceptable.

PROSECUTION

4–06 Any prosecution can only be for a C.U. offence. This means that the summons will be precisely that which would be appropriate for any allegation of excess weight, width, or length.

4–07   Normally, therefore, section 41 of the RTA 1988 will be used with regulation 7 (length), regulation 8 (width), and regulation 80 (weight) of the C.U. Regs.

4–08   The C.U. Regs., however, do contemplate certain departures from the normal length and width restrictions and, for that reason, prosecutions may allege a breach of regulation 82 with Schedule 12 of the C.U. Regs. (Where the alleged offence reflects a substantial departure from the normal limits the advocate should determine whether or not the load had been notified as being "abnormal").

4–09   Occasionally the prosecution may allege that the dimensions of the load were such that there was a risk of danger, in which case the prosecution will be brought under section 40A of the RTA 1988. It may also be alleged that the vehicle was unsuitable for the purpose for which it was being used and the prosecution would then use section 41 of the RTA 1988 with regulation 100(3) of the C.U. Regs.

PROSECUTION EVIDENCE

Vehicle Inspector/Trading Standards Officer

4–10 Evidence will be given that the vehicle was weighed, and/or measured, with the result that it was found to exceed the C.U. Regs. limits. Evidence may be given that the weight of individual axles, or the complete load, exceeded those weights set out in the Notice of Movement and that, therefore, the exemption provided by the Notice has been lost. Equally evidence may be given that the width or length of the load exceeded the notified figures with the same loss of exemption.

Police evidence

4–11 In so far as the weight or dimensions of the vehicle and load are concerned the evidence of the police will be the same as that of the trading standards officers and vehicle inspectors. The police are, additionally, likely to

DEFENCE

consider the presence of, and position of, any markers that may be required by Schedule 12 of the C.U. Regs. They may also give evidence of the absence of, or unsuitability of, any statutory attendant, (Sched. 12). There may be evidence that, for reasons other than variations in the dimensions and weight of the load, the Notice of Movement has not been complied with. Evidence may be given that the vehicle was, for instance, off route.

Finally there can be evidence that the axles exceed the maximum **4–12** permitted weight regardless of the weight that was notified. The present absolute maximum is 16,500 kg and, with abnormal loads, it does some-times happen that this weight is exceeded.

DEFENCE

Weight

Large vehicles can be extremely difficult to weigh for purely practical **4–13** reasons. Very often the weighbridge can only be accessed with difficulty which may affect the accuracy of the result. Where the vehicle is longer than normal to accommodate the load it may not be possible to keep the vehicle on the level surface — if there is one — whilst the process of weighing is being carried out. Very ofen the weights imposed by the loaded vehicle substantially exceed the weights at which the bridge was tested and there may, therefore, be opportunities to challenge the accuracy of the weighbridge.

In any case in which there is substantial weight involved it is always worth **4–14** looking into the circumstances surrounding the weighing procedure. (See "Overloading" for more details.)

Axle weights

Any case which is based on an allegation of excess axle weights involving **4–15** an abnormal load should be scrutinised with great care. It is arguable that it would only be possible to check axle weights on a very large vehicle by using a dynamic axle bridge. In certain cases, although the concrete approaches to these bridges have to comply with strict criteria as to level, where the vehicle is longer than normal, it may well be that part of the vehicle is off these level areas whilst the weighing is being done. In such a case it may well be possible to challenge the accuracy of the recorded weight. The maximum axle weight in any circumstances is 16,500 kg and, where that weight is exceeded, it is particularly important to consider the way in which the enforcement officers achieved the weight.

Dimensions

Measuring a large object is, again, less easy than might at first appear. **4–16** Frequently only one officer will appear to give evidence about a process which must, of necessity, require at least two people. Regulation 81 of the C.U. Regs. sets out at length the way in which measurements have to be

19

taken, and it is arguable that two enforcement officers, conducting a roadside check, could never achieve the standards required by regulation 81. Very often the prosecution rely on comparatively small errors and it is reasonably easy to disturb their evidence on the issue of accuracy. Certainly it is worth making enquiries of the driver as to how the measurements were taken.

Notice of Movement

4–17 The prosecution often assume, mistakenly, that the validity of the Notice of Movement is a matter of general complaint. This is not correct. The Notice has to be directed to the appropriate authority where there is, as we have seen, substantial discretion. The only person, therefore, who can complain about a breach of the terms of the Notice is the issuing officer. It has to be remembered that the approval of the route depends upon the ability of the road, or bridge, to bear the weight. A notice might validate a movement at, say, 54,000 kg, on a road which will accommodate, say, 80,000 kg. It will readily be appreciated that, in that situation, an excess on the notified weight of a number of tonnes will be of no significance to the Highways and Bridges Authority particularly if they have the indemnity which the notice, of necessity, incorporates. Where the available prosecution evidence, perhaps tendered in the form of section 9 statements, suggests that there is no complaint from the appropriate authority, a valid defence must always be available. There is no requirement that the driver should carry a copy of the notice of movement although that complaint is sometimes made.

Assistants

4–18 The police sometimes complain that the statutory assistant does not hold a licence or is under age. The law requires only that the assistant should be competent. In principle, there is no reason why a reasonably experienced 16-year-old should not act as assistant.

MITIGATION

4–19 It is particularly important that the court should understand the circumstances in which these large loads come to be carried. It is all too easy for the prosecution to paint a picture of some enormous load let loose on the public roads without thought or care.

4–20   In almost every case the load is put on to the vehicle at the consignors premises. The haulier must depend on accurate information being provided. Where the load is a fabricated piece, whether in metal or concrete, the manufacturer should have precise knowledge of the weight and dimensions. The haulier notifies the movement in the light of that information which is, for whatever reason, sometimes wrong. When there is a massive error in weight or dimensions it may be that the driver should have been put on inquiry, but, where the errors are small, the driver may well not have any reason for concern.

The manufacturers of engineering and construction plant publish **4–21** detailed information about the dimensions and weight of each type of machine. There are books available that list the weight and dimensions of most of the machines that are in common use, together with the weight of any ancillary equipment such as buckets. Again the haulier must rely on the customer, who may be many miles away, to give accurate information not only about the basic machine but also about any ancillary equipment that may be attached to the machine. Fuel and water can make a substantial difference to the weight, as can mud or earth sticking to the tracks. Once again the driver should be trained to exercise reasonable skill and judgment but the variations may not be perceptible.

The problem with weight is that it is very rare to find a weighbridge on **4–22** the specified route, and even more rare to find a public weighbridge that can be accessed by a large vehicle. Departure from the route invalidates the Notice of Movement.

Provided that the court understands the problem, there should always be substantial mitigation available. In many cases it may be possible to run the argument that there is no moral blame and that an absolute discharge should be the appropriate decision following *Hart v. Bex* [1957] Crim.L.R. 622, DC.

CHAPTER 5

PERISHABLE FOODS

5–01 In accordance with the general increase in concern about all matters affecting the environment and the way we live, governments became anxious about the condition in which perishable foods were being carried. It was felt that whilst substantial deterioration in the condition of some perishable foods was immediately apparent to the recipient or purchaser, some deterioration was not so readily perceptible and unscrupulous traders or carriers could take advantage of the public. There was a move to set standards which would ensure that designated categories of perishable foods would be carried in conditions that would ensure that they would arrive with the consumer in a safe condition.

5–02 A number of governments, of which the U.K. was one, signed the International Carriage of Perishable Foodstuffs Act 1976. This Act gave the U.K. government access to the Agreement on the International Carriage of Perishable Foodstuffs and on the Special Equipment to be Used for Such Carriage. This agreement, which has so cumbersome a title, is known more generally as the ATP (Accord Transports Perishables).

5–03 The Act needs to be read with the International Carriage of Perishable Foodstuffs Regulations 1985 for it is these regulations that put flesh on to the bare skeleton of the Act. The effect of the legislation is to lay down the temperatures at which certain categories of foodstuffs must be maintained in the course of transit. To enable this to be done there are regulations covering the equipment that is used to carry the designated foodstuffs. The regulations require that the equipment used to carry the goods must be classified in the classes defined in paragraphs 1 to 4 of Annex 1 of ATP and conform to the standards required by paragraph 5 of that Annex.

5–04 The effect of all this is that a vehicle used to carry foodstuffs of a designated class must be certified as complying with the regulations and must be able to show that the required temperature was maintained throughout the journey. In some cases the required temperature may be as low as $-20°C$, in other cases, such as certain categories of meat, the temperature may be as high as $+7°C$.

5–05 The record of temperature is made by a thermograph. This device rotates a chart on which the time is recorded and on which, by means of a graph, the temperature is recorded minute by minute. The regulations permit a fluctuation in temperature of $3°C$ to accommodate certain technical operations. It will be clear that this legislation gives the opportunity to prosecute for a range of offences. Failure to have the appropriate certificate

of compliance, whether by reason of expiry of an existing certificate or a
failure to submit the vehicle for testing will give rise to prosecution, as will
a failure to maintain the required temperature or to ensure the proper
working of the thermograph. More seriously forgery of such a certificate or
of a thermograph record will also result in prosecution. There are other
grounds for prosecution between those extremes.

A prosecution may arise if the vehicle has been altered in a way that **5–06**
might affect its thermal efficiency, which is, of course, a question of fact.
The legislation requires that any relevant alteration be notified and, if
necessary, the equipment be submitted for a new test.

The advocate faced with a case of this sort needs only to understand the **5–07**
background against which this legislation came to be made. The offences
are necessarily simple and it should be easy to determine whether or not a
defence may run.

PROSECUTION

Prosecution is likely to be brought by the appropriate Trading Standards **5–08**
authority. Although the tests are within the control of the Department of
Transport, the nature of the offence is such that it falls neatly within the
general responsibilities of the Trading Standards officers.

Section 7 of the International Carriage of Perishable Foodstuffs Act 1976 **5–09**
creates three categories of offence:

> 7(1)(a) deals with the absence of a certificate of compliance or
> certification plate for the equipment,
> 7(1)(b) deals with the failure to exhibit the designated mark for the
> equipment,
> 7(1)(c) deals with the breach of any regulations made under the Act.

Sections 8 to 11 create separate offences the most serious being sections 9
and 10 which cover forgery of certificates of compliance and the making of
false statements.

The International Carriage of Foodstuffs Regulations 1985 create a **5–10**
number of offences primarily concerned with the testing and certification of
the equipment. By way of example, regulation 16 requires that the
certification plate shall be affixed in a certain way. Failure to comply with
that regulation would result in a prosecution under section 7(1)(c) for
failure to comply with regulation 16.

PROSECUTION EVIDENCE

These cases are likely to be prosecuted by Trading Standards officers. **5–11**
The regulations are implemented through "Certifying Officers" who are
appointed by the Secretary of State. This will normally be an appointment
which, for enforcement purposes, is an additional power similar to, for
example, the authority given to police officers to weigh vehicles.

Those offences which turn on the failure to display or hold the relevant **5–12**
certificates for the equipment should present no difficulty. However,
sections 9 and 10 are not less serious than any other allegation of forgery or

the making of a false statement, and one would expect the prosecution evidence to be compatible with an allegation of that sort.

5–13   Unfortunately the nature of the work is such that the opportunity to rely on false or forged documents is apparent.

DEFENCES

5–14   In the first instance it is always worth remembering that only an examiner "appointed under the Act" may inspect any transport equipment or premises for the purpose of renforcing this legislation. Whilst it may be something of a "defence by ambush" there is always the possibility that the relevant officer does not have, or did not have, the appropriate authority.

5–15   There are a number of certificates of compliance that are acceptable under the regulations. A certificate in an appropriate form issued by a signatory to the ATP or a member of the E.C. will be sufficient as well as a certificate issued by certain recognised authorities. A certified copy or duplicate of a plate will be sufficient for this purpose. A prosecuting officer may be mistaken as to the validity of a certificate particularly if it is issued out of a country other than the U.K.

5–16   Where the equipment has been altered and the prosecution allege that the alteration was notifiable it will be a question of fact. An operator may be determined that the alteration neither could, nor did, affect the thermal efficiency of the equipment and, if the argument is successful it is a defence to a prosecution on that ground.

5–17   Thermograph records present their own problems. Unlike tachograph records, they are not presently required to be identified to the vehicle and one thermograph record is very like another. (Given the possibility of substantial civil claims for damage or loss of a load as a result of deterioration, there is a great deal to be said for encouraging operators to adopt a system of identification.) However, as with tachograph charts, thermographs require to be "read" and there may be a defence on the grounds of a miss-reading by the enforcement authority in a case which turns on the failure to maintain the correct temperature.

5–18   The prosecution may be brought in the belief that the equipment falls within one type of transport equipment whereas the operator may maintain that, in fact, the equipment is within another category. Ultimately this is a question of fact, but measurements can be critical, and objective and expert measurement may support the defendant.

5–19   It is always possible that there is an error in identifying the appropriate category for the foodstuffs that are being carried. The regulations set out the various types of perishable foods using, inevitably, fairly broad categories. It is always worth looking at the legislation to check whether the right category of foodstuff has been identified by the prosecution and, equally importantly, the correct temperature band.

5–20   Where the allegation is of forgery or falsification of a document or certificate, the usual defences may be available.

Mitigation

Mitigation

There are two possible scenarios for the purpose of mitigation. The first **5–21** is administrative error, the second, mechanical failure or driver error. The failure to re-test a vehicle that already holds a certificate as the result of a failure to make a proper record of the due date for renewal is a familiar story.

It can sometimes be argued that the consignor wrongly identified the **5–22** load so that the operator was simply mistaken as to the nature of the goods that were being carried. The label or description on the packed goods may be misleading. The instructions may have been "faxed" to the operator and a shorthand description might have been used which gave the wrong indications.

The driver may have simply failed to carry out clear instructions that **5–23** were given as to how the load should have been carried. The driver, for his/ her part may be able to show that the goods were carried in accordance with the instructions and that it was the instructions that were wrong.

Thermographs can, of course, go wrong. The regulations require that the **5–24** temperature is checked regularly, but that does not mean that there cannot be a sudden failure. A prompt response to such a failure will clearly be the sort of mitigation that one might hope would give rise to an absolute discharge.

Where the allegation is that a forged certificate or other document such **5–25** as a thermograph record has been used, it may be possible to show that there was a simple mistake and that the right document did exist and that the mistake led to the wrong document being produced.

CHAPTER 6

OVERLOADING

6–01 Overloading is probably the most common offence committed by those who operate commercial vehicles. This reflects the fact that three agencies, the police, the trading standards departments, and the vehicle inspectorate all carry out weight checks on a routine basis. It also reflects the fact that the haulage industry is particularly vulnerable to this offence both because customers carelessly or deliberately misstate the weight of loads and also because certain types of overload, particularly on axles, are effectively undetectable by the operator of the vehicle or the driver.

6–02 The enforcement authorities who could, as a matter of law, prosecute those who cause or permit overloading, habitually confine their attacks to the driver and operator of the vehicle who, given the absolute nature of the offence, may be unable to do more than mitigate. The matter is exacerbated because the spectre of the overloaded "juggernaut" is constantly used by those opposed to the presence of these vehicles on the public roads, and that public anxiety appears, on occasions, to affect the decision of magistrates in relation to penalties.

6–03 It must be not be forgotten that a conviction for overloading must be notified to the relevant traffic commissioner who can respond by removing the licence to operate the vehicle.

6–04 The offence is committed when an axle, or two or three compensating axles, impose a weight that is heavier than that permitted. "Compensating Axles" are axles that are connected in such a way that the weight imposed on them is divided equally between the axles. Theoretically, one compensating axle should never weigh more than the other.

6–05 The offence is committed when the weight of a rigid vehicle, including the towing unit of an articulated combination, exceeds the permitted limit. This is the "Gross" weight.

6–06 The offence is committed when the summated weight of the axles of an articulated vehicle, or a vehicle towing a trailer, exceed the maximum weight for that vehicle. This is the "Train" weight.

6–07 Perhaps surprisingly, overloading is a very technical offence even though it is disclosed by the simple act of weighing the vehicle or axle.

PROSECUTION

6–08 The prosecution of overloaded vehicles and trailers is authorised by section 41B of the RTA 1988. This will be used with either:

     (i) regulation 80 of the C.U. Regs.,

    (ii) regulation 78 of the C.U. Regs.,

  (iii) regulation 77 of the C.U. Regs.

(There are other regulations which might be used, but the circumstances would be unusual. Where, for instance, a vehicle was found to be loaded so heavily in relation to the capability of the vehicle or its suspension and wheel assemblies, it might be possible to prosecute under regulation 100(3) of the C.U. Regs. on the grounds that the use of that vehicle for the load was so unsuitable as to constitute a danger.)

Regulation 80 is the most common route to prosecution. It creates an **6–09** offence when the "plated weight" of the vehicle, trailer, or axle is exceeded. Subject to certain exemptions all commercial vehicles are required to be fitted with a Plate which sets out the maximum that can be imposed by either the vehicle or its axles in the U.K. Initially the vehicle will have a "Manufacturers Plate" (regulation 80(1)(a)), but that will be replaced by a "Ministry Plate" (regulation 80(1)(b)). The weights, in fact, are determined by reference to such things as the axle spacings, the suspension, and the size of the wheels.

Where there is no Plate then regulation 77, and, less commonly, **6–10** regulation 78, may be used. Sometimes, however, regulation 77 is used even though the vehicle is "Plated".

Prosecution Evidence

The police can stop a vehicle and direct it into a weighbridge where they, or **6–11** another enforcement authority, will carry out the weighing. Trading Standards Officers cannot stop a vehicle and will, therefore, rely on the police to perform that duty. They may, however, position themselves at a weighbridge and check vehicles as they arrive to be weighed. On occasions they will go to a weighbridge and examine copy weight tickets retrospectively and prosecute where an apparent offence is disclosed. Subject to those variations in procedure, prosecution evidence will be the same.

When the vehicle is weighed some record of the weight will be produced, **6–12** a copy of which will have been given to the driver. The nature of the initial record may vary slightly depending on the type of weighbridge used, but the driver will normally be given a certificate issued under the RTA 1988 confirming that the recorded weights are accurate. This weight will be compared with the "permitted weights" set out on the plate fixed to the vehicle or trailer. When the plated weight is exceeded, there is likely to be a prosecution, although, nationally, there is a tolerance of 5 per cent unless that tolerance exceeds 1,000 kg. (In some areas a figure of 10 per cent is used, although that is still subject to the 1,000 kg limit.)

There are four types of weighbridge that are used for enforcement **6–13** purposes and it is helpful to understand the differences between them.

The first type is a single metal plate normally set into a concrete **6–14** surround with a concrete run off at each end. These weighbridges may be raised from the surrounding ground level to protect them from dirt and water. The plate length may be as short as 20 ft, although modern bridges tend to be 60 ft to accommodate an articulated vehicle. Typically they will have a digital display combined with the ability to print a ticket recording the weights.

6–15 The second type is a metal plate weighbridge that has been split into three or five independent sections. A bridge of this type will either use all the sections together to produce the Gross or Train weight, or will use the sections independently to record the weight of each axle or group of compensating axles. These types of bridge are normally referred to as "split-plate" weighbridges.

6–16 The third type of weighbridge is a "Dynamic Axle" weighbridge. Here the vehicle is driven at a slow speed across a metal plate which is about 3 ft in width without stopping. The weight of each individual axle is recorded and this will disclose any axle weight offence and, by summating the results, any Gross or Train weight overload.

6–17 The fourth method of weighing, which is used rarely at the moment because of continuing problems with the Code of Practice for its use, is the mobile weigh pad. These pads, which resemble industrial bathroom scales, are placed under each wheel or pair of wheels on a vehicle and the individual readings are taken which are then summated to see whether or not either an axle or a Gross or Train weight offence is disclosed.

6–18 The prosecution will, therefore, adduce the Certificate of Weight as evidence, together with any record of interview that may exist and will, sometimes, give evidence that the vehicle appeared to be overloaded because the tyres were distorted, or the suspension appeared to be entirely compressed, or that the vehicle appeared to be labouring.

6–19 The driver will normally have been asked whether s/he had weighed the vehicle or was going to a weighbridge. S/he may also be asked what instructions had been given about the duty to weigh the vehicle. Sometimes the driver may have consignment notes or similar documents that indicate that the load was too heavy. Experience suggests, however, that such notes will do no more than suggest that the weight of the load should have been legal and will, therefore, raise questions about the recorded weights.

Defences

6–20 In the first instance the prosecution has to show that the vehicle was in the overloaded condition on the public road. Some "private" weighbridges are set at a distance from the highway, and particularly when trading standards officers have collected tickets from a weighbridge rather than seen the vehicle being weighed, it may be possible to argue that there is no persuasive evidence that the vehicle was on the public road in a overloaded condition.

6–21 This argument may be possible wherever the weighbridge is sited if the load can, by reason of its nature, move freely in the vehicle, and the alleged offence relates to axle weights, or is based on the summation of axle weights. Clearly liquids will move, some more freely than others, but so can dry, solid, materials such as sand, grain, coal dust, etc. The act of braking or going up or down an incline may well produce some movement in a load. It has to be remembered that the act of bringing the vehicle to the weighbridge will inevitably involve a number of stop/start manoeuvres each of which may result in some movement of the load.

This movement can only affect the axle weights, but if the offence alleged **6–22** is an "axle weight" offence, or if the Gross or Train overload is based on the summation of the axle weights, then the effect can be significant.

The weighbridge itself may not be accurate. To assure the public of the **6–23** accuracy of weighbridges that are used for enforcement purposes the Department of Transport has issued three Codes of Practice which are generally available (they are also printed as appendices to this work; see at pp. 107, 184, 189 and 195). Two of these relate to "plate" weighbridges, the third deals with "dynamic axle weighers". That relating to "weigh pads" has yet to appear. The requirement is that a weighbridge used by enforcement authorities should be tested at intervals of not more than six months or, if it is used only occasionally, it should be tested as soon as possible after the weighing that has led to the prosecution. All weighbridges have a tolerance. Plate weighbridges will be required to be accurate to not more than ± 30 kg, dynamic bridges to ± 150 kg.

The prosecution will normally produce certificates from the appropriate **6–24** trading standards officer confirming the date of tests that have been carried out in which the accuracy of the bridge is confirmed. The courts have tended to see the six month interval as being critical, and it is always worth checking the dates. There is, however, a curiosity because, if the bridge was tested on, say, May 1, the weighing that led to the prosecution was carried out on July 1, and the case appeared in court on September 1, the test would be good. In the event that the case was not heard until after November 1, and there had been no second test, or the second test is at an interval of more than six months, the bridge would be out of test.

The testing procedure for a dynamic weighbridge is complex and is set **6–25** out in the Code. Three or four different types of vehicle of a known weight are passed 10 times over the bridge, the tenth run being at a speed which is too fast for the bridge to accommodate. The summated weight on each run is compared with the static weight and, if the figure is within the ± 150 kg tolerance, the bridge will be considered to be accurate. These test results, which will normally be produced by the prosecution, are always worth considering. It is not uncommon for a weighbridge to produce results which, although within the permitted tolerance, are always heavy compared with the static weight. Where the defendants vehicle is of a different configuration to, or heavier than, those tested, something may be made of the apparent prejudice.

Examination of the recorded weights of compensating axles during these **6–26** tests may also be worthwhile. It is not uncommon for there to be differences in excess of 1,000 kg between the weights of compensated axles and, if there is no explanation from the Trading Standards Officer who conducted the weighing it may be possible to challenge the accuracy of the test. It is worth noting that one of the reasons for setting the ± 150 kg tolerance was to accommodate some limited variation between compensating axles.

6-27 The level of the surface surrounding the weighbridge plate may be critical if axle weights are to be achieved accurately. Dynamic axle site will be surveyed against the limits established by the Code. Public, and Private, weighbridges used for enforcement purposes may have surrounds that are less than level and, where axle weights are in issue, it is a check that should always be made. Drivers are often well aware of any slope, pothole, or other problem that affects a particular bridge.

6-28 The Codes of Practice also set out the procedure that should be followed when a vehicle is weighed. The normal formula used by a prosecution witness is to say "and the vehicle was weighed in accordance with the Code of Practice". The reality is that the Code is frequently neither followed nor, in fact, well known to the witness. It may well be worth taking the witness through the Code to ascertain whether the Code was followed. A fundamental error, for instance, is to allow the driver to keep the engine running whilst the vehicle is being weighed.

6-29 There are two statutory defences to be found in section 41B(2)(a) of the RTA which provides for a defence where:

1. The vehicle was weighed at the start of the journey and the excess weight found in the enforcement check does not exceed the permitted weight by more than 5 per cent. (This should be distinguished from the "tolerance" of 5 per cent. In the case of the statutory defence it arises if the excess is not more than 5 per cent even if that figures exceeds 1,000 kg.)
2. That the vehicle was on its way to the nearest weighbridge.

Note: In the case of defence 1 it is not clear whether the defence can be maintained if the excess weight of 5 per cent, or less, existed at the point of loading. Given that there is the national tolerance of 5 per cent, and given that all weighbridges are tested to a tolerance rather than to a precise figure, there seems to be no reason why there should not be that same tolerance at the start of the journey. The probable reasons for the statutory tolerance was the recognition that a vehicle which travels into the rain may increase its weight simply because of the weight of the additional water, but there is no such statutory qualification.

6-30 In the case of defence 2 the weighbridge must be the nearest in any direction. Even if, to arrive at the nearest weighbridge, the vehicle has to travel in the opposite direction to that of its intended delivery point, then so be it.

6-31 When a large vehicle is travelling under the provisions of the STGO and the approved route does not allow the vehicle access to a weighbridge this may support a defence on the grounds that the vehicle could not be weighed.

6-32 The final defence arises in the case of axle overloads checked on a dynamic weighbridge where the vehicle is carrying loads of live animals, or loads that swing from hooks inside the vehicle. In these cases movement will affect the result as an axle passes over the beam of the bridge by imparting additional dynamic energy to the vehicle. It is arguably impossible to obtain an accurate axle weight by the use of a dynamic bridge where the load is free to move inside the vehicle.

MITIGATION

The most common ground for mitigation arises when either the consign- **6–33** ment notes that accompany the load, or the information given to the operator or driver, specify the weight in an amount that would be legal.

Modern vehicles have a design capability that is almost always in excess **6–34** of that permitted by the law. The average six axle ("six wheel") articulated vehicle, limited to 38 tonnes in the U.K. will operate at least 44 tonnes if not more. This "design weight" will be shown on the plate, but this weight is, again, the result of a formula, and the real safe weight may be much higher. This means that the driver may be justified in saying that s/he had no indication from the way in which the vehicle performed that it was carrying an illegal weight. Clearly there is an element of objectivity in this; it might be difficult to accept the drivers lack of suspicion if the overload is vast.

This point is particularly important if the driver has no access to the load. **6–35** Some loads present health and safety or, hygiene, problems and the driver is not allowed to have contact with the load. Some loads are sealed into containers, or into the load carrying compartment of the vehicle or trailer, by the consignor and, again, the driver may not interfere with the seal.

Because this is an "easy" mitigation the courts are increasingly looking **6–36** for evidence to confirm that the driver or operator was understandably misled. Where the operator is seeking to put the responsibility for the decision as to whether the load should be weighed or not on to the driver, evidence should be adduced to confirm written or oral instructions and training that may have been given. Ideally evidence of disciplinary action, including dismissal, should be available. A letter of complaint written to the consignor following the discovery of the overload is also useful. Specific problems can occur when the original load is to be delivered to various points. The transfer of weight on a commercial vehicle is not an exact science and the driver may well make a judgment about the weight which is as understandable as it is wrong.

The driver might well be called to give evidence both as to his/her **6–37** experience as a driver and also as to the reasons for the decision to proceed without weighing the load.

There are two things to remember. The first is that parliament did not **6–38** require that no loaded vehicle should proceed onto a public road unless it had been, or was going to be weighed. There is, therefore, no absolute duty to weigh the vehicle. This leaves the driver and operator with a high duty of care which must be less than the absolute duty and courts should be encouraged not to see the offence as "absolute" when considering the penalty.

The second point to remember is that there are very few "public" axle **6–39** weighbridges across the country. As we have seen, obtaining accurate axle weights is a difficult exercise unless an axle bridge is used, and, where the axle overload is not excessive having regard to the real capability of the axle(s) in question, the point may well assist mitigation.

CONSULTANT ENGINEER'S COMMENTS

6–40 It may be unsafe to weigh a load which has its own dynamic on a dynamic weighbridge. A particular example would be in the case of a vehicle carrying a liquid load which can move in the container with comparative freedom. The viscosity of the load and the way in which the tank on the vehicle is baffled may be relevant factors, but a weighing of this sort should always be questioned. Similar problems may arise when a hanging load, such as clothes or meat, can move within the vehicle.

6–41 Passenger vehicle operators need to remember that, on a trip to a french hypermarket, for instance, the "luggage" acquired by their returning passengers may cause weight problems which did not exist at the outset of the journey.

6–42 A consulting engineer asked to express a view about an overloading case depends on the quality of the information that is available about the circumstances of the weighing. Drivers should be trained to understand the weighing process and the faults that can arise and, in particular, should understand when it is right to draw the enforcement officers attention to factors that might affect the accuracy of the weight. An example of this would be where the driver feels that braking in the course of a journey, or climbing and descending hills, may have caused the load to shift within the body of the vehicle. Some loads such as dry sand or ash are particularly prone to this effect.

CHAPTER 7

DANGEROUS SUBSTANCES

Given the enormous range of substances of all sorts that can be described **7–01** as dangerous, and the public concern that these substances should not be brought into contact with the public if at all possible, it is not surprising that the relevant legislation is extremely complex. In the first instance the nature of the substance has to be determined, and then, if it is identified as dangerous, the extent of that danger having regard, amongst other things, to the amount that is to be transported. It then has to be determined if the method by which this dangerous substance is to be transported provides adequate safety.

The advocate needs to have access to the European Agreement for the **7–02** International Carriage of Dangerous Goods by Road 1968, more shortly known as ADR (Accord Dangereux Routiers). As this is an agreement, it has no legal force in the U.K., but is incorporated in the relevant U.K. legislation of which there is a great deal. (The Road Traffic (Carriage of Dangerous Substances in Packages etc.) Regulations 1992; the Road Traffic (Carriage of Dangerous Substances in Road Tankers and Tank Containers) Regulations 1992; the International Carriage of Dangerous Goods (Rear Marking of Motor Vehicles) Regulations 1975, and the Carriage of Dangerous Goods by Road and Rail (Classification, Packaging and Labelling) Regulations 1994 [the 1994 Regs.] are the most relevant. Drivers are also affected by the Road Traffic (Training of Drivers of Vehicles Carrying Dangerous Goods) Regulations 1992).

The E.U. is conscious of the fact that there is this plethora of domestic **7–03** legislation throughout the Community and it is hoped that a harmonising directive, which will cover domestic as well as E.C. traffic, will be available in early 1997 which will then need to be incorporated by Parliament into the U.K. legislation.

It must, however, be remembered that certain substances attract their **7–04** own regulations. Corrosive Substances, Carbon Disulphide, Organic Peroxides, and Inflammable Liquids, being a sample of such separately controlled products. There should be no difficulty in identifying such a substance in the light of the requirements of Annex A to ADR which, with other legislation, requires dangerous products to be identified as being dangerous by the producer or consignor. As a general rule the product information should always be obtained from the client before attempting to find one's way through the maze of legislation. So much depends on a correct identification of the substance which, in the light of the Chemicals (Hazard

Information and Packaging for Supply) Regulations 1994 (known as CHIP 2) is now required to be described both accurately and in detail. The latest version of CHIP, CHIP 97, which must be complied with by May 31, 1998, seeks to deal with the anomalies of categorisation in the earlier versions.

7–05 Although ADR must always be the theoretical starting point for any examination of the carriage of dangerous goods it is merely a European agreement forming a contract between those countries which are signatories. The U.K. is a signatory and has incorporated all the relevant parts of the ADR into the various pieces of legislation. The advocate will find, however, that there is a direct reference to the ADR in the various regulations, particularly when certificates are required.

7–06 ADR estabishes four main areas of obligation. Vehicles and tank containers must be suitable and tested by a designated inspecting organisation and have fire extinguishers, tool kits and at least one "chock" for use as an emergency brake; the vehicles must carry appropriate markings; the driver must be trained and have with him/her a "tremcard" (traffic emergency card) identifying the product in writing with information on the nature of the load and details of emergency contacts; and the vehicle must be parked "safely" (this, in practice, means as far away from the public as is possible).

7–07 Dangerous substances are defined in the 1994 Regulations at regulation 2 and Schedule 1. Schedule 1 also establishes the appropriate visual indicator for the product to which must be added the appropriate "code". This is an area of astonishing complexity and it will be an unusual advocate who is equipped to cope with the complex chemical substances. Happily prosecutions normally follow alleged failures of duty and only rarely will the argument turn on the nature of the product when, no doubt, the services of an industrial chemist or explosives expert will be required.

7–08 Prosecutions for breaches of these regulations are becoming increasingly frequent due to an increased expertise on the part of the enforcement authorities combined with an increasing awareness of the problems that can arise. Drivers are found who are driving without the appropriate certificate to show that they have been trained, the wrong markings are displayed or there are no marker boards, items of equipment, such as fire extinguishers or tremcards, are missing, a greater amount of a prescribed substance is being carried than is allowed under the regulations, or the vehicle or tank container has not been tested for suitability. A carrier who is prepared to undertake work of this sort without trained drivers or suitable vehicles is at a commercial advantage. A vehicle that is unmarked may, for instance, be allowed to go through a tunnel when, if the real nature of the load were disclosed, the transit would be forbidden. A prosecution under these regulations is potentially very serious and, inevitably, is clouded by the obvious emotional overtones resulting from the possible results of a disaster which is frequently contemplated by the prosecution. Before advising on a case of this sort the defence advocate needs to be satisfied both that s/he understands the real nature of the offence and that s/he can, when putting the matter to the court, put the offence fairly in the context of reality. This is particularly important in the light of the substantial duty of care placed on the carrier by the various regulations.

PROSECUTION

These regulations all derive from orders made under section 15(1) of the **7–09** Health and Safety at Work etc. Act 1974. Prosecutions are, therefore, brought under section 33(c) of that Act in conjunction with the appropriate regulation.

It would be impossible to list every available offence given the complexity **7–10** of the regulations. Therefore, by way of example only:

— Road Traffic (Carriage of Dangerous Substances in Packages etc.) Regulations 1992,

regulation 7(1) (operator fails to ensure that the driver has "adequate information" about the — 7(1)(a), identity of the substance; 7(1)(b) quantity to be carried; 7(1)(c) the nature of the hazards created by the substance and the action to be taken in an emergency concerning it).

regulation 10(1) (operator fails to ensure that, on a vehicle carrying a dangerous substance, there is adequate fire-fighting equipment).

— Road Traffic (Carriage of Dangerous Substances in Road Tankers and Tank Containers) Regulations 1992,

regulation 16(1) (driver of a road tanker fails to ensure that all openings or discharge valve are properly secured).

regulation 19(1) (operator or, 19(2), driver fails to ensure that hazard warning panels are properly displayed).

— Road Traffic (Training of Drivers of Vehicles Carrying Dangerous Goods) Regulations 1992,

regulation 4 (operator fails to ensure that the driver has received adequate training).

regulation 10(1) (driver fails to produce to police officer or goods vehicle examiner a relevant certificate).

PROSECUTION EVIDENCE

It will be clear that the prosecution evidence must be precise in relation to **7–11** the offence which has been charged. Effectively all the potential offences turn on the carriage of a hazardous substance and the substance must, therefore, be identified as a hazardous substance. In those cases where the offence depends on the quantity carried then, of course, the quantity must also be established. Some of the offences appear to be simple issues of fact. The failure to carry fire-fighting equipment for instance is a simple "did s/he, or didn't s/he" question, but, of course, if the load does not require extinguishers to be carried there is no offence.

Prosecution Witnesses
The police, Vehicle Inspectorate, and Health and Safety Officers (who may **7–12** be Trading Standards Officers) may all prosecute but some regulations restrict those who may lay information in respect of particular offences.

7–13   Regulation 10(1) of the Road Vehicles (Training of Drivers etc.) Regulations 1992 permits prosecution by either the police or a Goods Vehicle Examiner and no one else.

Defences

7–14 There will always be a defence if the nature or amount of the substances has been wrongly identified. The opportunity for error is wider than one might imagine, for instance the categorisation of explosives is not easy, and, although a court may be alarmed by the apparent failure to adequately protect explosives in transit, expert evidence may suggest that the substance was harmless in the form and manner in which it was being carried.

7–15   Equally the regulations themselves present problems to a prosecutor. The opportunity to prosecute under the wrong regulation, or for the wrong offence is enormous and the charge should always be checked against the legislation. Sometimes the picture painted by the prosecution of some potential cataclysm is far from the reality but courts will be affected by the contemplation of disaster and, given the substantial penalties that may be available the defence advocate should leave "no stone unturned". The emotional overtones which can always affect these cases, particularly if the prosecution paints a picture of wide scale destruction, can be diluted by calling expert evidence even when the circumstances of the case might not point to the need to use an expert.

7–16   Many of the regulations do include the potential for a defence based on the argument that it was not "reasonably practicable" to avoid the commission of the offence. This defence is, however, less than easy. Section 40 of the Health and Safety at Work etc. Act 1974 places the burden of proof squarely on the defendant. The question as to what was meant by the phrase "so far as is reasonably practicable" was considered in the case of *Martin v. Boulton and Paul (Steel Construction) Ltd* [1988] I.C.R. 366. The test is not simply whether steps were physically or financially possible, the degree of risk has to be considered against the sacrifice that would have to be made. The problem with this is that the test leaves the matter as a subjective issue for the court and, as has already been seen, there is room in these cases for some emotional reaction.

7–17   Depending on the gravity of the matter, thought should always be given to the use of an "expert". Quite apart from the other reasons already considered, it is particularly important that the advocate should be confident in his or her knowledge of the product and the attached risks. This is particularly true when complex chemical products are in issue. Subtle changes in the make-up of a product can have a significant effect on the hazardous nature of a product, but the court may well need expert evidence to understand the case.

7–18   Intervention by a third party may provide a defence in very limited circumstances. Section 36 of the Health and Safety at Work etc. Act contemplates third party fault but, if that is to be a defence, it must be established by the relevant regulation.

CONSULTANT ENGINEER'S COMMENT

MITIGATION

The most obvious mitigation arises if the substance has been miss-described 7–19 either as to its nature or as to its quantity. Markings may have been lost in the course of a journey. Items such as fire extinguishers may be stolen.

In cases of this sort there can be a substantial difference between the 7–20 position of the operator and that of the driver. The driver must be trained and carry the appropriate certificate. This imposes a high degree of care on the driver, as was the intention, but conversely, protects the employer to a degree if the error or mistake should have been seen by the driver. The driver is trained to understand hazard markings and has a duty to inspect the load before it is carried. Driver failure may, therefore, be an effective mitigation.

Intervention by a third party may also be first class mitigation. The 7–21 prosecution have a discretion, in most cases, to prosecute both the third party and also the "innocent" carrier. One would hope that, in a case of that sort, the carrier who was caught as the result of the act of a third party would be given an absolute discharge.

The driver may simply have failed to carry out his duties in the required 7–22 manner. Commonly drivers forget to collect or change the "tremcard" that they are required to carry even when the correct card is available. Commonly drivers display Hazard Warning Panels that are less than legible as the result of frequent use, even when clear panels are available.

Mitigation in these cases is particularly difficult, but of enormous 2–23 importance to the client. As with any technical mitigation the advocate must be comfortable with the argument that is being advanced to the court and that requires an understanding of the background to the case. The advocate's confidence will communicate itself to the court and, in cases where there is, in the mind of the court, a real concern as a result of the incident or for the possibility of danger, this can make a very significant difference to the result.

CONSULTANT ENGINEER'S COMMENTS

The Petroleum, Chemical, and Explosives industries have an enviable 7–24 record of safety which reflects the very high levels of training that are provided in every sector of these industries.

Cases in which there has been a failure to comply with the regulations or 7–25 an accident are almost always the result of carelessness or negligence. The two major enforcement agencies in this field may be expected to display expert knowledge. They are the Health and Safety Executive and the Environment Agency.

The greater number of prosecutions of this type of offence arise where 7–26 mixed loads are carried. Operators who specialise in bringing together loads for one destination (groupage) are particularly vulnerable to prosecution. Although it may appear that there was negligence on the part of the driver or loader, there is room for error in both the description of the load and the markings.

7–27   Although these cases are absolute in nature, careful investigation of the circumstances may result in a substantial opportunity to mitigate the offence.

CHAPTER 8

DANGEROUS VEHICLES

Commercial vehicles and passenger vehicles are not often found to have **8–01**
parts with jagged metal edges, the normal situation in which the owner of a
car is prosecuted for having a vehicle in a dangerous condition. Commercial
vehicles and coaches can be dangerous if they are substantially overloaded,
have tyres inflated to the wrong pressure or which are being run at the
wrong speed, or have brakes, steering mechanisms, or other systems that
are substantially out of adjustment. These cases are, of course, extremely
serious, and present difficulties because the decision to prosecute is usually
based on a subjective view. In a case involving tyres every effort should be
made to ensure that the tyres are identified and kept. One situation which
does give rise to prosecutions of this sort is where the vehicle or coach is on
a road which is unsuitable for the vehicle, usually as a result of its height,
width or weight. Some prosecuting authorities appear to consider that this
is an easier route to conviction possibly reflecting the subjective nature of
the allegation.

PROSECUTION

These cases were usually prosecuted under regulation 100(3) of the C.U. **8–02**
Regs. This provides that "no motor vehicle or trailer shall be used for any
purpose for which it is so unsuitable as to cause or be likely to cause danger
or nuisance to any person in or on the vehicle or trailer or on the road".
Whilst that route is still available to the prosecution they may now choose
to prosecute under section 40A of the Road Traffic Act 1988. Section
40A(a) creates an offence if the "condition of the motor vehicle or trailer,
or its accessories or equipment is such that the use of the motor vehicle or
trailer involves a danger of injury to any person".

PROSECUTION EVIDENCE

There is no real technical problem with a prosecution under this regulation **8–03**
so far as the prosecuting authorities are concerned. The case will normally
be brought by the police. The grounds should be clear from the summons,
and will suggest that, by reason of excess weight or dimensions, or some
inadequacy of system, the vehicle was dangerous. To send a high vehicle,

say a double-decker bus, down a road with a low bridge would create the offence, so far as that vehicle would be concerned. To load a vehicle beyond its capability, or to run a vehicle with one of its systems so damaged or inadequate as to make the use of the vehicle dangerous would amount to an offence. It might be seen, for instance, as being appropriate to use this regulation to prosecute for a defective braking system if there was a problem with the formal evidence that would normally support a prosecution of that sort. A prosecution under this regulation might be brought where a vehicle was considered to be dangerously overloaded if there was a technical problem with the evidence of weight. To run a vehicle at a speed or weight beyond the rating of the tyres would also support a prosecution. To run a vehicle carrying inflammable substances without the appropriate safety systems would also create the offence. Tyres that are under-inflated may become excessively hot with the danger of a "blow-out", as may the tyres on twin wheels that touch the side-walls because of excess weight on the vehicle. A coach that is overloaded, or which has loose seats, or locked or obstructed emergency exits may also attract a prosecution under this regulation. A prosecution may also be brought if it is considered that the vehicle is unsuitable for the load that is being carried by reasons of, say, the dimensions of the load. A load with a high centre of gravity, for instance, may be unsafe on a goods vehicle with the load bearing platform at the normal level.

DEFENCES

8–04 The first question to be asked is whether or not the identification of the "danger" by the prosecution is justified. It is correct to say that, for instance, tyres on twin wheels that touch may become hot with the result that one or both of the tyres will "blow-out". This possibility depends on the length of the journey, the weather conditions and the speed of the vehicle. On a comparatively short journey on a cool day in an urban environment there is arguably no danger.

8–05 The prosecution may suggest that the vehicle was loaded to a dangerous level by comparing the weight of the vehicle on the occasion of the offence with the "plated" weight. The design weight of the vehicle, however, is likely to be higher than the permitted weight in the U.K., and a comparison of the weight with that design weight may well produce a much less alarming result. It is equally true that tyre manufacturers are likely to have built in a margin of safety when rating the tyres for speed and weight and, where the allegation relates to danger resulting from the over stressing of the tyres, it is always worth asking the manufacturers for a view.

8–06 On an inspection of a vehicle it may be found that one or more of the leaves in a spring were found to be broken with the result that, in the mind of the prosecution, there was imminent danger. Again, whilst it is true that a broken spring may be dangerous, the fracture of one or more springs does not necessarily constitute a dangerous condition. Many mechanical commercial suspensions, as opposed to air suspension systems, incorporate up to three main leaves, and the fracture of one of these may well be accommodated by the system. The guide issued to vehicle examiners suggests that, where a number of intermediate leaves are broken, the position may be dealt with by a delayed prohibition. This interpretation makes it clear that there is no immediate danger in that case.

Where the vehicle is inspected off the public road there may well be an **8–07** argument that the condition may not have existed whilst the vehicle was on the public road. Equally, if the driver stops the vehicle as soon as the fault becomes apparent, thereby avoiding any danger, it would be difficult for the prosecution to argue that there was a likelihood of danger.

There is a particular problem with a prosecution under section 40A. This **8–08** section contemplates an offence either as the result of the use of a motor vehicle, or of the use of a trailer or of the equipment. The prosecution must correctly identify the "target". Should the summons allege an offence following the use of a motor vehicle when, in fact, it was the trailer that was at fault, the case should be dismissed. Whilst there may be an application to amend it is certainly arguable that a new information is being laid which, if it is out of time in relation to the offence, should not be permitted.

MITIGATION

As with many problems encountered in the operation of commercial or **8–09** passenger vehicles, dangerous situations can arise in the course of a journey. Mitigation can result in an absolute discharge if there is evidence available of a good system of maintenance at appropriate intervals, supported by a system enabling the driver to report any defects. Ideally there will be evidence of driver training, together with evidence of disciplinary action, if there is driver or fitter error.

In serious cases it may be useful to call expert evidence to confirm that **8–10** the fault might arise without the operator or driver being culpable. In some cases involving problems with the load or route, the drivers subjective judgment may not be unreasonable, even if the result was dangerous. Equally a driver may decide to continue a journey with a faulty vehicle believing that the length of the journey or the chosen speed would avoid any danger.

In these cases it is important to try to ensure that the court understand **8–11** the reality of the problem. It is only too easy for the court to see only the potential for serious injury or fatality if the prosecution choose to describe a scenario in which injury is the inevitable result. The "if there had been a stationary car . . ." approach is used all too often in cases in which there neither was a stationary car nor was it likely that there would be one.

CONSULTANT ENGINEER'S COMMENTS

A defect in any part that is relevant to the safety of a vehicle can result in a **8–12** prosecution for using a dangerous vehicle. A fractured leaf spring or loose wheel nuts may, for example, be deemed to constitute a dangerous vehicle.

Issues of this sort are particularly appropriate for a consulting engineer. It should be remembered that there is a substantial difference between a failure that has resulted from a long standing condition, suggesting a failure of the maintenance system, and a failure that has occurred perhaps in the course of the journey during which the failure became apparent.

8–13   Certain defects may be the result of design error or a part failure. By way of example there were a series of cases in which the "prop-shaft flange coupling" became loose at the gearbox because the retaining nuts were defective. This result in a "Recall Notice" being sent out. In cases where there may be a similar explanation, the chassis number of the vehicle should be obtained and a search made with the Vehicle Inspectorate to ascertain whether or not a "Recall Notice" has been issued.

CHAPTER 9

LENGTH AND WIDTH

Although there are basic dimensions to be found in the C.U. Regs., the **9–01** variety of vehicles and vehicle combinations produces some variation in the relevant maximum measurements. It also produces complex regulations that provide opportunities for errors to be made, both by the operators of vehicles and by the various prosecuting authorities although it is unusual for errors to be made when considering the dimensions of a vehicle or trailer. The main problems arise when the excess length or width is caused by the dimensions of the load. It is, therefore, important to correctly identify the category of vehicle that is the subject of any proceedings before making any decision about the appropriate course of action. Where the legal maximum appears to have been substantially exceeded, the vehicle may be moving under the Motor Vehicles (Authorisation of Special Types) General Order 1979 (STGO) when different criteria apply.

Accurate measurement is essential. There is no discretion available, the **9–02** offence either is, or is not, committed.

PROSECUTION

The prosecution must be brought under section 42 of the RTA 1988, the **9–03** regulations having been made under section 41(2)(a).

Regulation 7 of the C.U. Regs. deals with excess length of the vehicle. A **9–04** table appended to regulation 7(1) divides vehicles and trailers into 13 categories setting out the appropriate maximum length in each case. The maximum length for a commercial vehicle is 18 m (draw bar combination). The longest passenger vehicle being 18.35 m (articulated bus).

Regulation 8 of the C.U. Regs. deals with excess width of the vehicle. A **9–05** table appended to regulation 8(1) contemplates eight categories of vehicle although the width that is generally applicable is 2.55 m. Refrigerated vehicles may be 2.60 m wide to accommodate the necessary insulation.

Regulations 81 and 82 of the C.U. Regs. deal with loads that are longer **9–06** or wider than the vehicle on which they are being carried. (Regulations 81 and 82 need to be read with Schedule 12 of the C.U. Regs.).

The summons will normally include a reference to the dimension which is **9–07** alleged to have been exceeded, even if the precise sub-section is not mentioned. There may be a reference to the alleged failure to comply with Schedule 12 suggesting, for instance, that marker boards were omitted or that there was no attendant.

9–08 Because these offences depend, in the main, on measurement, there will be evidence of the dimension of the vehicle or its load. In some cases the amount of any overhang may be critical. When the case turns on the dimensions of the load, however, evidence may additionally be given that the requirements of Schedule 12 of the C.U. Regs. have not been complied with, and that, therefore, the movement of a vehicle and load that would otherwise have been legal under the provisions of regulations 81 and 82, was, in fact, unlawful. Schedule 12 is a very complex schedule but its main requirements are:

> (i) Advance notice to the police.
>
> (ii) The need to have an attendant.
>
> (iii) The need to mark projections.

9–09 Regulation 82(7) sets out the circumstances in which requirements of Schedule 12 have to be met by the use of a table appended to regulation 82(7) and the prosecution will have to show that they have correctly identified that part of the schedule which has not been met by relating the schedule to the measurements on which they rely.

9–10 The case for the prosecution may well depend, therefore, not on a complaint that the vehicle/load was too long or too wide, but on a complaint that the marker boards were not of the required dimensions or in the required form, and photographs may be adduced to support the complaint. It may be alleged that the attendant was unsuitable or that there had been no advance notice to the police.

9–11 Where a prosecution is based on an allegation that the vehicle, with or without its load, is too long or too wide the summons is frequently wrong. Both regulation 7 and 8 incorporate tables which establish different criteria for different types and combinations of vehicles and trailers, and it is important to establish whether or not the defendant's vehicle has been correctly identified in the table in addition to checking that the right section and regulation have been used.

9–12 The position is doubly complicated when it is the dimensions of the load that have led to the prosecution. Regulation 81 is effectively an explanatory regulation which supports regulation 82, but it, in turn, must be read with the definitions of "overall length", "overall width", and "overhang", contained in regulation 3 of the C.U. Regs. Not only are the points between which measurements may be taken defined with great clarity, but there are a number of items which are not to be incorporated in any measurement. Possibly the most surprising of these exceptions being the wing mirrors ("driving mirrors") which are not to be included in any measurement of width.

9–13 The legislation treats measurement as being a precise science; the prosecution rarely do. It is common for measurements to be taken

44

pragmatically by hooking or holding one end of a tape measure to some part of the vehicle or load, and then reading the distance at the other end of the tape. Looking at regulation 81(b) by way of example it provides that "the width of any lateral projection shall be measured between longitudinal planes passing through the extreme projecting point of the vehicle on that side on which the projection lies and that part of the projection furthest from that point". Add to that the requirement in regulation 3(2)(h) that any sheeting or other readily flexible means of covering or securing a load shall be excluded and the difficulties faced by the prosecution become apparent.

The driver of the vehicle should be asked to give as much information as **9–14** possible about the way in which the measuring was done. Frequently, although two officers are involved in the check, only one will appear in court and it may not be the one who was at the "working" end of the tape. In the event that the officer giving the evidence did hold that part of the tape which indicated the distance, it may be possible to query the position of the person at the other end of the tape. When measuring the length of the vehicle it is critical that the vehicle be in a straight line. The regulations offer no discretion (regulation 81(e)).

Overhangs cause even greater problems for the prosecution. Not only is **9–15** an overhang likely to be more difficult to measure, but, again, the regulations establish very precise criteria. Regulation 81(h)(i) refers specifically to the definitions in regulation 3(2). The point is that, whatever the magnitude of the alleged excess measurement may or may not be, the court should not be allowed to exercise a discretion which the law does not contemplate. The evidence of the measurement should be precise beyond doubt: in the event that the measurements were obtained outwith the statutory provisions, the court should be asked to reject the prosecution's case. It should be remembered that when a vehicle that may be 18 m long is being measured, a slight deviation from a straight line may have a dramatic effect on the recorded length. It is, for this reason, effectively impossible to measure accurately the length of an articulated or draw-bar vehicle parked on a bend, however slight.

Schedule 12, Pt. 1, para. 2 deals with the need to have an attendant on **9–16** the vehicle in certain circumstances. This "attendant" is not a "second man". There is no age criteria, the test is one of competence and there is no reason why a teenager should not act as an attendant if s/he has sufficient experience. The prosecution have been known to base a case on the proposition that the attendant should be the holder of a relevant driving licence.

Schedule 12, pt. 1, para. 1(a) deals with the giving of notice to the police **9–17** and the information that should be contained in the notice. It also confirms that the police have a wide discretion in relation to both the timing and detail of the notice. In court, it is important that any complaint about the notice, or the absence of a notice, is given by the appropriate officer, who will normally be the "abnormal loads" officer. Evidence from other officers will inevitably be hearsay.

9–18   Schedule 12, Pt. 1, paras 3 and 4, deal with the dimensions and placement of end and side markers and the circumstances in which they are required. Yet again this is a very technical regulation and the prosecution may fall into error.

MITIGATION

9–19 The difficulties faced by the prosecution are substantially less than those faced by the operator and the driver of the vehicle. Whilst ignorance of the law can be no defence, ignorance of regulations of this complexity is effectively universal. Even when the law is understood, the operator and driver may have to rely on information from the consignor, who may not be as precise in measurement as the law requires.

9–20   It is, of course, the driver who is at the front line and who has to make a decision about the amount of overhang or the length of the vehicle and load, and s/he may simply not have the opportunity to measure the load accurately. A subjective decision that leads to a minor breach of the law might well allow an absolute discharge to be sought.

9–21   Commonly drivers elect to proceed without markers. Usually one of three explanations is offered. The first is that the consignor gave no indication that the load was oversize, and the driver formed the subjective view that the load was legal as it was. The second is that, whilst the markers were available the driver simply did not bother to fix them. This is, of course, of no assistance to the driver, but may get the operator an absolute discharge. The third is that there were no markers available and the driver marked the load by means other than those contemplated in Schedule 12, or simply elected to travel without markers.

9–22   A great deal will depend on the information that was, or should have been, available to the driver and operator, and how valid was the subjective decision of (usually) the driver.

9–23   It should be remembered that the failure to mark long or wide loads is, potentially, very dangerous. Mitigation needs to be handled with care.

CHAPTER 10

WHEELS

When a wheel, or pair of wheels, leave a moving vehicle, they accelerate **10–01** away and develop a great deal of energy. Severe injuries and damage can result; fatal accidents are not uncommon. Unfortunately, notwithstanding the increasing technology of commercial vehicles, wheels do still become detached, particularly those on the near side of the vehicle.

There are four main causes of wheel loss: human error, forces created by **10–02** the movement of the vehicle, failure of the studs, and dirt trapped between adjacent metal surfaces.

The offence is absolute and there are minimal opportunities to defend a **10–03** summons based on wheel loss.

PROSECUTION

Wheel loss will be prosecuted under the RTA 1988. There are two sections **10–04** available to the prosecutor.
  (i)   section 40A,
  (ii) section 42, which authorises prosecution where there has been a
        failure to comply with regulation 100(1).
It is self-evident that a wheel which has come off, or which is loose, is not in good and efficient working order and, subject to the one technical issue that will be discussed, it is inevitable that a plea of "guilty" will be entered.

PROSECUTION EVIDENCE

Vehicle Inspector
A Vehicle Inspector may give evidence that it was discovered, in the course **10–05** of a check, that one or more of the wheel nuts were loose. It would be unusual for a Vehicle Inspector to be first on the scene following a wheel loss, although the police might well seek assistance if they felt that technical expertise was required.

Police
A police officer may choose to give non-expert evidence of the condition of **10–06** the wheels where there has been a loss. When an officer arrives at the scene of an incident and the vehicle is found to have wheels, or a wheel, missing,

s/he may simply elect to rely on that evidence. Where the incident is serious or, for other reasons, the officer feels in need of technical support, the Vehicle Inspectorate, or a qualified police officer, or civilian aide may be brought in.

10–07   Evidence is likely to be directed to the condition of the nuts, studs, or the holes in the wheel centre through which the studs pass. The prosecution will suggest that the greater the wear to the thread on the studs, the longer the fault has been in existence. This argument will be particularly strong if the holes in the wheel centre are significantly enlarged. In many cases photographs will be taken, and the studs and nuts retained.

10–08   Wheel loss can also occur if there is a failure on the axle or in the brake drum assembly.

DEFENCE

10–09 There will rarely be an available defence. Probably the only possible ground will arise when the summons is wrongly worded. The summons might suggest that the nuts had been inadequately tightened when the factual evidence is to the effect that the bearing assembly collapsed. Rarely the wrong section may be used.

MITIGATION

10–10 In many cases of wheel loss it is possible to look to the court for an absolute discharge.

10–11   Human error is still the most likely cause of wheel loss but the daily inspection of the wheels by the driver is a standard requirement. Where an employer can show that the driver was properly instructed and had the opportunity to inspect the wheels, it may be appropriate to ask the court for a discharge. Where the driver insists that the wheels were inspected prior to the journey and saw no fault, other explanations should be considered.

10–12   In the case of twin wheels, it is possible for a small particle of dirt to be trapped between the flat metal surfaces and, in the course of a journey, that particle may break down, with the result that the tension on the nut is minimally reduced, allowing movement to generate. Enquiries should be made to ascertain when the wheels last needed attention. Conversely, once a wheel has been removed, to repair a puncture for instance, the nuts do need to be checked for tension after a short time, and one should have evidence that that was done.

10–13   The nuts can stretch. Constant applications of a torque wrench can cause metal fatigue which, in turn, can allow a nut and stud, that appear to be adequately tightened, to loosen and this can happen in the course of a journey.

10–14   Deterioration of the stud and elongation of the hole in the wheel centre can happen in a remarkably short period of time. The driver may well be accurate when s/he confirms that the wheels appeared to be in good order before the journey began.

The maintenance records for the vehicle should be available with any **10–15** separate records of wheel checks if there are separate inspections by an independent tyre company.

The Institute of Road Transport Engineers have long recognised the **10–16** "Lost Wheels Mystery" and have now published a long report detailing the various causes of wheel loss. It is particularly a matter in which the evidence of a consulting engineer may be both relevant and helpful.

Wheel loss is particularly an issue of "moral blame" and it will often be **10–17** possible to seek an absolute discharge following the *Hart v. Bex* ([1957] Crim.L.R. 622, DC) line of decisions.

CONSULTANT ENGINEER'S COMMENTS

It is a matter of fact that a set of wheel nuts on a wheel can be tightened to **10–18** the correct torque, the vehicle may then not move and, half an hour later, one or two of the nuts will have slackened to a slight extent. The problem of wheel security needs to be seen against this background.

The daily checks that drivers are expected to carry out should never be **10–19** seen as a cosmetic exercise. Drivers should be trained to carry out those checks and, in the contest of a discussion on wheel security, trained to recognise the signs that suggest that wheel nuts may be loose.

In many cases where the loss of wheels has been investigated it has been **10–20** found that, due to the presence of some foreign material, such as paint rust or dirt, the mating surfaces between twin wheels has been contaminated with the result that the clamping force has been lost. Most specialist tyre companies, having changed, or repaired, tyres, leave a note in the cab confirming that work has been carried out and reminding the driver to check the torque after no more than 50 km of movement.

CHAPTER 11

TYRES

11–01 The technology of tyres is constantly changing. The construction and tread pattern of a tyre can affect the fuel consumption of a vehicle, the specification of that part of the tyre which carries the tread pattern clearly affects the likely life of the tyre, but also affects the performance of the tyre in different work conditions. The composition of the material out of which the tyre is made is constantly changing.

11–02 To give adequate advice to someone who faces prosecution for a tyre offence it is helpful to have some understanding of the way in which a tyre is made. The modern commercial tyre has a "body" which is a smooth round form of some rubber compound which is braced and strengthened by "body cords" which lie just under the rubber compound and which determine the shape of the tyre when it is inflated, and also determine the strength of the tyre to withstand distortion when the tyre is in use.

11–03 On to this "body" is placed a thick band of a different rubber compound into which the tread pattern is cut. This bond between the "body" and the tread compound will normally be achieved by some form of heat process. The fact that this bond can fail, although not commonly, is all too apparent if one drives along the roads of this country when the tread bearing portion of commercial tyres may be seen at the edge of roads following separation. On the other hand it has to be remembered that the tyres on a single axle may have to bear loads in excess of 20 tonnes as a result of the hammer effect of the wheels of a loaded vehicle passing over a bump in the road surface.

11–04 To protect the weaker "body" of the tyre from road shocks, there will normally be a series of mesh bands, usually between five and seven in number, in the middle of that part of the tyre in which the tread is cut. These bands will be stacked one on top of the other with a thin layer of compound between each layer. The mesh will be made of either nylon, or, perhaps more commonly, metal. The strips are called either breaker strips or shock strips.

11–05 Commercial tyres usually have sufficient depth in the tread compound to enable a new tread pattern to be cut into the tyre once the original pattern has been worn to the legal limit. Some method of determining when this point has been reached will have been built into the tyre. The manufacturer will issue a book which demonstrates the appropriate pattern for the re-cut. Re-cutting can be done in any workshop by using a simple hand tool, but is also done by specialised tyre suppliers. Remoulding is a different process in which that part of the tyre that carries the tread is replaced.

There are specific circumstances in which commercial vehicles and **11–06** trailers are used which may result in tyre damage, and, where the complaint arises as a result of damage, rather than wear, it is always worth making some enquiry. Wear will normally affect the whole of that part of the tyre which is in contact with the road. Damage will normally affect only a small part of the tyre surface or the walls of the tyre.

Damage may result from sharp objects on a site, particularly when **11–07** chunks of the tread surface have been removed or when there are cuts on the tyre surface, or in the wall. A patch on the tyre surface may also be worn by sudden and fierce braking, particularly when the vehicle is unladen, or by, say, an intermittent failure of the ABS system. Commonly trailer tyres may be damaged if the trailer is rotated on the spot. This is a common problem when trailers are put onto ferries by vehicles owned by the ferry company which are used to manoeuvre trailers.

"Blow outs" and bulges in the tyre wall are nearly always sudden, rather **11–08** than long term failures.

Anyone faced with a prosecution for a tyre offence should be urged to **11–09** keep the tyre so that it can be examined by an expert, if that seems to be necessary. The tyre should be identified before it is removed from the vehicle, preferrably marked with tyre chalk, and then kept in a safe place.

Because of the technical progress achieved by the manufacturers the **11–10** C.U. Regs. have never been entirely up to date. It can be argued that some new tyres do not meet the criteria set out in regulation 27, particularly in relation to the application of regulation 27(1)(g).

Prosecution

Proceedings will normally be brought under section 41 of the RTA 1988 **11–11** with regulation 27. This is a complex regulation running to six sub-sections. Regulation 27(1) deals with the various defects giving rise to a prosecution and it is worth setting it out in full:

> 27.—(1) Save as provided in paragraphs (2), (3) and (4), a wheeled motor vehicle or trailer a wheel of which is fitted with a pneumatic tyre shall not be used on a road, if —
>
> (a) the tyre is unsuitable having regard to the use to which the motor vehicle or trailer is being put or to the types of tyres fitted to its other wheels;
>
> (b) the tyre is not so inflated as to make it fit for the use to which the motor vehicle or trailer is being put;
>
> (c) the tyre has a cut in excess of 25 mm or 10% of the section width of the tyre, whichever is the greater, measured in any direction on the outside of the tyre and deep enough to reach the ply or cord;
>
> (d) the tyre has any lump, bulge or tear caused by separation or partial failure of its structure;
>
> (e) the tyre has any of the play or cord exposed;
>
> (f) the base of any groove which showed in the original tread pattern of the tyre is not clearly visible;

(g) either —

> (i) the grooves of the tread pattern of the tyre do not have a depth of at least 1 mm throughout a continuous band measuring at least three-quarters of the breadth of the tread and round the entire outer circumference of the tyre; or
>
> (ii) if the grooves of the original tread pattern of the tyre did not extend beyond three-quarters of the breadth of the tread, any groove which showed in the original tread pattern does not have a depth of at least 1 mm; or

(h) the tyre is maintained in such condition as to be fit for the use to which the vehicle or trailer is being put or has a defect which might in any way cause damage to the surface of the road or damage to persons on or in the vehicle or to other persons using the road.

(2) Paragraph (1) does not prohibit the use on a road of a motor vehicle or trailer by reason only of the fact that a wheel of the vehicle or trailer is fitted with a tyre which is deflated or not fully inflated and which has any of the defects described in sub-paragraph (c), (d) or (e) of paragraph (1), if the tyre and the wheel to which it is fitted are so constructed as to make the tyre in that condition fit for the use to which the motor vehicle or trailer is being put and the outer sides of the wall of the tyre are so marked as to enable the tyre to be identified as having been constructed to comply with the requirements of this paragraph.

(3) Paragraph (1)(a) does not prohibit the use on a road of a passenger vehicle (not being a bus) by reason only of the fact that a wheel of the vehicle is fitted with a temporary use spare tyre, unless the vehicle is driven at a speed exceeding 50 mph.

(4)(a) Nothing in paragraph (1)(d) to (g) applies to —

> (i) an agricultural motor vehicle that is not driven at more than 20 mph;
>
> (ii) an agricultural trailer;
>
> (iii) an agricultural trailed appliance; or
>
> (iv) a broken down vehicle or a vehicle proceeding to a place where it is to be broken up, being drawn, in either case, by a motor vehicle at a speed not exceeding 20 mph.

(b) Nothing in paragraph (10(f) and (g) applies to —

> (i) a three-wheeled motor cycle the unladen weight of which does not exceed 102 kg and has a maximum speed of 12 mph; or a pedestrian controlled vehicle; or
>
> (ii) a pedestrian controlled works truck.

(c) Nothing in paragraph (1)(g) applies to a motor cycle with an engine capacity which does not exceed 50 cc.

[(d) With effect from January 1, 1992, paragraph 1(f) and (g) shall not apply to the vehicles specified in sub-paragraph (e) of this paragraph but such vehicles shall comply with the requirements specified in sub-paragraph (f) of this paragraph.

(e) The vehicles mentioned in sub-paragraph (d) are —

    (i) passenger vehicles other than motor cycles constructed to carry no more than 8 seated passengers in addition to the driver;

    (ii) goods vehicles with a maximum gross weight which [does] not exceed 3500 kg; and

    (iii) light trailers not falling within sub-paragraph (ii); first used after January 3, 1933.

(f) The requirements referred to in sub-paragraph (d) are that the grooves of the tread pattern of every tyre fitted to the wheels of a vehicle mentioned in sub-paragraph (e) shall be of a depth of at least 1.6 mm throughout a continuous band [comprising] the central three-quarters of the breadth of tread and round the entire outer circumference of the tyre.]

(5) A recut pneumatic tyre shall not be fitted to any wheel of a motor vehicle or trailer if —

(a) its ply or cord has been cut or exposed by the recutting process; or

(b) it has been wholly or partially recut in a pattern other than the manufacturer's recut tread pattern.

(6)(a) In this regulation —

"Breadth of tread" means the breadth of that part of the tyre which can contact the road under normal conditions of use measured at 90 degrees to the peripheral line of the tread;

"original tread pattern" means in the case of —

a re-treaded tyre, the tread pattern of the tyre immediately after the tyre was re-treaded;

a wholly recut tyre, the manufacturer's recut tread pattern

a partially recut tyre, on that part of the tyre which has been recut, the manufacturer's

recut tread pattern, and on the other part, the tread pattern of the tyre when new, and

any other tyre, the tread pattern of the tyre when the tyre was new.

"tie-bar" means any part of a tyre moulded in the tread pattern of the tyre for the purpose of bracing two or more features of such tread pattern;

"tread pattern" means the combination of plain surfaces and grooves extending across the breadth of the tread and round the entire circumference of the tyre but excludes any —

    (i) tie bars or tread wear indicators;

    (ii) features which are designed to wear substantially before the rest of the pattern under normal conditions of use; and

  (iii) other minor features; and

  "tread wear indicator" means any bar, not being a tie bar, projecting from the base of a groove of the tread pattern of a tyre and moulded between two or more features of the tread patterns of a tyre for the purpose of indicating the extent of wear of such tread pattern.

 (b) The references in [this regulation] to grooves are references—

  If a tyre has been recut, to the grooves of the manufacturers recut tread pattern;

  and

  If a tyre has not been recut, to the grooves which showed when the tyre was new.

 [(c) A reference in this regulation to first use shall, in relation to a trailer, be construed as a reference to the date which is six months after the date of manufacturer of the trailer.]

Note: for car and light vans and trailers up to 3.5 tonnes the tread depth (regulation 27(1)(g)) must not be less than 1.6 mm.

11–12 The prosecution could also use section 40A of the RTA 1988, but it would still be necessary to justify the complaint, which would mean that one of the defects contemplated in regulation 27 would have to exist.

PROSECUTION EVIDENCE

Vehicle inspectors

11–13 The very technical nature of some of the offences set out in regulation 27 gives more opportunity to V.I.s to prosecute the tyre offences. They are more likely to notice mismatched tyres, or, perhaps, tyres that are under-inflated. Where the prosecution depends on the recorded measurement of, say, tread depth they should have the figures available that justify the complaint. In fact a practice seems to have developed in which the police will prosecute for worn, cut, or damaged tyres, the V.I. concentrating on mechanical defects.

11–14 The V.I.'s evidence should be recorded on a P.G.9, the formal notice to the driver of the defect, and this document will always form the basis of a prosecution by a V.I.

Police evidence

11–15 The police commonly prosecute tyre offences and, in particularly, those arising under regulation 27(1)(c), (d), (e) and (g). These are all offences in which the condition of the tyre should be immediately apparent, and which require, therefore, only a modicum of investigation. Whilst some police office are now authorised to issue P.G.9s, the majority are not, and the evidence will normally be derived from the officers pocket book. The standard observation is to the effect that, when the tyre was examined "no tread was visible" or, more interestingly, "the tyre was worn and the body cords were clearly visible". The officer may say that, for a variety of reasons, no number could be obtained from the tyre, although the make will usually be known. The court may be told that the edges of the "cut" were worn smooth suggesting that the defect had existed for some time.

The police and V.I.s do sometimes prosecute on the basis that the tyre is **11–16** unsuitable (regulation 27(1)(a)). All tyres have both speed and weight ratings and it is not uncommon, particularly on wheeled plant, for a vehicle to be travelling at a speed greater than that permitted for the tyres.

DEFENCE

Perhaps the first thing to consider is the time that elapsed between the **11–17** investigation and the decision to issue the summons. It is common for defendants to fail to realise that the threat of prosecution was serious and, therefore, to scrap the tyre or, perhaps, to send it to be remoulded. Excessive delay may amount to an abuse of process particularly if the investigation is less than adequate.

The very technical nature of the regulation means that it is common for **11–18** the wording of the charge to be either inconsistent with the regulation or the alleged facts. In practice it may be found that the summons does not identify the precise sub-section of the regulation, but uses the language of the sub-section.

Regulation 27(1)(c) and (g), both require measurement and it is surpris- **11–19** ing how often these measurements are simply not taken. Regulation 27(1)(c) needs to be considered with care as the police frequently treat the 25 mm criteria in that sub-section as the standard. In fact it is not, the alternative test is "10 per cent of the section width of the tyre", which may well be more than 25 mm.

Tread depth is clearly a question of measurement although police officers **11–20** will rarely attempt to measure it. When measurements are taken the police have available two or more extremely accurate devices which depend on a hard metal probe of the prescribed length. These devices should have a certificate confirming the accuracy. The more common device, that is operated by manually pushing a probe into the tread, is not likely to be accurate.

The defence should press for a dismissal of the charge if the evidence of **11–21** the measurement is unsatisfactory.

The officer will sometimes maintain that it was impossible to measure the **11–22** depth of the tread as none could be seen. This is a separate offence, regulation 27(1)(f), and depends upon the officers knowledge of what should have been there in the first place. Very often the officer will simply be unable to give any clear evidence as to the original tread pattern. The advocate should consider regulation 27(6)(a) which provides that, where the tyre has had a re-tread, or been recut, it is the new pattern that should be considered and manufacturers recut patterns are often very different to those that were on the new tyre.

Regulation 27(1)(g) turns upon exposure of the "ply or cord". The reality **11–23** is that it is rarely the ply or cord that is exposed, more commonly it is the "shock strip" or "breaker strip" and the exposure of this material does not create an offence. This is an unattractive defence, but it has to be remembered that the tyre would need to have substantial damage for the ply or cord to be exposed unless it is on the side walls and perhaps the parliamentary draughtsman intended to exclude the "shock strip". This offence will really only appear where there has been very local damage to the tyre tread or the tyre is effectively bald.

11–24 Any client who is particularly vulnerable to this type of charge should be urged to mark and keep any tyre about which there is a complaint. It is not unknown for police officers to deny that the tyre produced to the court is the one that was examined. This denial can only be challenged if the evidence trail from the check to the production of the tyre is sound.

11–25 Depending on the gravity of the matter to the client it may well be worth calling an expert witness, perhaps from the manufacturer or one of the national tyre distributors.

MITIGATION

11–26 As with all construction and use offences, the best mitigation is based on persuasive evidence from the defendant that there is a maintenance system designed to prevent vehicles running in an unsafe condition. Those operating fleets of goods vehicles or coaches will be expected to have a system of regular tyre checks. This system should be supported by a drivers defect reporting system with drivers being required to carry out those daily checks that are now considered normal. This check by the driver will certainly include a visual examination of the tyres. This evidence should demonstrate that the defect could only have occurred in a short space of time.

11–27 Many tyre defects do occur in a very short space of time in any event. Separation or partial failure of the tyre or its structure is unlikely to be apparent until the bulge, lump or tear appears (regulation 27(1)(d)). A driver may well set off believing that the tyres are sound only to find that there has been a failure in the course of the journey. Some damage can only be impact damage or the result of severe spot wear. Cuts, lumps taken out of the tread, and patches of wear on the tread are examples of this type of thing. The condition of the rest of the tyre will usually be a good guide as to whether it was sudden damage or not.

11–28 Where the evidence suggests that the damage occurred during the journey then, of course, the court can be asked to find special reasons for not endorsing the drivers, or owners licence, on the grounds that s/he could not reasonably have been aware of the defect. Additionally, both for the driver and employer, the court should be pressed to give both an absolute discharge, following *Hart v. Bex* [1957] Crim.L.R. 622, DC, on the basis that, if they could not have been aware of the defect there could be no moral blame.

CONSULTANT ENGINEER'S COMMENTS

11–29 Investigating officers at the scene of road traffic accidents involving heavy goods vehicles often appear to have difficulty in distinguishing the difference between tyre condition that was the result of the accident and the previous condition of the tyre. When wheels "lock up" due to heavy braking the wheels on one or all of the trailer axles can "tramp", an effect caused by the differential in the braking effort. This will cause a number of "flat spots" on the affected tyres.

Expert examination of the scene of an accident should indicate the cause **11–30** of these "flat spots", but an inexperienced examiner may consider that the wear demonstrates a series of unrelated tyre defects resulting in a series of prosecutions.

Tyres are no less important than any other maintenance records. A **11–31** consultant engineer would hope to find a record of the history of any tyre available for inspection. This record would confirm dates on which the tyre was inspected as well as records of any re-grooving that may have occurred.

The average tyre pressure for a car is 28 lbs per square inch compared **11–32** with an average commercial vehicle pressure of 100,000 lbs per square inch. The instant deflation of a commercial vehicle tyre, sometimes known as a "blow out", may be the result of a manufacturing defect and it is absolutely essential that the tyre is retained for proper analysis.

Large commercial vehicles engaged in tight manoeuvres often create **11–33** scrub on tyres. This effect is particularly apparent on trailer tyres as their turning radii does not allow the axles to follow through. This results in scrub on the external or internal edges. This, in turn, can effect the flexibility of the sidewalls.

Effective mitigation may turn on the analysis of the damage to the tyre **11–34** combined with an examination of the historic records.

CHAPTER 12

GOODS AND PASSENGER CARRYING VEHICLE OPERATORS LICENSING SYSTEM

PUBLIC INQUIRIES BEFORE TRAFFIC COMMISSIONERS AND LICENSING AUTHORITIES

12–01   A practitioner may be asked to represent an operator at a public inquiry before the local traffic commissioner or one of his deputies. Such inquiries, which deal with applications for operator's licences variations to such licences and consideration of disciplinary action against a licence, are of a quasi-judicial nature.

12–02   Goods and Passenger Vehicle Operator Licensing is a system of quality control, first introduced under the Transport Act 1968, to replace the quantity controls which, at that time, existed. Very briefly, the system is that a standard national or international operators' licence is required to carry other peoples' goods or passengers for hire or reward, though in the latter case standard licences are required for passenger-carrying vehicles above a certain seating capacity. Restricted Operator's licences allow the carriage of goods in connection with the operator's trade or business (*i.e.* own account operations, and the carriage of passengers on passenger carrying vehicles below a certain carrying capacity). In addition, in the latter case the authorisation on the licence cannot exceed two vehicles and the carriage of passengers by the vehicles authorised must not provided the operator's main source of income.

12–03   The current legislation is contained in the Goods Vehicles (Licensing of Operators) Act 1995 and the Public Passenger Vehicles Act 1981.

12–04   There are currently eight traffic commissioners based in traffic area offices in various parts of the country. The Scottish Traffic Area is situated at J Floor, Argyle House, 3 Lady Lawson Street, Edinburgh EH1 9SE. Both the North Western and the North Eastern Traffic Areas are situated at Hillcrest House, 386 Harehills Lane, Leeds LS9 6NF. Both the West Midland and the South Wales Traffic Areas are situated at Cumberland House, 200 Broad Street, Birmingham B15 1TD. The Eastern Traffic Area is situated at Terrington House, 13–15 Hills Road, Cambridge CB2 1NP. The Western Traffic Area is situated at The Gaunt's House, Denmark Street, Bristol BS1 5DR. The South Eastern and Metropolitan Traffic Area is situated at Ivy House, 3 Ivy Terrace, Eastbourne BN21 4QT.

12–05   Operator's licences are granted "as a right", provided that the applicant satisfies the required criteria. Applicants must show that they have sufficient financial standing to enable them to safely maintain and operate the vehicles, that they have adequate maintenance arrangements, that they have systems in place to ensure compliance with the law, and that they are of good repute and fit persons to hold a licence. The latter criteria is judged by reference to any previous convictions and past conduct in the transport industry.

Traffic commissioners have wide-sweeping and quite draconian disciplin- **12–06** ary powers. These range from the complete revocation of an operator's licence, its suspension in whole or part, or its curtailment, down to a formal warning for the operator concerned.

In cases where a decision is made to revoke the licence, the com- **12–07** missioner also has the power to disqualify an operator, or the directors of a limited company, from holding or obtaining an operator's licence in any traffic area for whatsoever period he feels fit.

The matters which traffic commissioners may take into account in **12–08** deciding upon a grant, refusal, variation, revocation or suspension of an Operator's Licence are spelt out in the legislation. It also lays down those who have a statutory right of objection, namely the police, the trade associations, trade unions and local authorities. In addition, since 1982 occupiers of land in the vicinity of an operating centre have had the right to make representations on environmental grounds against an application for or a variation of an Operator's Licence.

Public inquiries before traffic commissioners essentially fall into two **12–09** types. Disciplinary hearings, including licence applications where there is an unsatisfactory history, and those dealing with the environmental provisions. Normally, a commissioner will give an oral decision at the end of the proceedings. However, in more complex cases he will reserve judgment and announce it in writing at a later date.

DISCIPLINARY CASES

Normally, traffic commissioners consider exercising their disciplinary **12–10** powers for basically two reasons. First, the operator's record in relation to the maintenance of his or her vehicles. Secondly, because of convictions for road traffic offences of the operator, any employees and, if a limited company, its directors or officers.

A traffic commissioner may revoke, suspend or curtail an operator's **12–11** licence on any of the following grounds:
1. That the operator made a false statement or a statement of expectation for the purpose of obtaining a licence that has not been fulfilled.
2. That the operator has failed to keep to an undertaking recorded on the licence.
3. That any condition on the licence has been contravened.
4. That prohibition notices have been issued to an operator's vehicle because of their mechanical condition.
5. That vehicles have been used whilst still the subject of a prohibition notice.
6. That convictions have been recorded against the operator.

    7. That the operator is no longer of good repute or of the required financial standing.

    8. That there has been a material change in circumstances since the licence was granted.

12–12   Before exercising any of his displinary powers a traffic commissioner must give the operator notice in writing of the public inquiry. That notice, which colloquially has become known as the "call up letter" sets out the various actions he is considering taking and his grounds for doing so. Issues not raised in the call up letter should not be the subject of evidence or action at the public inquiry.

12–13   The procedure at the public inquiry is very similar to that in a magistrates court with two essential differences. The first is that evidence is not given under oath. Secondly, the commissioner acts in an inquisitorial manner, rather like an examining magistrate. In effect, he acts as both prosecutor and as judge. In disciplinary proceedings, he will normally call evidence from the Department of Transport Vehicle Inspectorate both about the operator's maintenance record and about the record of convictions. On occasions he may call evidence from police officers and representatives of the local vehicle taxation office. Any such witnesses are open to cross-examination by the advocate representing the operator.

12–14   Where disciplinary action has been taken, a traffic commissioner, if so requested, has the power to stay the implentation of his decision pending the determination of any appeal to the appellant body, the Transport Tribunal. If a traffic commissioner refuses to stay his decision, the operator has the right to ask the Transport Tribunal for a stay. However, the Tribunal have made it clear that, in seeking to obtain a stay from the Tribunal, it is extremely important to show that there are arguable grounds of appeal that offer a reasonable prospect of success.

CASES INVOLVING THE ENVIRONMENTAL PROVISIONS

12–15   For some years now operators of heavy goods vehicles have been subject to environmental provisions in relation to their operating centres. As a result, the days of wagons operating off pub car parks, spare pieces of land or being kept in residential areas have long gone. Broadly, traffic commissioners have the power, where any objection or representation has been made on environmental grounds, to refuse a licence application in respect of a place to be used as an operating centre on the grounds, first, that the parking of vehicles used under the licence at or in the vicinity of the place in question could cause adverse effects on environmental conditions in the vicinity of that place; or, secondly, that the place in question would be unsuitable for use as an operating centre of the holder of the licence on other environmental grounds.

12–16   In addition to applications for goods vehicle operator's licences being published in the official publication "Applications & Decisions", which is produced fortnightly by each of the eight Traffic Areas in the country, they also have to be advertised in a newspaper circulating in the locality of the operating centre.

Statutory objectors, and in practice in environmental cases it is almost **12–17** always a local authority, are empowered to object "on the ground that any place which, if the licence is granted, will be an operating centre . . . is unsuitable on environmental grounds for use as such. The Act also states ". . . any person who is the owner or occupier of land in the vicinity of any place which, if the licence is granted, will be an operating centre . . . may make representations against the grant of the application on the ground that that place is unsuitable on environmental grunds for use as such, provided that any adverse effects on environmental conditions arising from that use would be capable of prejudicially affecting the use and enjoyment of the land."

Generally, representors are held to be in the vicinity of an operating **12–18** centre if they are within "sight, sound or smell", though the Transport Tribunal have ruled that people living on or near approach roads to an operating centre may also be "in the vicinity", even though they are not near enough to hear, see or feel any environmental effects emanating from the operating centre itself.

Representors can complain only about the effects on their own property **12–19** and not about the effects on the highway or the environment generally. It is only adverse environmental effects emanating from the activities connected directly with the operation of the authorised vehicles that can be taken into account, and not those emanating from other uses of the site.

Where a site not previously used as an operating centre is involved, the **12–20** commissioner can refuse an application where he is satisfied that the operating centre is unsuitable on environmental grounds. In all cases, he has the power to impose conditions relating to the operation of the authorised vehicles from the site. The type of conditions that can be imposed relate to the number, size and type of vehicles, the parking arrangements, the times of operation, and the means of ingress and egress.

Any restrictive conditions imposed on the use of an operating centre only **12–21** apply to vehicles authorised on that particular licence at that operating centre. The environmental effects a commissioner can take note of include noise from the movement of authorised vehicles in and out of, and inside, the operating centre itself; noise from maintenance work being carried out on the authorised vehicles; noise from the loading and unloading of authorised vehicles; the visual impact of the parking of the authorised vehicles; fumes, vibration and dust caused by authorised vehicles; diesel seepage; and flooding caused by the washing-off of authorised vehicles.

However, road safety is not an issue that can be considered under the **12–22** heading "environmental", though a commissioner is entitled to consider it as a separate matter when deciding upon the suitability of the site as such for use as an operating centre. Again, planning matters such as green belt, areas of outstanding natural beauty, and the absence of planning permission, are not considered to fall under the heading "environmental".

Where there is an objection from the highway authority, the commis- **12–23** sioner also has to take account of the suitability of any private road or track linking the operating centre to the public road, but not the suitability of the public road beyond where it is joined by the private track or road.

12–24   Where a commissioner is reviewing an operator's licence, following complaints from neighbouring residents or a local authority, and there is no material change in the use of the operaring centre, and in cases of an application for a new licence where there is no material change compared with the use of the site under a previous licence, a commissioner's powers are more limited. S/he is unable to refuse a new licence in such circumstances, unless s/he is not satisfied about the parking arrangements. If the commissioner proposes to impose restrictive conditions in order to protect neighbouring residents, s/he has first to give the operator the opportunity to make representations about the effects on his or her business of any such conditions, allowing him or her time for consideration and to take advice. Where the operator makes such representations, the commissioner is required to give them "special consideration".

12–25   The procedure generally adopted in such cases is for the advocate for the operator to outline briefly what it is that is being sought. It is then for the representors and/or objectors to make their case. Any witnesses called are subject to cross-examination in the normal manner. On the completion of the case by the representors/objectors, it is for the applicant to call evidence in rebuttal. Again, witnesses are open to cross-examination. At the end of the applicant's case, final submissions are made, with the advocate for the applicant having the final word.

THE TRANSPORT TRIBUNAL

12–26   Appeals against decisions made by traffic commissioners are made to the Transport Tribunal, which is situated at 48/49 Chancery Lane, London WC2A 1JR. The Transport Tribunal is a Court of Record with the same authority and standing as a Crown or County Court. Its president is a senior circuit judge, who sits with two members drawn from the transport world. English and Welsh cases are normally heard in London, whilst those emanating from Scotland are heard in Edinburgh. The procedure adopted is unusual to those with experience of Crown Court appeal procedures. Whereas in the Crown Court the evidence is heard afresh, even if it differs from that given in the lower court, the Transport Tribunal will only hear fresh evidence if it can be shown that that evidence was unavailable at the time of the hearing before the traffic commissioner.

12–27   Proceedings before traffic commissioners are taped which results in a complete transcript of the proceedings being available. The appeal hearing before the Transport Tribunal takes the form of a reading of the transcript of the proceedings before the traffic commissioner by all parties, including the Tribunal, and then each party arguing the points it wants the Tribunal to decide. Consequently, the appeal is decided on the evidence that was before the traffic commissioner at the time of his or her hearing of the case. The commissioner's decision will only be interfered with in cases where it becomes clear that the conclusion reached by the commissioner was a perverse conclusion and/or one to which no reasonable commissioner, properly directing himself about the law and the facts of the case, could have come. The Tribunal has made it plain that the weight to be given to any relevant factor is a matter for the traffic commissioner and not the Tribunal, as it is the commissioner who sees and hears the witnesses, whilst the Tribunal only sees a transcript of the evidence.

The Transport Tribunal is not bound to follow its own previous decisions, **12–28** but it does normally do so unless it can be cogently argued that their earlier decision was wrong.

Decisions of the Transport Tribunal can only be appealed on a point of **12–29** law. Such appeals in England and Wales lie with the Court of Appeal and in Scotland with the Court of Session.

Offences

Offences include using a vehicle that is the subject of a restricted operators **12–30** licence for hire or reward and failing to display an operator's licence identity disc. Operating goods, or passenger carrying vehicles that fall within the scope of the licensing system without the authority of an operator's licence, is an offence. Such offences can be committed in a number of ways. The first is by operating more vehicles than the licence held by the operator authorises. The third, which applies to goods vehicles only, is a little more complex. Goods vehicle operator's licences have licence identity discs that are vehicle specific, similar to a vehicle excise licence. To obtain a licence identity disc the operator has to supply the traffic commissioner with the registration number of the vehicle to be used, and that is recorded on the licence. That process is known as specifying a vehicle. If a licence authorises more vehicles than the operator has specified, the balance is known as a "margin". If an operator has a margin on his licence he can acquire or hire an additional vehicle and put it on the road straight away. The operator is allowed a month's grace in which to specify the vehicle concerned on the licence. However, if the vehicle is operated beyond the month from the date of its acquisition without it being specified, then an offence is committed.

Mitigation

In the latter case it would be good mitigation to point out that the operator **12–31** is not gaining any unfair advantage in that he or she is not operating more vehicles than are, in fact, authorised on the licence.

Operation without licence authority can sometimes arise when a business **12–32** has failed and a new business is being set up to carry on the work. The process of acquiring an operator's licence takes time, and in mitigation it can be pointed out that the offence(s) were committed to preserve the contracts and keep the employees in work.

CHAPTER 13

DRIVERS' HOURS AND TACHOGRAPHS

13–01 The legislation dealing with drivers' hours and tachograph offences is probably some of the most complex that advocates will have to deal with. The most common offences that are come across are breaches of E.C. regulations, which are made offences in this country by various enabling legislation. Offences contrary to the provisions of sections 96, 97, 98 and 99 of the 1968 RTA are the most likely to be come across. The E.C. Rules are contained in E.C. Regulation 3820/85 — drivers hours, E.C. Regulations 3821/85 and 3314/90 — tachographs, the Community Drivers' Hours and Recording Equipment (Exemptions and Supplementary Provisions) Regulations 1986 (S.I. 1986 No. 1456), the Community Drivers' Hours and Recording Equipment Regulations 1986 (S.I. 1986 No. 1457), the Drivers' Hours (Harmonisation with Community Rules) Regulations 1986 (S.I. 1986 No. 1458), the Community Drivers' Hours and Recording Equipment (Exemptions and Supplementary Provisions) (Amendment) Regulations 1987 (S.I. 1987 No. 805) and the Passenger and Goods Vehicles (Recording Equipment) Regulations 1991 (S.I. 1991 No. 381).

13–02 Less common are offences against what are known as the domestic drivers' hours and records regulations. The Domestic Rules are contained in section 96 of the Transport Act 1968 (Part VI) (as amended), the Drivers' Hours (Goods Vehicles) (Modifications) Order 1970 (S.I. 1970 No. 257), the Drivers' Hours (Passenger and Goods Vehicles) (Modifications) Order 1971 (S.I. 1971 No. 818), the Drivers' Hours (Harmonisation with Community Rules) Regulations 1986 (S.I. 1986 No. 1458), the Drivers' Hours (Goods Vehicles) (Modifications) Order 1986 (S.I. 1986 No. 1459), the Drivers' Hours (Goods Vehicles) (Exemptions) Regulations 1986 (S.I. 1986 No. 1492), and the Drivers' Hours (Goods Vehicles) (Keeping of Records) Regulations 1987 (S.I. 1987 No. 1421).

13–03 Because of the complexity it is necessary to look at the requirements of the legislation in some detail.

13–04 A tachograph is basically a speedometer which is able to record time, speed, distance, work, rest and breaks from driving. The record it produces is contained on a circular chart which shows a 24-hour period, divided into five minute intervals. There are three recording styli, which record speed, distance and driver mode by compressing the waxed surface of the chart to make traces. There are four sections on the chart. The speed recording section has concentric lines representing a 20 km per hour speed range. The driver mode section records the driver's activity, *i.e.* driving, rest or other work. The distance section records the distance travelled in the form of V's and inverted V's, each completed side of a V representing five kilometres travelled. The central area of the chart is known as the centre field, and it is here that the driver is required to make manual entries. The details which the driver is required to enter are his or her name in full, the vehicle registration number, the date of the start and finish of duty, the odometer readings at the start and finish, and the places where they started and finished.

Following accuracy tests at a recognised calibration centre, a plaque is **13–05** fixed on or near to the tachograph and the complete isntallation sealed. It is a requirement that tachographs should be inspected every two years at an approved calibration centre to ensure that the equipment is working properly, and they must be recalibrated every six years.

Subject to a number of exemptions which we will deal with later, all **13–06** vehicles used for the carriage of goods on journeys for hire or reward, in or between E.C. and AETR (the European Agreement concerning the work of crews of vehicles engaged in International Road Transport) Member States, the permissible maximum weight of which, including any trailer or semi-trailer, exceeds 3.5 tonnes, are subject to the E.C. tachograph and drivers' hours regulations.

On the passenger carrying side, the E.C. regulations apply to vehicles of **13–07** 10 seats or more, including the driver, on international journeys other than to the Republic of Ireland, including private use, and vehicles of 18 seats or over on both national and international journeys, including business and private use.

Definitions

The regulations contain a number of statutory definitions which are as **13–08** follows:

Carriage by road — any journey made on roads open to the public of a vehicle, whether laden or not, used for the carriage of passengers and goods.

Vehicles — motor vehicles, tractors, trailers and semi-trailers defined as follows—

Motor vehicles — a mechanically propelled vehicle circulating on the road, other than a vehicle running on rails, and normally used for carrying passengers or goods.

Tractor — a mechanically propelled vehicle specially designed to pull, push or move trailers, semi-trailers, implements and machines, with an unladen weight not exceeding 7,370 kg.

Trailer — a vehicle designed to be coupled with/drawn by a motor vehicle or tractor.

Semi trailer — a trailer without a front axle, coupled in such a way that a substantial part of its weight and the weight of its load is borne by the tractor or motor vehicle.

A specialised breakdown vehicle — a vehicle which is specially equipped with some form of crane for lifting/towing purposes for the removal of broken down vehicles or mobile plant from the point where the breakdown occurred.

Driver — any person who drives a vehicle regularly or occasionally, or who is carried in the vehicle in order to be available for driving, if necessary.

Conductor — anyone who travels with a driver on a vehicle and whose duty it is to issue and check tickets.

A day — successive period of 24 hours beginning with the resumption of driving after the last weekly rest period.

Note: The European Court ruled, in two judgments, in June 1994, that the phrase "each period of 24 hours" in Article 8(1) of E.C. Regulation 3820/85 means any period of 24 hours commencing at the time when the driver activates the tachograph following a weekly or daily rest period. Where the daily rest period is taken in two or three separate periods the calculation must commence at the end of the period of not less than eight hours (*Van Swieten B.V.* Case C–313/92, and *Michielsen v. Geybels Transport Service N.V. (GTS)* Case C–394/92).

Week — the period between 00.00 hours Monday to 24.00 hours Sunday.

Break — a period of at least 15 minutes when the driver is not driving or doing other work.

Rest — any uninterrupted period of at least one hour during which the driver may freely dispose of his time.

Daily rest period — any period of at least eight consecutive hours during which the driver can freely dispose of his time.

Driving — being at the controls of a vehicle for the purpose of controlling its movement, whether it is moving or stationary, with the engine running.

Duty — other periods of work, including work for another employer not concerned with driving or other periods of availability to the employer.

International journey — a journey to or from another country or Member State, including that part of the journey in the U.K.

Maximum permissible weight — the maximum authorised operating weight of the vehicle fully laden.

Live animals — cattle, sheep, swine, goats, horses, and any kind of mammal (except man), poultry, any kind of four footed beast which is not a mammal, any fish, reptiles, crustaceans and any other cold blooded creatures of any species.

Carcasses — dead poultry and part carcasses (not such things as frozen chicken portions, sausages or packaged lamb chops, etc.).

Animal waste — slaughterhouse scraps and offal (not such things as organic chemical compounds, skins and hides if *en route* to be processed into shoe leather).

Regular service — a service which provides for the carriage of passengers at specified intervals along a specified route, passengers being taken-up and set-down at predetermined stopping points. It does not have to be a service for the general public. It may be a service provided exclusively for a particular category of passengers. A service may be varied according to the needs of those concerned and still remain a regular service.

EXEMPTIONS

The following vehicles and/or operations are exempt from the E.C. **13–09** Regulations (see Article 13 of E.C. Regulation 3820/85 and the Community Drivers' Hours (Exemptions Etc.) Regulations 1986 (S.I. 1986 No. 1456)).

1. Vehicles not used on the public road.
2. Vehicles with a maximum authorised speed not exceeding 30 km per hour.
3. Vehicles used by or under the control of the civil defence, fire services and armed forces responsible for maintaining public order.
4. Vehicles used in connection with the drainage, flood protection, water, gas and electricity services, highway maintenance and control, refuse collection and disposal, telegraph and telephone services, the postal authorites for the carriage of mail, radio and television services and the detection of radio or television transmitters or receivers, or vehicles which are used by other public authorities for public services, and which are not in competition with professional road hauliers.
5. Vehicles used in emergencies or rescue operations.
6. Specialised vehicles used for medical purposes.
7. Vehicles used for transporting circus and fun-fair equipment.
8. Specialised breakdown vehicles.
   Note: This exemption does not cover vehicles used to collect cars from auction even if they are not roadworthy.
9. Vehicles undergoing road tests for technical development, repair or maintenance purposes, and new or rebuilt vehicles which have not yet been put into service.
10. Vehicles used for non-commercial carriage of goods for personal use.
11. Vehicles used for the collection of milk from farms and the return to farms of milk containers or milk products used for animal feed.
12. Vehicles used by the agricultural, horticultural, forestry or fishery undertakings for the carriage of goods within a 50 km (31 mile) radius of the place where the vehicle is normally based, including local administrative areas, the centres of which are situated within that radius.
    Note: In the case of fishery undertakings, the exemption applies only to the carriage of live fish, or a catch of fish from the place of first landing to the place where it is to be processed.
13. Vehicles used for the carriage of animal waste or carcasses which are not intended for human consumption.

14. Vehicles used for the carriage of live animals from farms to local markets and vice versa, or from markets to local slaughterhouses.
15. Vehicles used as shops at local markets or for door-to-door selling, specially fiited for such uses. Specialised vehicles in this context are vehicles specially constructed or adapted to carry/distribute the commodity being sold, as distinct from a vehicle that could be used for general purposes.
16. Vehicles used for mobile banking, exchange or savings transactions, for worship, for the lending of books, records or cassettes, for cultural events or exhibitions, specially fitted for such uses.
17. Vehicles with a maximum permissible weight of not more than 7.5 tonnes used for the carriage of material or equipment for the driver's use in the course of his or her work within a 50 km (31 mile) radius of the place where the vehicle is normally based, provided that the driving of the vehicle does not constitute the driver's main activity.
18. Vehicles operated exclusively on islands not exceeded 2,300 square km in area, which are not linked to the rest of Great Britain by a bridge, ford or tunnel open for use by motor vehicles.
19. Vehicles with a gross vehicle weight (gvw), including batteries, of not more than 7.5 tonnes, used for the carriage of goods and propelled by means of gas or electricity.
20. Vehicles used for driving instruction with a view to obtaining a driving licence, but excluding instruction on a journey connected with the carriage of a commercial load.
21. Vehicles operated by the Royal National Lifeboat Institution.
22. Vehicles manufactured before January 1, 1947, or preserved for their historic interest which were first made more than 25 years ago, do not carry more than nine passengers including the driver and are used non-commercially, *i.e.* not for hire or reward, whilst travelling to and from museums, rallies or other places where the vehicles are to be displayed or to and from their place of maintenance and repair.
23. Vehicles propelled by steam.
24. Vehicles used by health authorities as ambulances to carry staff, patients, medical supplies or equipment.
25. Vehicles used by Local Authority social services departments to provide services for the elderly or physically or mentally handicapped.
26. Vehicles used by H.M. coastguard and lighthouse services.
27. Vehicles used by harbour or airport authorities if the vehicles concerned remain wholly within the confines of ports or airports.
28. Vehicles used by British Rail and other transport authorities when engaged in maintaining railways.
29. Vehicles used by the British Waterways Board when engaged in maintaining navigable waterways.
30. Tractors used exclusively for agricultural and forestry work.

31. Vehicles used for the carriage of passengers on regular services where the route covered by the service in question does not exceed 50 km.
32. Vehicles of between 10 and 17 seats used on the domestic leg of an international journey, provided that the vehicle does not leave the U.K.

EXPLANATION OF TERMS

Daily Driving Limit
The daily driving limit is nine hours, which can be increased to 10 hours **13–10** twice a week, taken between two consecutive daily rest periods or between a daily rest period and a weekly rest period.

Continuous Driving
A driver has to take a break of 45 minutes after $4\frac{1}{2}$ hours continuous **13–11** driving, unless he or she begins a daily or weekly rest period. The 45 minutes can be taken as one continuous break or as a combination of breaks of not less than 15 minutes distributed over the $4\frac{1}{2}$-hour driving period or at the end of that period, which aggregate at least 45 minutes in total. During such breaks the driver is not allowed to carry out other work. Waiting time and time not devoted to driving spent on a vehicle in motion, on a ferry boat or train, is not regarded as other work for this purpose. In December 1993 the European Court ruled that if a driver had taken 45 minutes break, either as a single break or as several breaks of at least 15 minutes during or at the end of the $4\frac{1}{2}$-hour driving period, the calculation should begin afresh, without taking account of the driving time and breaks previously completed by the driver. The court also ruled that the calculation of the driving period begins the moment the driver sets in motion the tachograph and begins driving (*Kevin Albert Charlton, Raymond Edward William Wilson and James Huyton* Case C–116/92).

Where "regular services" have a lay-over in Central London, defined as **13–12** Camden, Islington, Westminster, Kensington and Chelsea, or within or near to Digbeth Coach Station, Birmingham; Marlborough Coach Station, Bristol; Wellington Street Coach Station, Leeds; Oxpens Coach Park, Oxford; Victoria Bus Station, Nottingham; and St Margarets Bus Station, Leicester; the minimum break can be reduced to 30 minutes as long as it is not possible to take a 15 minute break elsewhere and the maximum driving period is no more than four hours.

Fortnightly Driving Limit
A driver is not permitted to drive for more than 90 hours in a fortnight. **13–13**

Daily Rest Period
A driver must take a daily rest period of not less than 11 consecutive hours, **13–14** which can be reduced to nine hours not more than three times in any one week. Any reduction must be compensated for by an equivalent period of

rest being added to a daily or weekly rest period before the end of the following week. As an option, a daily rest period of 12 hours may be taken, split into two or three periods, one of which must be of at least eight hours and none of which must be less than one hour.

13-15 In June 1994 the European Court ruled that if the daily rest period is split in such a manner, then the 24 hour period commences at the end of the period of rest that lasts a minimum of eight hours (*Van Swieten B.V.* Case C–313/92). It also ruled that "daily working period" comprises the driving time, all other periods of work, the period of availability, breaks in work, and, where the driver divides his daily rest into two or three separate periods, such a period provided it does not exceed one hour; that the "daily working period" commenced at the time when the driver activated the tachograph following a weekly or daily rest period, or where the daily rest is divided into separate periods, following the rest period of at least eight hours; that it ended at the beginning of a daily rest period, or if the daily rest was divided into separate periods, at the beginning of the rest period extending over a minimum of eight consecutive hours; and that the term "day" must be understood as equivalent to the term "period of 24 hours" (*Marc Michielsen and Geybels Transport Service N.V. (GTS)* Case C–394/92).

13-16 Where vehicles are double-manned each driver is required to have a daily rest period of not less than eight hours during each period of 30 hours.

13-17 A driver must take a weekly rest period after six daily driving periods. However, the weekly rest period may be postponed until the end of the sixth day if the total driving time over the six days does not exceed the maximum corresponding to six daily driving periods, usually 56 hours (*Kelly v. Shulman*, QBD, April 28, 1988).

Weekly rest period

13-18 A driver must take a weekly rest period of 45 consecutive hours. That period can be reduced to 36 consecutive hours if the rest is taken where the vehicle or the driver are normally based, and to 24 consecutive hours if taken elsewhere. Where the weekly rest period is reduced it must be compensated for *en bloc* in conjunction with a daily or weekly rest period before the end of the third week following the week in which the reduction occurs. A weekly rest period which begins in one week and continues into the following week can be attached to either of those weeks.

13-19 On the passenger-carrying side, in the case of non-regular international and national services, the weekly rest period may be postponed until the end of the twelfth day, if the total driving period does not exceed the maximum fortnightly driving period of 90 hours. This postponed rest period must be added to that following week's weekly rest period.

Journeys by ferry boat or train

13-20 Where part of the vehicle's journey is by ferry boat or train the following rules apply:

   (i) The rest period may be split, with part being taken on land preceded or followed by a period of rest taken on the boat or train. The rest period must only be interrupted once and two hours must be added to the total rest time. The interruption to the rest period must be as short as possible and must be no more than one hour before embarkation or one hour after embarkation. Customs formalities being included in the embarkation and disembarkation procedures.

  (ii) During both parts of the rest period the driver must have access to a bunk or couchette.

 (iii) Any time spent on board not counted as part of the rest period is regarded as a break from driving or other work.

 (iv) The rest period or break on board the ferry boat or train is deemed to have started once the driver is free to leave the vehicle and it continues until he is instructed to rejoin the vehicle prior to disembarkation.

The daily rest period may be taken in the vehicle, provided that it is **13–21** equipped with a bunk and it is stationary. This provision means that it is an offence for a driver to take a rest period, as distinct from a break, on a moving vehicle.

EMERGENCY PROVISIONS

In cases of emergency, provided that road safety is not jeopardised and in **13–22** order to reach a suitable stopping place, the driver may depart from any of the E.C. drivers' hours rules only to the extent that is necessary to ensure the safety of persons, or the vehicle or its load. The driver is required to indicate the nature of any such departure and the reason for it on the tachograph chart.

In November 1995 the European Court ruled that drivers of vehicles **13–23** carrying high security loads cannot depart from the E.C. drivers' hours rules to get to a secure stopping place when it is known that the journey cannot be undertaken within the permitted hours' limits before the driver set out (*Alan Geoffrey Bird* Case C–235/94).

The E.C. regulations prohibit payments to drivers in the form of bonuses **13–24** or wage supplements which are related to the distance travelled and/or the amount of goods carried, unless the payments are of such a kind that they do not endanger road safety.

PROSECUTION

Summary offences involving the use of tachographs
Both employer and driver can be prosecuted for using a vehicle when the **13–25** recording equipment does not comply with the regulations in respect of construction, installation, use and testing, and when the seals are not intact.

Offences committed by drivers

13–26 Drivers can be prosecuted for the following offences:

1. Using dirty or damaged charts.
2. Failing to attach a damaged chart to the chart replacing it.
3. Failing to ensure that the tachograph is kept running continuously whilst on duty.
4. Failing to ensure that the time recorded was the same as that of the country of the vehicle's registration.
5. Failing to operate the switch mechanism to record separately driving time, periods of work and rest (known as the "mode switch").
6. Failing to enter, either manually or automatically, the various periods of time on the record sheet after being away from the vehicle.
7. Failing to enter surname and first name on the centre field of a chart.
8. Failing to enter the date and place where the use of the vehicle begins and ends on the centre field of the chart.
9. Failing to enter the registration number of the vehicle on the centre field of the chart.
10. Failing to enter the odometer reading at the start and end of the use of the vehicle on the centre field of the chart.
11. Failing to enter a change of vehicle on the centre field of the chart.
12. Failing to produce a chart to an enforcement officer.
13. Failing to return a completed chart to the employer within 21 days.
14. If employed by more than one employer, failing to notify to each of them the name and address of the other.

Offences committed by employers

13–27 Employers can be prosecuted for the following offences:

1. Causing or permitting offences committed by drivers.
2. Failing to issue sufficient record sheets to a driver.
3. Failing to issue sufficient record sheets of an approved type for the type of tachograph installed in the vehicle.
4. Failing to ensure that the driver returns the charts within 21 days of their completion.
5. Failing to produce tachograph charts, which the employer is obliged to retain for a period of 12 months.

13–28 The employer is required to organise work in such a way that drivers can comply with the regulations. The regulations require employers to make periodic checks to ensure that the regulations are complied with, and if there are breaches, to take steps to prevent any recurrence. There is no requirement on the employer to check every single tachograph record.

13–29 The employer is liable to conviction if it can be shown that he has caused and permitted offences by drivers.

Either way offences

The most serious cases that practitioners are likely to come across are cases **13–30** where it is alleged that drivers have made false entries in tachograph records and that their employers have either caused, aided, abetted, counselled or procured, or conspired with them to do so. Such offences are either way matters, and if convicted at the Crown Court a defendant is liable to a term of imprisonment not exceeding two years and/or an unlimited fine.

Where the falsification takes place abroad the offence of making a false **13–31** entry in a tachograph record, and the associated causing, aiding, abetting, counselling and procuring offences are outwith the jurisdiction of British Courts. However, it has become the practice of prosecuting authorities in such circumstances to lay charges under the Forgery and Counterfeiting Act 1981 alleging the use of a false instrument.

Methods of falsifying tachograph charts are many and varied. One of the **13–32** most common is to insert a switch into the electronic system. Such switches, colloquially known as "magic buttons" when operated prevent the tachograph from functioning with the exception of the clock. The effect is to produce a tachograph record that shows the vehicle as being stationary, with the driver at rest, when, in fact, it is being driven. A similar effect can be achieved by the removal of a fuse, known in the industry as a "fuse pull".

One of the simplest forms of falsification is the insertion of a fictitious or **13–33** false name on the centre field of a tachograph record, what is known as a "ghost driver". Other common methods include opening the tachograph head and either winding forward or winding back the clock, running which the tachograph head open or with no chart in the tachograph, the use of two charts in the one day with the driver producing the most appropriate one when requested to produce his chart by an enforcement officer.

For some time proceedings were not brought in connection with the **13–34** falsification of tachograph records whilst the driver was out of the country because of problems over jurisdiction.

However, the practice has now evolved in such cases of bringing **13–35** proceedings under section 3 of the Forgery and Counterfeiting Act 1981. The basis for that is the assertion that the false tachograph record is a false instrument and that its production to either the employer or an enforcement officer is an attempt to deceive.

The only authority for this practice is the unreported case of *Osman,* **13–36** *Mills and Chalker*, December 9, 1993 (92/6361-2-3/Z4) before the Court of Appeal, Kennedy L.J., in an *obiter dicta*, said that there had to be an intention both to induce someone to accept the instrument as genuine and an intention that the other person should act or choose not to act to his own or someone else's prejudice. A driver unquestionably used the tachograph chart when he passed it to his employer. If the employer was also a person who was aware of the falseness of the document, then it seemed to them that the intention of the driver would be the intention of inducing somebody in the shape of the inspector, if the inspector ever came to look at it, to accept the tachograph chart as genuine and, by reason of so accepting it, to do or not to do some act to his own or any other persons' prejudice within the meaning of that phrase. Alternatively, if the employer were not, on the face of it, a party to the arrangement, in that the employer did not know that the tachograph chart was false when it came into his possession, then it would seem, on the face of it, that the intention on the part of the driver would be to induce the employer to accept it as genuine, and, by reason of so accepting it, to do or not to do some act to his (the employer's) own prejudice.

PROSECUTION EVIDENCE

13–37 It is often part of the prosecution case, when operators face allegations of permitting drivers' hours offences, that particular types of bonus payments encourage drivers to commit such offences. A number of attempts to prosecute operators summarily for making such payments have been defeated following arguments that there is no such offence in English law. However, there is as yet no definitive decision on the issue, as it has not yet been argued before a higher court.

DEFENCES

13–38 A person is not liable for conviction for failing to have recording equipment complying with the regulations where it can be shown that the vehicle in question was proceeding to a place where a tachograph was to be installed and calibrated. In cases where the equipment is not functioning properly, a person is not liable for conviction when it can be shown it is not reasonably practicable for the equipment to be repaired by an approved fitter or workshop and that temporary written records, usually on the back of a tachograph chart, were being kept. In the case of broken seals, a person is not liable to be convicted where it is shown the breaking or removal of the seal was unavoidable, it was not reasonably practicable for the seal to be replaced by an approved fitter or workshop, and that, in all other respects, the equipment was being used in accordance with the provisions of the regulations.

13–39 In the majority of cases it will be clear, whether the driver has committed the offence alleged or not. However, there are a number of points worth bearing in mind. First, any driving that is not on the public road does not count towards the total driving time, though it cannot be counted as rest and is regarded as "other work". Examples of off-road driving include driving within quarry premises and on landfill sites.

13–40 Guidance on what constitutes a public road was given by the Divisional Court in the case of *DPP v. Cargo Handling* 1991, when they ruled that the roads at Heathrow Airport owned by the British Airports Authority were "open to the public" for the purposes of E.C. tachograph regulations. The Court rejected defence arguments that "roads open to the public" meant roads maintainable and manageable at public expense, and that the public did not have access to the roads at Heathrow Airport, as access was limited to those who were going to the Airport on business and it was prohibited to use the roads as a short cut. Leggatt L.J. said that, as a matter of English, the phrase "roads open to the public" meant roads to which the public had access. Public expense could not be introduced into that concept. Although the roads at Heathrow were subject to various restrictions, thousands of people used them every day and there was evidence that they were open to sightseers. The fact that most visitors were there on business did not mean they were not members of the public. It was a random selection of people and vehicles who might require business access to the Airport. In no sense were the roads private. There were no barriers or obstructions to prevent access by visitors.

Secondly, if a driver fails to take the required amount of break or rest, **13–41** the driving periods are aggregated. However, in so doing the times spent in taking rest or breaks, though insufficient to count legally, does not form part of the aggregated driving time.

Causing or permitting are not absolute offences. Merely because the **13–42** driver has committed an offence does not automatically mean the employer is guilty of causing or permitting it. Causing requires a far higher standard of proof than permitting and for this reason it is allegations that the employer permitted offences by drivers that the practitioner is more likely to come across. Causing requires a positive mandate to the employee to commit offences. In *Redhead Freight v. Shulman, The Times*, May 12, 1988 the Divisional Court held that a company, which, at the very least, shut its eyes to the fact that an employee was not filling in his tachograph records, could not be said to have caused the employee not to use the tachograph in accordance with the regulations. Although there was acquiescence in the failure to keep records which could amount to permission, it fell short of a positive mandate or any other sufficient act required for the offence as charged.

To be guilty of permitting the employer has to have guilty knowledge, **13–43** actual or imputed. In *Knowles Transport v. Russell* [1975] R.T.R. 87, Melford Stevenson J. said that the very essence of the offence was that there shall be knowledge. Whether or not there is actual knowledge or not is usually clear, but the question of imputed knowledge is more difficult. Knowledge is not imputed by mere negligence but by something that can be described as recklessness. That principle is restated in the 1985 case of *Patrick William Coggins v. the Licensing Authority for Goods Vehicles in the Metropolitan Traffic Area* (CO/590/84). It can be compared with the offence of reckless driving. The prosecution have to show that the employer turned a blind eye to the obvious for the offence to be committed. Though only persuasive, it has been held in the case of *Ancliff BLT Ltd* in the Manchester Crown Court that negligent carelessness on the part of a traffic manager does not impute knowledge, provided that the company employed someone who was apparently responsible and qualified for that appointment.

The leading authorities on causing and permitting include *James & Son* **13–44** *Ltd v. Smee* [1955] 1 Q.B. 78; [1954] 3 All E.R. 273; *Grays Haulage Ltd v. Arnold* [1966] 1 All E.R. 896; *Hill & Sons (Botley & Denmead) Ltd v.*

Hampshire Chief Constable [1972] R.T.R. 29; and *Ross Hillman Ltd v. Bond* [1974] R.T.R. 279.

13–45   In such cases it is helpful if the defence can show that there is a system for checking tachograph records and that action is taken when breaches are found, producing, for example, copies of any disciplinary letters or written warnings issued to drivers.

MITIGATION

13–46 In mitigation, it is often worth pointing out the fact that a driver is said to have, for example, driven for say 18 hours, does not mean that he has done so without taking any rest. It often means that what he is really guilty of is failing to organise his rest properly. It must be remembered that "daily driving" does not mean the driving in a day but the driving between two daily rest periods. If a driver does not take the required amount of daily rest, the next day's driving is added to the previous day's, and because the driver has not had the required amount of rest, albeit say 10 or 15 minutes short, he is regarded as having been on duty for two days. Similarly, it is often worth making the point that the regulations are complex, and difficult for drivers to understand and apply from a practical point of view. An example is the difficulty a driver engaged on multi-drop delivery work will have in working out his compliance with the $4^1/_2$-hour driving rule.

13–47   A point often worth making is that the transport industry is perhaps the only one where people are penalised for working hard.

13–48   A further point worth making in mitigation where operators have been convicted of offences against the E.C. Regulations is that the matter does not end with the criminal court. Convictions have to be reported by the operator to the traffic commissioner for the Traffic Area in which he or she is based within 28 days. The commissioner will then, in exercising his function of licensing authority, consider whether to revoke, suspend or curtail the operator's licence of the person concerned.

DRIVER'S HOURS – DOMESTIC RULES

13–49 Cases that involve breaches of what are known as the domestic drivers' hours rules are comparatively rare, but do crop up from time to time.

13–50   The domestic drivers' hours rules apply to drivers of vehicles exempt from the E.C. Regulations on journeys within the U.K.

13–51   The domestic drivers' hours rules do not apply to:

    (i) Drivers of vehicles used by the armed forces, the police and fire brigades.

    (ii) Drivers who always drive off the public roads.

    (iii) Private driving not in connection with any employment.

    (iv) Drivers of vehicles of less than 10 seats used for public service or utility purposes; or for business use (*e.g.* crew bus).

    (v) Drivers of vehicles of less than 18 seats used for private purposes.

(vi) Drivers of vehicles made before January 1, 1947, or vehicles preserved for their historic interest which were first made more than 25 years ago, do not carry more than nine passengers including the driver in the case of passenger-carrying vehicles and are used non-commercially, *i.e.* not for hire or reward whilst travelling to and from museums, rallies or other places where the vehicles are to be displayed or to and from their place of maintenance and repair.

Under the domestic rules a driver must not drive for more than 10 hours **13–52** in a day, including driving under the E.C. rules. After driving for 5½ hours a driver must normally take a break of at least 30 minutes, in which the driver is able to obtain rest and refreshment. However, a driver can drive for 8½ hours, as long as breaks from driving totalling at least 45 minutes are taken during the driving period and a 30 minute break, in which the driver is able to obtain rest and refreshment, is taken afterwards. In addition, a driver must not be on duty for more than 16 hours in any working day (spreadover), including work other than driving and off-duty periods during the working day. A daily rest period of 10 consecutive hours must be taken between two working days. However, that can be reduced to 8½ hours up to three times a week. There must be at least one period of 24 hours rest in any fortnight — defined as two weeks in a row, Monday to Sunday. A driver is exempt from the daily duty limit on any working day when he does not drive, or if he does not drive for more than four hours on each day of the week. If a driver drives for more than four hours for up to two days in any week he is still exempt from the rules, but on each of those two days all working duties must start and finish with a 24 hour period, 10 consecutive hours of rest must be taken immediately before the first duty and immediately after the last duty and the rules on driving time and spreadover must be complied with.

Drivers of light vans not exceeding 3.5 tonnes permissible maximum **13–53** weight and dual purpose vehicles are only subject to the 10 hour daily driving limit when engaged solely in certain professional activities such as:

(a) Doctors, dentists, nurses, midwives and vets.

(b) Services of inspection, cleaning, maintenance, repair, installation or fitting.

(c) Commercial travellers.

(d) The AA, RAC or RSAC.

(e) Cinematograph or radio and television broadcasting.

Under the domestic rules, the limits may be exceeded when there are:

(i) Events which cause or are likely to cause danger to the life or health of one or more individuals or animals, a serious interruption in the maintenance of public services for the supply of water, gas, electricity, drainage, telecommunications or postal services; or serious interruption in the use of roads, railways, ports or airports.

(ii) Events which are likely to cause such serious damage to property that it becomes necessary for immediate action to be taken to prevent such danger or interruption occurring or continuing.

13–54   A day is defined in the domestic rules as any period of 24 hours.

13–55   A written record must be kept by the driver of a vehicle that has been driven beyond a radius of 50 km from its operating centre or for more than four hours within a radius of 50 km of its operating centre.

13–56   Written records are kept in the form of a weekly sheet contained in a record book (Driver's Hours (Goods Vehicles) (Keeping of Records) Regulations 1987). The book must have:

(a) a front cover which details the dates on which the book was first and last used, the name and address of the driver, the name(s), address(es), and telephone number(s) of the employer(s) and the Operator's Licence number(s);

(b) instructions specifying how a driver is to complete the record sheet;

(c) notes for the guidance of both employers and drivers on the use of the book; and

(d) weekly sheets in duplicate divided up into boxes for the entry of information relating to the driver's activities of each day of the week in the prescribed format.

13–57   The number of weekly sheets each book must contain is not specified, but the book must be of at least A6 size or larger. It is the duty of the employer to issue drivers with a record book, having first of all entered on the front cover the employer's name, address, telephone number and Operator's Licence number before the book is used. In the case of an owner driver the address must be the address of his or her place of business. If the driver has more than one employer, the first employer is required to issue the record book. Drivers must only be issued with one record book at a time.

13–58   Where the employer is not the employer who issued the record book, that employer has a duty to require its production by the driver, so that necessary information can be entered on the front cover.

13–59   It is the duty of the driver to complete the remaining entries on the front cover and record on the weekly sheets the details of the activities undertaken each day. The entries must either be made in ink or in ball point pen. The driver must ensure that the duplicate copy is made. Once a driver has made an entry in a weekly record sheet, he or she must not make any entries in another record book until all the weekly sheets in the first record book are completed.

13–60   It is an offence to erase or obliterate any entry once made in a driver's record book. If a correction is required, it should be made by striking the original entry through in such a way that it is still readable, and writing the appropriate correction adjacent to the entry that has been struck through. Any such correction must be initialled by the person making it.

13–61   Drivers must have in their possession their current record book, including all unused record sheets, at all times when on duty. They have a responsibility to produce their current record book for inspection whenever required to do so by an authorised inspecting officer, the employer who issued it, or by any other person by whom they are employed at any time during the currency of the record book.

On completion of the weekly sheet, the driver is required to return it to **13–62** the employer within seven days, or earlier if required by the employer. The employer has a duty to check the weekly sheet, sign both the sheet and the duplicate, detach the duplicate copy and return the record book to the driver before his or her next period of duty.

In the case of an owner driver, he or she must detach the duplicate sheet **13–63** within seven days of its completion and deliver it to his or her business address.

The driver is required to retain completed record books for 14 days after **13–64** the employer has signed the last weekly record sheet in the book and returned it to the driver, before handing it in to the employer as soon as reasonably practicable after the end of the 14 day period. If the driver leaves the employment of the employer who has issued a record book before it is completed, the driver is required to return the incomplete book, including all the unused weekly record sheets, to that employer.

The employer has a duty to preserve intact the completed record books **13–65** and the detached copies for 12 months after the completed books are handed in by the driver. In the case of an owner driver, the period is 12 months from the day on which the record book was completed or ceased to be used.

The regulations provide for the use of a tachograph in lieu of written **13–66** records, but in such cases all the provisions in relation to the use of tachographs must be complied with.

The employer should keep a register of all record books issued to drivers. **13–67**

Drivers of exempt passenger-carrying vehicles, not required to keep **13–68** records, must still observe the hours and rest rules.

Defences

The same principles apply in relation to offences of causing and permitting **13–69** breaches of the domestic drivers' hours and records regulations as apply to similar offences in relation to the E.C. regulations. As we have already seen, causing or permitting are not absolute offences. Merely because the driver has committed an offence does not automatically mean the employer is guilty of causing or permitting it.

Mitigation

Where defendants are guilty of breaches of the domestic regulations, **13–70** similar points in mitigation can often be made, as can be made in relation to defendants guilty of breaches of the E.C. regulations.

CHAPTER 14

VEHICLE EXCISE DUTY

14–01 In general terms there should be few problems arising out of the taxation of a commercial vehicle. The charge for Vehicle Excise Duty (VED) is based on the Gross or Train weight of the vehicle which is ascertained from the plate fixed to the vehicle. (This used to be referred to, for obvious reasons, as the "plated weight" but the Finance Act 1995 introduced the concept of "revenue weight", which is defined in an extremely complex provision at Schedule 4, Pt. IV, para. 26). The fact is that, for all practical purposes, the relevant information is still set out on the plate. The relevant law is found in the Vehicle Excise and Registration Act 1994 (VEA), as amended by the Finance Act 1995 (F.A.). Specifically the rates of duty are set out in Schedule 1 to the VEA subject to the alterations achieved by Schedule 4 to the F.A. Traditional grounds for prosecution are the non-payment of duty, the fraudulent use of a disc, or the forgery of a disc. Where commercial vehicles are concerned, however, there may be other problems. The allegation may be that the vehicle is taxed at the wrong rate, either because there is an issue as to the relevant weight, or because there is an issue as to the nature of the vehicle. Before dealing with a prosecution of this type it is essential to be clear about the type of vehicle that was being used and the purpose for which it was being used.

PROSECUTION

14–02 All Vehicle Excise Duty cases are brought under the powers contained in the VEA. Section 29(1) creates an offence if a person uses, or keeps on a public road, an unlicensed vehicle. Section 37(1) creates an offence where the duty paid is less than that which should have been paid either at the outset, or as a result of changes to the vehicle, or as a result of the purpose for which it is being used whilst a licence is in force.

14–03 Section 44 creates an offence if a person forges, fraudulently alters, fraudulently uses, or fraudulently lends to another, the disc or other document relating to the taxation of the vehicle. (Sections 30 and 38 allow an additional penalty to be imposed on the keeper of the vehicle calculated against the appropriate rate of duty. This calculation can result in very high "back duty" claims.)

PROSECUTION EVIDENCE

General

Section 52 provides that certain statements shall be admissible in any **14–04** proceedings. Effectively this covers any certificate issued by the DVLC at Swansea but, if there is doubt as to whether a particular certificate is admissible, then the detail is contained in section 52(2).

Prosecutions are normally brought by the police, although officials from **14–05** the relevant regional licensing office may also prosecute.

Vehicles Excise and Registration Act 1994, s.29

The prosecution will adduce evidence to show that the vehicle was being **14–06** used on a "public road" to support the case against the user, or will call evidence to show that the vehicle was being kept on a public road to support a case against the keeper. The arguments as to what is, or is not, a public road are well known but, nonetheless, the prosecution should have evidence to establish that fact in cases where the vehicle is not on, or being kept on, an obvious road. Recently the test has altered and the mere fact that a notice is displayed indicating that he land is private will not be sufficient to prevent the place being described as public if, as a matter of fact, the public do have general access.

Evidence as to the rate of duty and as to the fact that the duty was **14–07** unpaid will normally be given by certificate (section 52), although the prosecution should have evidence to confirm the rate that is alleged to be appropriate.

Evidence as to the identity of the user or keeper will either be by way of **14–08** a recorded interview, or by details provided by that person following a demand made under section 46 of the VEA.

Buses are taxed against the seating capacity and the detail is set out at Pt. **14–09** III of Schedule 4 to the F.A.

Vehicle Excise and Registration Act, s.37

The prosecution has to demonstrate that the rate of duty that has been paid **14–10** is wrong having regard to the nature or use of the vehicle. There are five possibilities:

(1) The prosecution may adduce evidence to the effect that the vehicle was being used for the carriage of an exceptional load, having been taxed at the relevant goods vehicle rate. Exceptional load is defined in Schedule 1, Pt. VI, para. 6(3) to the VEA.

(2) The prosecution may adduce evidence to the effect that the vehicle was carrying goods for hire and reward having been taxed as if it were not so used, the defendant having relied on the provisions of Schedule 1, Pt. VIII, para. 16(1)(b) to the VEA.

(3) The prosecution may adduce evidence to the effect that the suspension or tyre size of the vehicle has been altered so as to increase its relevant revenue weight thereby attracting a higher rate of duty.

(4) The prosecution may adduce evidence to show that an articulated vehicle taxed at the preferential rate for six axle operation was operating on fewer axles thereby attracting a higher rate of duty.

(5) The vehicle may have been taxed as a special vehicle, and the prosecution may seek to show that the vehicle was not in fact special and should, therefore, have been taxed as a goods vehicle.

Vehicle Excise and Registration Act 1994, s.44

14–11 The circumstances in which the offence of forgery or fraudulent use is committed are self-evident. The prosecution will produce the offending disc and will say either that it was displayed on the wrong vehicle or that, it has in some way been altered or, currently, that it is a copy.

DEFENCE

Vehicle Excise and Registration Act 1994, s.29

14–12 The usual defence arises from the defendant's determination that the vehicle was not kept on a public road. Recent decisions, many of which arose out of cases involving drinking and driving, have eroded the arguments that used to be available. Broadly, if the public have access to the site, with or without permission, the court is likely to find that the place is public, unless the access can only be achieved by trespass. The temporary placing of the vehicle in a public place will afford no defence unless the circumstances make it possible to run a *de minimis* argument.

14–13 A recent problem has resulted from the large areas of roadworks on motorways and major roads. Is a vehicle on one of these sites, where it may remain for a considerable time, on a public road? The test is the degree of annexation. Where the site boundary is marked by cones and tape it probably remains public. Where large concrete boundary blocks are used to delineate the site boundaries it is probably not a public place.

14–14 A second argument that is frequently advanced is to the effect that, because of the mechanical condition of the vehicle, it is not, in reality, a vehicle and is not, for that reason, liable to duty. There are a number of cases on this point and the position changes on a fairly regular basis. The simple fact that the vehicle needs repair will not be sufficient to avoid the charge, some critical part of the vehicle must be missing, the replacement of which requires something more than simply putting it back.

14–15 Faced with a defendant who wishes to advance either of these defences, the advocate should check on any current decisions.

14–16 There can be a defence if the duty has been paid but no disc has been received. It must be possible to show, either that the cheque for the duty has been paid into the appropriate account, or that cash has been accepted. "The cheque is in the post" is not a defence to this charge.

14–17 There can also be a defence if a cheque for the appropriate duty is tendered but refused.

Vehicle Excise and Registration Act 1994, s.37
It is possible to own a commercial vehicle and to use it for purposes other **14–18**
than for hire and reward or in the course of a trade or business. The fact
that the vehicle is obviously a commercial vehicle is not, of itself, sufficient
to bring it into the class of duty that would otherwise be appropriate having
regard to its revenue weight.

Obviously the owner of a vehicle of special interest may simply wish to **14–19**
drive it, possibly to shows, possibly just as an afternoon's activity. The police
may seek to say that the vehicle, whilst empty when it was stopped, has
been used to carry goods but that is an issue of fact. More problems arise
when the vehicle is used to carry goods and the defendant seeks to deny
that that is being done, either for hire and reward, or in the course of a
trade or business. A person might, for instance, carry a roundabout to a
fête to be used for charitable purposes, or carry, say, a steam engine of one
sort or another to a steam fair in pursuance of a hobby. In either of these
cases the defence to a claim for higher duty should succeed.

There can be a technical defence if the summons contains no information **14–20**
as to the taxation class that the prosecution allege is appropriate. The
defence should be left in no doubt as to what the prosecution consider to
be the correct category of duty.

Perhaps surprisingly, alterations to the suspension or tyre size can affect **14–21**
the revenue weight. It is common practice for operators to have their
vehicle down-plated, thereby saving duty, when the full carrying capacity of
the vehicle as designed is not required. Conversely, although less commonly, the revenue weight of the vehicle can be increased by manipulating
the suspension, which will increase the relevant duty. Whilst these matters
are extremely technical, they are issues of fact. In complex cases the
assistance of a consulting engineer may be helpful.

In an endeavour to encourage the use of six-axled articulated vehicles **14–22**
(three axles on the towing vehicle, the "tractor", and three on the trailer, a
"tri-axle trailer"), which are, because of the axle loadings, more environ-
mentally acceptable, a reduced rate of duty was introduced. The problems
arise when the tractor, taxed to six axles, is coupled to a tandem axle trailer.
The simple defence arises when the trailer, whether on one or two axles, is
empty. In this case there can be no claim to the higher rate of duty that
would be appropriate to a 38,000 kg vehicle on five axles. There was a
question as to whether, if the Train weight, that is to say the combined
weight of the articulated tractor and trailer, were kept below the weight
that would be appropriate for a vehicle with fewer than six axles at the rate
of duty paid, there would be no offence. That defence is clearly not
available although, in terms of mitigation, an absolute discharge would
appear to be appropriate.

The more difficult defences arise in cases involving "special vehicles". **14–23**
Historically, it was recognised that there are vehicles which, because of
their purpose, spend comparatively short periods of time on the public road
and that, in the circumstances, it would be unjust if the owners were
required to pay the rates of duty that would be applicable to a vehicle of
similar size operating for hire and reward, or in the course of a trade or

business. The most obvious example being the showman's vehicle which, in the course of a season, moving from fair to fair, may cover no more than 200 miles. Agricultural vehicles are another obvious example.

14-24   These special vehicles were covered in the VEA at Schedule 1, Pts. IV, V, VI, VII and VIII, para. 14, but this part of the VEA was radically altered by Schedule 4 to the F.A., and, in any case involving special vehicles the two acts need to be read together.

14-25   There are two scenarios. The first involves vehicles which are specifically identified and which attract argument. The second involves vehicles which are not specifically identified, but which may attract duty under paragraph 14 of Part VIII of Schedule 1 to the VEA which also can attract argument.

14-26   Certain specific categories of vehicle are identified in Schedule 1, the most important of which are as follows.

Recovery vehicles

14-27   Recovery vehicles are identified in schedule 1, Pt. V of the VEA although the rate of duty was altered by paragraph 11 of Part IVA of Schedule 4 to the F.A.

14-28   Despite the apparently clear definition at paragraph 5(2), cases continue to appear in the reports, arising from arguments as to what is, or is not, construction or adaptation, for the purpose of this section. A Crown Court has held that a vehicle with a box body equipped as a workshop to facilitate repair and recovery of a disabled vehicle can fall within the definition of paragraph 5(2), but that must be seen as an extreme case. It is a situation that is constantly changing and the advocate should try to be as objective as possible.

14-29   Paragraph 5(3) contains traps for the unwary operator. To be a recovery vehicle it must be being used for the recovery of a disabled vehicle. More importantly perhaps, it must not be used simply to take a disabled vehicle to be scrapped, nor must it be used to take a vehicle from a place of repair to premises where it will be scrapped.

Vehicles used for exceptional loads

14-30   These vehicles are covered by Part VI of Schedule 1 to the VEA, although it must be read with paragraph 12 of Part IVA of Schedule 4 to the F.A. The definition is found in paragraph 6(3) of Part VI but in simple terms, when the combination of the vehicle and its load is such that, either by reason of its size, or by reason of its weight, it cannot comply with the Construction and Use Regulations, it will be a vehicle used for exceptional loads. There is no question here of normal use: one journey with a large or heavy load will attract the high rate of duty which operators of these vehicles have to pay.

14-31   There is one exceptional case. The Motor Vehicles (Authorisation of Special Types) General Order 1979 (STGO) permits the use of a C and U vehicle, where the only problem arises as a result of the width of the load. It is not unknown for prosecutions to be brought on the basis that a vehicle carrying a light but wide load should attract the high rate of duty. Reference to the exception in the STGO should persuade the prosecution to abandon the matter.

Locomotives

It is important to understand the concept of a "locomotive". Locomotives **14–32** and motor tractors are brought into the scope of Part VI by paragraph 6(1)(b). Certain very large loads are carried on a free-standing trailer (a trailer with axles, or, more probably, sets of axles at each end). These trailers are pulled by vehicles which carry no load other than ballast weights, which are designed to make the braking efficiency of the towing vehicle compatible with the weight of the trailer that is being towed, and it is these vehicles that are described as locomotives.

A large number of commercial vehicles have a design capability that **14–33** enables them to operate both as C and U vehicles and also under the STGO. To avoid the high rate of duty, the vehicle must be brought with the scope of the C.U. Regulations, subject to the one exception.

Finally, where the allegation that the vehicle was outwith the C.U. **14–34** Regulations is based on the dimensions of the load, remember to consider whether the accuracy of the measurements can be challenged.

Showmen's vehicles

Showmen's vehicles attract a reduced rate of duty and there are prosecu- **14–35** tions based on an allegation that the vehicle is not, in fact, owned by a showman. The courts will accept membership of the Showman's Guild as evidence that a person is a showman. Evidence of presence at a fair, or series of fairs, may also be sufficient, but that is less persuasive. A different problem arises with showman's haulage vehicles. These vehicles which are normally used to pull trailers which are rides, are sometimes found to have accessories for the ride being carried. This immediately brings them into the goods vehicle category with the relevant rate of duty. Paragraph 14(5) of Schedule 1, Pt. IVA of the F.A. varied the rates of duty for showman's vehicles.

Works trucks

Works trucks are dealth with in Schedule 1 of the VEA, at Part IV, under **14–36** the heading "Special Machines", a title that was altered by the F.A. to "Special Vehicles". The rate of duty was also altered to the basic goods vehicle rate, but it is still a substantial saving against the duty that would be payable under the standard tables. It is difficult to understand why these vehicles continue to cause problems. They are defined in the VEA, Sched. 1, Pt. IV, para. 4(6), and although there is no definition of immediate vicinity, it seems to be generally accepted that the distance must be no more than 1,000 yds.

14–37   Each of these cases turns on issues of fact and a defence will always be available if the defendant can show that the vehicle, for whatever reason, did not fall within the higher category of duty. These matters are not simple in argument, and it is worth remembering that a lay bench may require considerable assistance if they are going to follow the argument. In some cases a model of the vehicle in question may make all the difference.

14–38   The second category of vehicles entitled to a reduced rate of duty are those contemplated in paragraph 14 of Part VIII of Schedule 1 to the VEA, as amended by paragraph 14(16) of Part IVA of Schedule 1 to the F.A. Paragraph 14 reads as follows:

A vehicle which:

   (a) is constructed and adapted for use and used for the conveyance of a machine or device and no other load except articles used in connection with the machine or device,

   (b) (deleted by Finance Act 1995),

   (c) (deleted by Finance Act 1995),

is chargeable with vehicle excise duty at the rate which would be applicable to it if the machine or device were burden even if it is built in a part of the vehicle.

14–39   There are a growing number of vehicles that, arguably, come within the scope of this paragraph and it may be helpful to consider some examples, although a list could never be exhaustive.

14–40   The modern roadsweeper is a vehicle which has the ability to wet the road by using a spraybar fed from a water container, to brush the road using mechanically driven brushes, and, by using a vacuum facility, to take the resulting debris into a container.

14–41   Environmental considerations have brought into being a comparatively new range of vehicles which incorporate a high-pressure water-jetting facility using water carried on the vehicle, the operation of which requires the operators to be specially trained, a vacuum facility, and a container to carry the resulting wet debris. Note: these machines must be distinguished from "street cleansing" vehicles defined at paragraph 16 of Part VIII of Schedule 2 to the VEA.

14–42   Certain types of cement-mixing vehicles carry the dry ingredients in separate hoppers together with water and/or additives in separate tanks to the point of delivery, where the cement is mixed in a mixer also carried on the vehicle to the required specification at the point of delivery. (The Court of Appeal in the 1996 case of *DPP v. David Anderson t/a Spotmix* CO/372/96, held that such a vehicle was not a goods vehicle and should be taxed under para. 14.)

14–43   A similar vehicle is used to deliver various animal foods to farms where, with the assistance of a vehicle mounted mill, feed can be presented to the required recipe.

14–44   Tower wagons, whose exemption from duty contained in the VEA, at paragraph 17 of Part VIII of Schedule 2, was removed by the F.A., are tightly defined in Schedule 17(2), have, in their new guise as "mobile access platforms", taken on a range of functions which, it may be argued, do not fall within the Schedule 17(2) definition. Nonetheless, they are not, on any test, goods vehicles.

Prosecutions are frequently brought against vehicles of this type on the **14–45** basis that they are goods vehicles and should be taxed at the appropriate rate. That rate being the rate for the "Gross Vehicle Weight" (GVW) at which the chassis/cab of the vehicle was designed to operate.

The prosecution will ascertain the GVW from the plate that will be **14–46** affixed to the vehicle either by the manufacturer or subsequently at a vehicle testing station. Certain of these vehicles may have been altered after some time operating as goods vehicles and will, therefore, carry a historic plate.

Certain vehicles, however, are exempt from Plating, the exemptions **14–47** being set out in the Goods Vehicles (Plating and Testing) Regulations. The material exemption being found at Schedule 2(4) which reads "Engineering plant and plant, not being engineering plant, which is moveable plant or equipment being a motor vehicle or trailer (not constructed primarily to carry a load) especially designed and constructed for the special purpose of engineering operations".

In the "*Spotmix*" case, the court had no problem in finding that, where a **14–48** vehicle exempt from plating carried a plate, for whatever reason, the plate should be ignored.

To defend a prosecution in this type of case, therefore, it is necessary to **14–49** form a view as to the relationship between the load-carrying capacity of the vehicle and the purpose for which it was intended. In many cases the answer may seem to be obvious, but, in cases of doubt, it may be helpful to consider whether it would make commercial sense to hire a vehicle of that type to carry the load which is on the vehicle either before, or at the conclusion of, its operation. The point being that the operational costs of vehicles of this sort are such that the hire charge would be disproportionate considered against the cost of hiring a standard goods vehicle to remove a comparative load.

Mitigation

Unhappily the usual reason for the non-payment of duty is lack of money. **14–50** Large commercial vehicles have a high rate of duty, and, where profit margins are small, if indeed they exist. The perception that other uses for the money could be found is common.

The best mitigation is found when the offender can point to some **14–51** administrative problem with a prompt payment of the outstanding duty when the error was discovered. There can be good mitigation if the error has arisen because of a misunderstanding as to the class of vehicle. The complexity of the law is such that, once one moves away from the standard vehicle, there can be entirely understandable mistakes.

Because the claim for back duty can be so high, a successful mitigation **14–52** can be highly effective in cost terms and any relevant and proper argument should be considered.

CHAPTER 15

MITIGATION

15–01 Mitigation is possibly the most important function of the advocate dealing with commercial vehicles. It is inevitable that there will be mechanical failures, that axles, if not vehicles, will be overloaded, and that tyres will be damaged whilst the vehicle is moving on the road. On the other hand, those concerned with the operation of commercial vehicles look for skilful and informed mitigation and that, in turn, requires knowledge of the subject.

15–02 The first problem faced by the advocate is the lack of public sympathy for those who drive and operate commercial vehicles. Uniquely in Europe the public in the U.K. have never accepted the importance of the commercial vehicle to their quality of life. Coach operators have, until recently, enjoyed a better reputation, but that has been substantially eroded following a series of accidents.

15–03 Inevitably, that attitude is reflected by magistrates and, to a lesser extent, judges, who are being asked, not only to understand arguments about technical engineering matters, but also to exercise a neutral judgment notwithstanding a prejudice that appears to be almost inevitable.

15–04 Conversely the drivers and operators of these vehicles face a situation in which a single conviction attracting a high penalty can lead to a disciplinary enquiry held by the traffic commissioner for the region, in which they hold a licence for the vehicle in question, which, in turn, could result in the loss of either the driving or operators licence.

15–05 The advocate has to be able to give the court sufficient technical information to enable the argument to be understood without losing the court's interest. This, in turn, requires the advocate to have sufficient knowledge to appear confident with the argument that is being advanced. Cases involving drivers' hours, for instance, require the advocate to have sufficient understanding of tachographs to enable him or her to assist the court, not only to follow the marks made on the tachograph disc, but also to see the record in the context of complex legislation. In fact the opportunity to seek an absolute discharge will often arise if the advocate can recognise the opportunity.

15–06 In cases where a guilty plea is necessary in a case involving mechanical failure, the first decision to be made is whether or not the failure could have occurred in the course of the journey. The need to protect the employer will always be of paramount importance where the advocate is instructed by the employer, and a decision may have to be made as to whether the defect should have been seen and reported by the driver. The second decision to be made is whether or not expert evidence is required. This depends on the advocate's view as to whether or not the court will accept the mitigation without independent support, and this, in turn depends on the nature of the offence, and, perhaps, some knowledge of the court.

Mitigation following a prosecution for Wheel Loss, for instance, will **15–07** almost always benefit from independent expert evidence if an absolute discharge is the required result; particularly as a court may understandably consider that wheels will only come off if someone fails to fasten them on securely.

Perhaps the most common argument in support of an application for an **15–08** absolute discharge is that of "no moral blame". In the case of *Hart v. Bex* [1957] Crim.L.R. 622 the court observed that prosecutors should consider whether, before prosecuting an absolute offence, the circumstances required that proceedings be issued, and, in the event that proceedings were issued, suggested that there should be no imposed penalty where there was no moral blame.

Overloading cases frequently arise in circumstances that are outside the **15–09** control of the driver or operator, and the *Hart v. Bex* argument can be particularly useful. There are, however, some signs that, although the *Hart v. Bex* principle remains good, the courts are requiring very high standards before they will give an absolute discharge. Written instructions to drivers dealing with the circumstances in which a load should be weighed should be seen as a minimum requirement, the court may expect evidence to show that written instructions have been supported by disciplinary action.

It should be remembered that the law does not require that every goods **15–10** vehicle be weighed before setting-out on to the public road. This, arguably, results in a position in which, whilst there is a very high duty of care, it is not an absolute duty, and should not be a standard that is beyond achievement.

Mitigation is also relevant where there has been some error by a third **15–11** party in relation to the repair of a vehicle. This is not simply, and familiarly, to escape endorsement, but to also avoid a conviction that might affect an operators' licence.

CHAPTER 16

THE POSITION IN SCOTLAND

16–01 While Scotland has its own legal system the applicability of the various statutes and regulations controlling the use of commercial vehicles, and indeed R.T. law in general, is no different in Scotland than elsewhere in the U.K. Differences can, however, sometimes be seen in the interpretations placed on the statutes and regulations by the Scottish courts and it is important that the Scottish practitioner is aware of these differences, when they exist. It is trite to say that English decisions, while they may be of persuasive authority in Scotland, are not binding on the Scottish courts.

16–02 The pressures on the enforcement authorities and the political sensitivity of proper and regulated maintenance of commercial vehicles, particularly those involved in carrying passengers, are matters of equal relevance in Scotland. The practitioner can expect little or no sympathy from the courts if they seek to justify their client's offence on economic grounds. The financial pressures on the commercial vehicle operator have increased substantially in recent times and the indications are that the rate of increase will not subside in the foreseeable future. One major contributor to this increase in financial pressure has been increased maintenance costs. Busier roads and faster vehicles both lead to more accidents – more accidents, particularly those involving fatalities, lead to greater scrutiny of vehicle condition and maintenance procedures, as well as the quality of the driving. It cannot be stressed enough how important it is that you know and understand, not only the client's business, but also the vehicle involved, the mechanical workings of the part allegedly at fault and the client's maintenance procedures: if something went wrong, know and fully understand why it went wrong. Those sitting in the Scottish courts are not mechanics or road haulage operators and neither are those who prosecute. Total comprehension of the issue by the defending solicitor can only be an advantage, whether in defence of the charge or in mitigation.

16–03 Reference has already been made to "causing and permitting" offences. The Scottish practitioner acting for commercial vehicle operators is often faced with charges alleging the operator "caused or permitted" one of their drivers to contravene a statute or regulation. Indeed, more often than not, the driver and operator appear on the same complaint. Such offences must be distinguished from "using" offences. "Using" offences tend to be absolute, but "causing and permitting" offences have to be looked at differently and, in Scotland, no causing and permitting charge can be considered without having regard to the judgment in *Smith of Maddiston*

Ltd v. Macnab 1975 S.L.T. 86. Essentially permitting, within the context of use and contravention of a statute or regulation, requires a state of mind and requires knowledge on the part of the person who permitted, not only the use of the vehicle, but its use in contravention. Actual knowledge need not be required. Knowledge can be imputed to the person who shuts his eyes to the obvious. Similar considerations apply to "causing". To cause involves some express or positive mandate from the person causing to the other person. Thus, causing or permitting requires knowledge, actual or imputed, not only of the use of the vehicle, but also its use in contravention of the relevant statute. The regulations covering driver's hours of work, rest periods and keeping of records are libelled against the employer on a causing or permitting basis and the prosecution, therefore, has to prove actual or imputed knowledge. These regulations are complex. When faced with such a charge, consideration msut always be given as to whether the vehicle in question falls within the regulations (*Baron Meats Limited v. Lockhart* [1991] S.C.C.R. 537; *Forganv.Hamilton* [1995] S.C.C.R. 733; and *Nicholls v. Carmichael* [1993] S.C.C.R. 991).

For an analysis of the various authorities dealing withthe question of **16–04** "use" of a vehicle see the case of *Valentine v. MacBrayne Haulage Limited* [1986] S.C.C.R. 692. The judgment in that case was to the effect that "use" could not extend beyond the driver of the vehicle and his employers.

Generally the offences which the practitioner will meet can only be **16–05** committed if committed on a public road or in a public place. As in England, what is regarded by the courts in Scotland as a public road or public place has been extended in recent years (*Thomson v. McPhail* [1992] S.C.C.R. 466; *Alston v. O'Brien* [1992] S.C.C.R. 238; and *Rodger v. Normand* [1994] S.C.C.R. 861).

The evidential requirements to secure a conviction in Scotland are **16–06** outwith the remit of this book, but it is worth mentioning that corroboration remains a requirement and this is something which must be addressed, particularly in causing and permitting situations where the evidence of knowledge often, if not always, comes from the operator's transport manager, or other employees of the operator.

As has already been noted, a conviction can impact on the operator's **16–07** licence and can lead to an appearance before the local traffic commissioner. While, on the face of it, the offence libelled may not be particularly serious and the court may be sympathetic the conviction, combined with others, may be sufficient to result in the traffic commissioner asking questions and exercising the punitive powers contained within the 1995 Act. While the appearance before the court and any financial penalty imposed, is, in itself, serious enough for the operator, it is often the traffic commissioners, and their powers, which are feared most. Any fine imposed by the court can pale into insignificance when compared with the financial implications of a suspension, revocation or curtailment, of the operator's licence.

APPENDIX 1

"P.G.9", TESTERS MANUAL CATEGORISATION OF DEFECTS

A1–01 When a vehicle is checked, whether at the roadside, or in the course of a multi-agency check, a vehicle inspector or specially authorised police officer will record the defects on a "Form P.G.9" [the P.G. standing for Passenger/ Goods]. It is this document that is likely to be produced to form the basis of the prosecution evidence where the proceedings are based on alleged defects in a vehicle.

A1–02 A P.G.9 is a "Prohibition Notice" and the issue of a P.G.9 will normally mean that the vehicle is either prohibited from continuing its journey, or is allowed to proceed only to a specific destination and at a controlled speed. On the left-hand side of the form the date, name and address of the owner/ operator or driver, registration number of the vehicle or identification number of the trailer, and the time at which the prohibition was issued are recorded.

A1–03 On the right-hand side the defects are listed, together with the nature of the prohibition, "I" for immediate and "D" for delayed; the type of check, "R" for roadside, etc.; the details of any exemption from the prohibition, thus turning the P.G.9 into a "delayed" prohibition; and the nature of the test to which the vehicle must be subjected. There is also a record as to whether the vehicle was laden or unladen.

A1–04 The defects will be sequentially numbered and will also have a further identification number at the end, for example:

"1 Offside rear spring anchor pin significantly loose on hanger bracket. T.M. 48.6"

A1–05 "48" is the I.M. number taken from the looseleaf guide. The Categorisation of Defects on Road Vehicles which is available from HMSO.

A1–06 T.M. 48.6 is the reference to the "Heavy Goods Vehicle Inspection Manual" which is known more commonly as the Testers Manual (T.M.) also available from HMSO (ISBN 011 551063 X).

A1–07 Normally the operator will be required to present the vehicle for a full test at an official Testing Station, either immediately, or within the time limit specified, if the prohibition is delayed.

A1–08 The information is always limited by the use of a technical shorthand, as can be seen in the example, and it is necessary to understand the relevance of the Testers Manual and the companion looseleaf book the Categorisation of Defects.

The Testers Manual lists each major part of a passenger vehicle, **A1–09** commercial vehicle, or trailer, and breaks each major component into its sub-groups. An example of the type of detail is contained in the chapter on Brakes (p. 3).

The Categorisation of Defects contemplates the faults that can occur in **A1–10** each of the items in the Testers Manual and categorises the faults according to their perceived seriousness. Major faults attract a recommendation that the vehicle be immediately prohibited, less serious faults attract a delayed prohibition.

There is a third possibility open to the vehicle inspector which is to issue **A1–11** a defect notice, P.G. D.N. This notice, as its name indicates, merely requires the operator/driver of the vehicle to put right a fault within a specified time. Although not impossible, a defect notice will rarely precede a prosecution.

The problem with the P.G.9 system is demonstrated in the example that **A1–12** has been used above. The phrase "significantly loose" is highly emotive. Any court advised that the condition of the part was such that the words "significantly loose" were appropriate is likely to impose a severe penalty. In fact, the phrase reflects the subjective view of the vehicle inspector who might either have been having a bad day or who might not be sufficiently familiar with the part in question.

One of the most common complaints is that there was found to be excess **A1–13** movement on the brake actuator, the mechanism by which the braking system applies effort to the brake shoes. The design of a brake actuator allows for some variation in the movement whilst maintaining adequate brake efficiency. The only test that is certain is to put the axle on a "rolling road" to measure the brake efficiency which is the test required by the definition of brake efficiency in regulation 3 of the C.U. Regs.

A P.G.9, for these reasons, should never be seen as a document that **A1–14** cannot be challenged. Ideally, of course, the owner of the vehicle would have the fault checked by his own engineer at the earliest possible moment, but, perhaps surprisingly, not all vehicle operators are competent mechanics and, in any event, may believe that the P.G.9 establishes the accuracy of its contents. The advocate should be prepared to prompt enquiry if there is an apparent problem. In serious cases a consultant engineer may be of substantial assistance.

APPENDIX 2

JURISDICTION

A2–01 It is inevitable, given the nature of commercial vehicle operation, that there will be, from time to time, jurisdictional issues arising from a decision to prosecute in a certain court. Whilst "factual" offences, such as Construction and Use offences, are clearly committed at the point at which they are discovered, offences of "record", such as "driver's hours offences" are clearly continuous in their nature and may well continue over long distances, and through different countries.

A2–02 Offences involving daily driving periods or hours of rest will have to be distinguished from cases of omission. The failure to return a tachograph chart to the operator or to insert a chart in the tachograph are offences which clearly occur at the place where the law requires that the action be taken. A failure to have a 45-minute rest in a 4½-hour driving period will occur at the point at which the 4½-hour driving period terminates, but may be discovered at some other place and some time later. It is common for a roadside check to result in prosecutions being brought for driver's hours offences which have occurred in different parts of the country, as the driver has carried out his/her employment. A working day in which the driver drove for an excessive period might have finished in Woking, the check that brought the offence to light might have been carried out in Carlisle some days later. In a strict application of the jurisdiction of the Carlisle court it might properly be argued that they could not deal with a case committed in Woking.

A2–03 The issue is dealt with in section 103(7) of the Transport Act 1968 which was substituted by section 3 of the Road Traffic (Drivers' Ages and Hours of Work) Act 1976. The section provides that:

> **3.** An offence under this Part of this Act may be treated for the purpose of conferring jurisdiction on a court (but without prejudice to any jurisdiction it may have apart from this sub-section) as having been committed in any of the following places, that is to say —
>
> (a) the place where the person charged with the offence was driving when evidence of the offence first came to the attention of a constable or vehicle examiner;
>
> (b) the place where that person resides or is believed to reside or be at the time when the proceedings are commenced; or
>
> (c) the place where at that time that person or, in the case of an employee-driver, that person's employer, or in the case of an owner-driver, the person for whom he was driving,

94

has his place or principal place of business or his operating centre for the vehicle in question.

Looking at the example of the Woking offence committed in Carlisle in **A2–04** the light of this section it would seem to be clear that if there were no offence committed within the jurisdiction of the Carlisle court the Carlisle magistrates could have no jurisdiction. The matter has to be looked in the context of section 1 of the Magistrates Courts Act 1980 which, at section 1(2)(b) gives jurisdiction "if it appears to the justice necessary or expedient, with a view to the better administation of justice, that the person charged should be tried jointly with, or in the same place as, some other person who is charged with an offence, and who is in custody, or is being or is to be proceeded against, within the area".

The issue was considered in great detail in the seminal authority on this **A2–05** point *R. v. Abergavenny Justices, ex p. Barratt* [1994] R.T.R. 98, DC and, as the matter is of continuing importance, it is worth setting-out the decision in full.

24 March 1993. Queen's Bench Division

REGINA v. ABERGAVENNY JUSTICES, EX P. BARRATT AND ANOTHER

Watkins L.J. and Rougier J.
Goods vehicle – Drivers' records - Jurisdiction – employed driver stopped and **A2–06** *vehicle tachograph records examined – information preferred and summonses issued against employers and previous driver in area where vehicle stopped – Employers' place of business and offences taking place in different area – Whether justices having jurisdiction – Tranport Act 1968, ss.96(11A), 97A, 103(7) – Magistrates' Courts Act 1980, ss.1(2), 2(1).*

Section 96(11A) [as inserted by section 4 of and Schedule 4 to the European Communities Act 1972 and amended by section 2(1) of the Road Traffic (Drivers' Ages and Hours of Work) Act 1976 and the Community Drivers' Hours and Recording Equipment Regulations 1986] of the Transport Act 1968 provides:

"Where, in the case of a driver of a motor vehicle, there is in Great Britain a contravention of any requirement of the applicable Community rules as to periods of driving or distance driven, or periods on or off duty, then the offender and any other person (being the offender's employer . . .) who caused or permitted the contravention shall be liable on summary conviction to a fine . . ."

Section 97A [as inserted by the Passenger and Goods Vehicles (Recording Equipment) Regulations 1979 and amended by the Community Drivers' Hours and Recording Equipment Regulations 1986] provides:

"(1) If an employed driver of a vehicle . . . fails —
  (a) without reasonable excuse to return any record sheet which relates to him to his employer within 21 days of completing it . . . he shall be liable on summary conviction to a fine . . .

(2) If the employer of drivers . . . fails without reasonable excuse to secure that they comply with subsection (1)(a) of this section, he shall be liable on summary conviction to a fine . . ."

Section 103(7) [as substituted by section 3 of the Road Traffic (Drivers' Ages and Hours of Work) Act 1976] provides:

"An offence under this Part of this Act may be treated for the purposes of conferring jurisdiction on a court (but without prejudice to any jurisdiction it may have apart from this subsection) as having been committed in any of the following places, that is to say – (a) the place where the person charged with the offence was driving when evidence of the offence first came to the attention of a constable or vehicle examiner . . . (c) the place where at that time that person or, in the case of an employee-driver, that person's employer . . . has his place or principal place of business or his operating centre for the vehicle in question . . ."

Section 1 of the Magistrates' Courts Act 1980 provides:

"(1) Upon an information being laid before a justice of the peace for an area to which this section applies that any person has, or is suspected of having, committed an offence, the justice may, in any of the events mentioned in subsection (2) below . . . (a) issue a summons directed to that person requiring him to appear before a magistrates' court for the area to answer to the information . . . (2) A justice of the peace for an area to which this section applies may issue a summons . . . under this section – (a) if the offence was committed or is suspected to have been committed within the area, or (b) if it appears to the justice necessary or expedient, with a view to the better administration of justice, that the person charged should be tried jointly with, or in the same place as, some other person who is charged with an offence, and who is in custody, or is being or is to be proceeded against, within the area, or (c) if the person charged resides or is, or is believed to reside or be, within the area . . ."

Section 2 provides:

"(1) A magistrates' court for a county . . . shall have jurisdiction to try all summary offences committed within the county . . . (2) Where a person charged with a summary offence appears or is brought before a magistrates' court in answer to a summons issued under paragraph (c) of section 1(2) above . . . the court shall have jurisdiction to try the offence . . .

The applicants were haulage contractors whose place of business was in Lancashire. On March 7, 1991 a police constable stopped one of their lorries in Gwent, when it was being driven by L, and examined its tachograph charts, some of which related to periods when it had been driven by the second applicant. As a result informations were laid in Gwent, not only against L, but also against the second applicant alleging, inter alia, that on March 7, 1991 on a specified road in Gwent the second applicant, being the driver of the lorry, had driven for more than $4\frac{1}{2}$ hours without observing a minimum break of 45 minutes on February 28, 1991, contrary to section 96(11A) of the Transport Act 1968, and against the first applicant alleging that on March 7, 1991 on the same road, being the employer of a crew member, he had failed, without reasonable excuse, to secure that the crew member returned any record sheet within 21 days of completion on March 7, 1991, contrary to section 97A of the Act of 1968. Though none of the offences alleged to have been committed by the applicants had taken place in Gwent, summonses were issued by the clerk to the Gwent justices and, following amendment of the summonses by deletion of references to March 7, 1991 and to the location, jurisdiction was assumed by justices in Gwent who convicted the applicant.

Held, granting the application, that the responsibility for determining the issue of jurisdiction fell on the single justice who considered whether a summons or warrant should issue, or on the clerk to the justices who performed a like function (p. 102); that the clerk to the justices had not paid sufficient regard to the important provisions in sections 1 and 2 of the Magistrates' Courts Act 1980 and section 103 of the Transport Act 1968, because the charges had grossly misstated the place where the offences charged had taken place (p. 102) and the charges had come before the justices on the sole jurisdictional basis that the alleged offences had all been committed within the geographical county of Gwent (p. 102); that the clerk to the justices gave no consideration to section 1(2)(b) of the Act of 1980 and that, even if he had done so, having regard to the whole of the circumstances and the nature of the charges, necessity and expediency demanded that they should be tried in Lancashire or Greater Manchester (p. 105); and that there was no avoiding the conclusion that at the material time the justices did not have jurisdiction to hear the charges (p. 106).

Per curiam It is of importance that an information states as well as can be where an offence is alleged to have taken place as well as the name and address of the party charged (p. 105).

Cases referred to in the judgment:
Reg v. Blandford [1955] 1 W.L.R. 331; [1995] 1 All E.R. 681, CCA.
Turf Publishers Ltd v. Davies [1927] W.N. 190, DC.

Application for judicial review
By notice dated February 28, 1992 the applicants, Graham Barratt and Stuart Barratt, sought judicial review of the decision of the respondents, Abergavenny Justices, that they had jurisdiction to hear and amend all the applicants' summonses.
The facts are stated in the judgement.

Mark Laprell for the applicants.
The justices did not appear and were not represented.
Malcolm Bishop for the Crown Prosecution Service.

Watkins L.J.: The applicants, Graham and Stuart Barratt, are father and son. They are haulage contractors, whose place of business is at

19 Heywood Hall Road, Heywood, Lancashire. They have several large lorries. The drivers of them include the applicant Stuart Barratt himself and a man called Longdon.

We have before us a challenge by the applicants to a decision by the respondents, the Abergavenny Justices, on February 12, 1992, at Abergavenny Magistrates' Court, to assume jurisdiction to amend and to hear charges against the applicants for breaches by Graham Barratt of section 97A and by Stuart Barratt of that and section 96(11A) of the Transport Act 1968. The justices found the charges proved and fined both applicants. The charge against Graham Barratt, un-amended, was that on March 7, 1991, on the A465 at Abergavenny, he, being the employer of a crew member of a vehicle to which section 97 of the Transport Act 1968 applied, failed, without reason-able excuse, to secure that the crew member returned any record sheet relating to him within 21 days of completion on March 7, 1991, contrary to sectin 97(1)(a). The amendment which was brought about to that charge consisted of the deletion of "On 07/03/91 on the A465 at Abergavenny."

The first eight of nine charges against Stuart Barratt alleged, as unamended:

"On 07/03/91 on the A465 at Abergavenny . . . being a driver of a motor vehicle namely an ERF lorry to which Article 7(1) of the Community Drivers' Hours Regulations applied drove for more than 4^1/$_2$ hours without observing a minimum break of 45 minutes on 28.2.91 contrary to section 96(11A) . . ."

As amended each of the first eight charges ceased to contain: "On 07/03/91 on the A465 at Abergavenny."

The ninth charge which Stuart Barratt faced related to the charge against his father as amended.

Longdon was dealt with properly, so it would seem, the court having jurisdiction to deal with him, for the offence which he was found to have committed undoubtedly took place in the county of Gwent. He was fined. The issue involved here clearly is whether, having regard to the informations and summonses, the court had jurisdiction to deal with and adjudicate upon them in any way. The statutory provisions going to this issue are as follows. Section 1 of the Magistrates' Courts Act 1980, as material, provides:

"(1) Upon an information being laid before a justice of the peace for an area to which this section applies that any person has, or is suspected of having, committed an offence, the justice may, in any of the events mentioned in subsection (2) below, but subject to subsections (3) to (5) below – (a) issue a summons directed to that person requiring him to appear before a magistrates' court for the area to answer to the information . . .
(2) A justice of the peace for an area to which this section applies may issue a summons . . . under this section – (a) if the offence was committed or is suspected to have been committed within the area, or (c) if it appears to the justice necessary or

expedient, with a view to the better administration of justice, that the person charged should be tried jointly with, or in the same place as, some other person who is charged with an offence, and who is in custody, or is being or is to be proceeded against, within the area, or (c) if the person charged resides or is, or is believed to reside to be, within the area . . ."

Section 2, as material, provides:

"(1) A magistrates' court for a county, a London commission area or the City of London shall have jurisdiction to try all summary offences committed within the county . . . (2) Where a person charged with a summary offence appears or is brought before a magistrates' court in answer to a summons issued under paragraph (b) of section 1(2) above . . . the court shall have jurisdiction to try the offence . . ."

The Transport Act 1968 (as substituted by section 3 of the Road Traffic (Drivers' Ages and Hours of Work) Act 1976) contains a provision bearing on the question of jurisdiction in relation to the commission of offences by the use of motor vehicles. That provision is contained in section 103, the interpretation section. Section 103(7) states:

"An offence under this Part of this Act" —

the offences here clearly do come under "this Part" of the Act —

"may be treated for the purpose of conferring jurisdiction on a court (but without prejudice to any jurisdiction it may have apart from this subsection) as having been committed in any of the following places, that is to say – (a) the place where the person charged with the offence was driving when evidence of the offence first came to the attention of a constable or vehicle examiner;" —

that does not apply here —

"(b) the place where that person resides or is or is believed to reside or be at the time when the proceedings are commenced;"—

that does not apply here —

"or (c) the place where at that time that person or, in the case of an employer-driver, that person's employer or, in the case of an owner-driver, the person for whom he was driving, has his place or principal place of business or his operating centre for the vehicle in question."

That is of application in the circumstances prevailing here, for the two applicants, as I have indicated, had their place of business and their homes, not in the county of Gwent, but in the county of Lancaster.

The time when the court's jurisdiction to entertain informations, and to issue summonses arising out of them, has to be considered is when the single justice or the clerk to the justices considers whether summonses should issue. That much is clear from *Turf Publications Ltd v. Davies* [1927] W.N. 190. That was a case concerned with the Ready Money Football Betting Act 1920 and with section 31(1) of the Criminal Justice Act 1925 which states:

"Where it appears to any justice necessary or expedient, with a view to the better administration of justice, that any person charged with any indictable offence, or with a summary offence, should be tried jointly with or in the same place as some other person who is charged with an indictable offence or a summary offence, as the case may be, and who is in custody or is being or is to be proceeded against within the jurisdiction of that justice, he may, notwithstanding that the person so charged is not within that jurisdiction, issue a summons or warrant against him."

That is similar, not in every respect but in most respects, to the provision which is contained in section 1(2)(b) of the Act of 1980. In the course of his judgment, Lord Hewart C.J. said, at p. 191:

"Section 31 did not give rise to any question whether the justices hearing the charge thought it necessary or expedient that the person should be summoned or charged with the offence although he was not within the jurisdiction. It obviously related to the jurisdiction to be exercised by the justice who issued the summons."

That authority, so far as I am aware, has never been doubted. It is to the plain effect the responsibility for determining the issue of jurisdiction falls fairly and squarely upon the single justice who considers whether a summons or warrant should issue, or upon the clerk to the justices who performs a like function at any relevant time.

Under the heading

"Commencement of proccedings; information, summons, warrant"

in *Stone's Justice Manual*, (1992, Vol. 1), p. 34, it is stated:

"Every information, summons, warrant or other document laid, issued or made for the purposes of, or in connection with, any proceedings before a magistrates' court for an offence, shall be sufficient if it describes the specific offence with which the accused is charged, or of which he is convicted, in ordinary language avoiding as far as possible the use of technical terms, and without necessarily stating all the elements of the offence, and gives such particulars as may be necessary for giving reasonable information of the nature of the charge."

That comes from rule 100 of the Magistrates' Courts Rules 1981. In the notes to that passage in *Stone* it is stated:

"The form of information should state the name and address of the party charged and of the person laying the information, and the offence, when and where it was committed, which must be within the court's jurisdiction."

The clerk to the justices here, and indeed any clerk to the justices who may deal with informations, before he or the single justice deals with the matter, must pay careful regard to, inter alia, the jurisdiction of the court, with well in mind the provisions of section 1 and section 2 of the Magistrates' Courts Act 1980 and section 103 of the Transport Act 1968.

There is no doubt whatsoever, in my view, that neither the clerk nor his staff paid regard to these important provisions, or if they did, their regard was insufficient. It was taken for granted, because the charges wrongly stated the offences to have been committed as the charges stated in the unamended form on the A465 at Abergavenny, that that was in fact the place where all offences had taken place. There could not have been a more gross misstatement of where the offences charged against both the applicants had taken place than that.

Section 1(2)(a) and (b) of the Act of 1980 clearly called for very careful scrutiny in the circumstances, as indeed did section 2(1). Upon the informations before us, there is no question but that the charges came before the justices on the sole jurisdictional basis that the alleged offences were all commited within the geographical county of Gwent. This was brought to the notice of the justices and their clerk, who was sitting with them on the material day, by the solicitor for the applicants who made appropriate submissions with regard to sections 1 and 2 and the case to which I have already referred, namely, *Turf Publishers Ltd v. Davies* [1927] W.N. 190. Notwithstanding the submissions which were made – there is a careful note of them agreed to in the main by the clerk to the justices – the clerk advised the justices that they could assume to have jurisdiction to deal with the charges against the applicants, and that they proceeded to do. The exact nature of his advice as recorded, and agreed to by him, was as follows:

"[The clerk] however then proceeded to advise the justices that it was his advice that the summonses themselves were issued correctly. They may have been issued on the basis of false information" —

I think the clerk takes issue with the word "false". Let the word "incorrect" be substituted therefore —

"but at the time of issuing them [the clerk] was not aware of the error. He issued them believing the offences to have been committed in Abergavenny and hence the summonses themselves were issued correctly. At the time the summonses were laid before the justices therefore the summonses were prima facie correct and once the justices had been seised of the cases they have jurisdiction."

The note also records the following:

"The prosecution then made another attempt to convince the justices by referring to section 103(7) and suggested that the place of the offence is not considered as important. If this section is applied it entitles proposed defendants to be brought to justice at any place provided section 103(7) applies."

That seems to be a very strange and confused contention in the circumstances. The only place in which the applicants could be proceeded against, putting aside the provisions of section 1 of the Act of 1980 altogether, was in Lancashire. If the advice of the clerk to his justices had been different, namely, that there had been an error in consideration by him of them before he signed the summonses and informations, it would have been too late for the prosecution to issue fresh summonses, for more than six months had elapsed by that time from the time when the offences were alleged to have occurred.

That it is very important indeed for consideration to be given to jurisdiction at the time I have mentioned emerges from observations of Lord Goddard C.J. in *Reg. v. Blandford* [1955] 1 W.L.R. 331. In that case consideration was given to provisions of section 1(2)(b) of the Magistrates' Courts Act 1952, provisions which are wholly similar to those which are in the Act of 1980 at section 1(2)(b). In concluding his judgment, Lord Goddard C.J. said at p. 335:

> "We desire, however, to emphasise that a justice acting under this subsection should bear in mind that it is not only the interests of the prosecution that are at stake but also the interests of the defendants. While it may be very convenient and economical from the point of view of the prosecution that they should be able to proceed in a particular county, it must be remembered that to bring a man, as in this case, from Hampshire to North Wales is a very serious matter. It would necessarily cause him considerable expense and might put very great difficulties in the way of the preparation and presentment of his defence and the calling of witnesses. We are not saying that any injustice or any undue hardship was caused in this case . . ."

The background to this affair is as follows. I take what I am about to say from the very helpful affidavit of Mr Griffiths who was the principal Crown prosecutor based at Newport. He informs us that the whole matter was set on foot by Police Constable Neale of the Gwent constabulary stopping a lorry driven by Simon David Longdon. Having regard to what he then discovered, he told Longdon that he was going to report him for possible summonses for offences to do with the tachograph charts which the constable had looked at. He informed him that there was at least a possibility, if not a high probability, that Longdon had been driving for longer hours than he was by law entitled to. The constable seized, not only tachograph charts which related to the driving of that vehicle by Longdon, but also tachograph charts which related to the driving of that vehicle on previous occasions by Stuart Barratt. From then on inquiries were made through the South Wales constabulary, various other sectors of the Gwent constabulary and the Greater Manchester constabulary.

Accordingly, when all the information from those various forces was assembled, it was decided that the charges already referred to in this judgment should be brought. Accordingly, informations were, as thought appropriate at that time, drafted at Pontypool in Gwent. According to modern technology, the informations were tramsitted from a computer console from police headquarters and received via the computer link to a computer console in the justices' clerks' department at Cwmbran, which is not very far from Abergavenny. There these informations appeared on the screen of the console.

102

Amongst the various equipment attached to the console, there were pro forma informations. On blank pro forma informations, the information which was sent by this computer link was printed out without human intervention. Thus we see, from the material before us, the original informations which emanated from the equipment in the magistrates' court.

Mr Griffiths goes on to say in his affidavit, and say very rightly, that what the clerk receiving the informations at the magistrates' court's office should then proceed to do would be to decide whether a summons should be issued, considering whether the offence alleged on the information is known to the law; second, whether there was jurisdiction in the court to hear the matter; and third, whether there had been due compliance with time limits. He goes on to say that, whilst it is conceded that the original summons relating to Stuart Barratt wrongly specified both the date and location of the alleged offence, the date of the offence is specified elsewhere in the summons, and that it is not possible, in any event, to specify an exact location of each offence because of their continuing nature.

It seems to me that what happened here, up to the point when the informations were transmitted to the magistrates' court, was that insuffucient regard was paid by the police to the jurisdiction of the court at Abergavenny. Here, in my opinion, was a need for the Gwent constabulary to pass the information it had about Longdon to the Greater Manchester police, for it was in that area that the bulk of the offences alleged here took place. Thus they occurred within the jurisdiction of the local police force and of the local magistrates' court, where the offence could be properly tried having regard to section 103(7) of the Transport Act 1968. The offences committed by Longdon almost pale into insignificance compared with the multiplicity of offences said to have been committed by Stuart Barratt.

However, whilst the police officers concerned took the decision they did and thus became exposed to criticism, there was still a vital duty to be performed at the magistrates' court by the clerk to the justices and his staff. It may be that on a cursory glance – it could only have been a cursory glance – the justices' clerk or a member of his staff could be said to be misled, by the words appearing on the informations:

"On March 7, 1991 on the A465 at Abergavenny,"
into thinking that there was no question here but that all of these offences had been committed in the geographical county of Gwent. If that was a proper assumption, then there can be no doubt that the justices would have had jurisdiction to hear the charges, but it was, in my view, by no means a proper assumption. One has only to look, with perhaps rather more than a cursory glance, at these charges to see that they contain not only wrong but also contradictory information. In the leading part of the information the date is stated to be March 7, 1991, and in a later part the date is expressed to be, looking at the first of the charges against Stuart Barratt, February 28, 1991.

That alone should have alerted the justices' clerk's staff and the clerk to the justices, that there was need for inquiry of the police as to what precisely was being alleged with regard to where the offences were committed. There should then have been a dialogue between the police and the clerk to the justices as to the particulars of the charges, so that the clerk could clear his mind as to whether or not, having regard to the statutory provisions, he could say, by looking at section 2(1) or section 1(2)(b) of the Act of 1980, that jurisdiction could be founded in the court at Abergavenny. That he did not consider section 1(2)(b) is, I think, beyond doubt. He admits that he did not. If he had considered it, it seems to me, having regard to the whole of the circumstances and the nature of the charges, the accumulation of them and so on, that he could have come to no other conclusion than that it was not expedient nor necessary that these applications should be tried at Abergavenny. Necessity and expediency, it seems to me, demanded that they should be tried in the county of Lancaster or Greater Manchester, as the case may be.

My conclusion is that there was unhappily here, for the reasons which I have explained, a failure by both the police and the clerk to the justices to pay sufficient regard to the question of the court's jurisdiction to hear these summary offences. Very different provisions apply to indictable offences. To those no further reference needs to be made.

Mr Bishop, who has appeared here on behalf of the Crown Prosecution Service, has submitted that the clerk, notwithstanding that he gave no thought to section 1(2)(b) of the Act of 1980, gave proper advice to the justices for a number of reasons. He points in his skeleton argument, expanded on by him in his submissions to the court, to the fact that it is stated, with regard to the content of an information, that the charge need not be in formal language. Indeed, an information can be laid orally, so that it is not necessary, he says, for an information to state where the offence was committed. I disagree with that as a general proposition. It is usually necessary for the information to state where the offence was committed. However, with regard to offences under the Transport Act 1968, which appear from a study of tachographs, they might be committed here or somewhere abroad. Accordingly section 103(7) was brought into force to allow of the prosecution of those offences committed, no matter where, to be made in the area where the business which owns the relevant lorry is being conducted or has its headquarters, or where the owner of the lorry lives, as the case may be.

It is, therefore, of importance that an information states as well as can be where an offence is alleged to have taken place as well as the name and address of the party charged.

Mr Bishop then points to the words used in section 1(2)(a) of the Act of 1980:

> "(a) if the offence was committed or is suspected to have been committed within the area . . ."

"Suspected", it is submitted, means "believed". Any study of the offences here, as set out in the informations, could lead no one to believe that they had been committed in the county of Gwent. Mr Bishop points to the fact that Longdon was within the jurisdiction of the court. That is undoubtedly right. Longdon was the applicants' driver at the material time and he did undoubtedly commit offences within the county, but the fact that he was properly dealt with means nothing unless the clerk of the justices, when he was considering the informations and deciding whether summonses should issue against the applicants, gave thought to the provisions of section 1(2)(b) and used his discretion as to necessity and expediency to cause persons other than Longdon, *i.e.*, the applicants, to be tried along with him at Abergavenny.

For reasons which I have already explained, the fact that Longdon was charged and properly dealt with is of no account, as no attention was paid to section 1(2)(b) by the clerk to the justices.

Mr Bishop relies on section 123 of the Act of 1980. That is a well known provision. It has nothing to do with this case, however. It deals with objection taken to the form or content of any summons or warrant. We are dealing here, not with the defect in form or content of any summons or warrant, in relation to evidence, for example, but with what was fundamentally a question of jurisdiction.

There are other points taken by Mr Bishop which do not need to be addressed, save this one. He says that it did not really matter how the applicants appeared before the justices at Abergavenny, nor that they appeared there because the clerk to the justices was wrong, mistaken in thinking that the offences had been committed in the county of Gwent, if there was some other lawful route by which they could have come before the justices, and there was, namely, under section 1(2)(b) of the Act of 1980. That was sufficient to clothe the justices with jurisdiction. I disagree with that. One cannot know what the clerk would have thought if he had addressed his mind to section 1(2)(b). He may very well have come to the conclusion, giving the matter careful thought, that it was neither necessary nor expedient for people from Lancashire to come from their headquarters with all their records to Gwent to be tried for offences which are wholly un-connected with the geographical county.

Mr Laprell contends that this contention had consistently been made before the matter came before the justices. The solicitor then acting for the applicants made a forceful representation to the clerk to the justices on the telephone about jurisdiction, but to no avail. In my judgment, this unfortunate chapter of errors, commited by police officers, the clerk and his staff, has led to a situation in which it seems to me there is no avoiding the conclusion that the justices, at the material time, did not have jurisdiction to hear these charges.

It does matter by which route defendants appear before justices where jurisdiction is in issue. Especially does it matter, in a case such as this, where the only proper way in which they could have come before the justices was via section 1(2)(b) of the Act of 1980 or section 103 of the Act of 1968 and no consideration was given to either of those provisions. For these reasons I would let certiorari go and quash the convictions.

Rougier J. I agree. In the world of computers there is a slogan which goes to the acronym of GIGO, which stands for garbage in/garbage out. This unfortunate case serves as a warning to justices' clerks and their staff that, although computers properly used can greatly accelerate the administration of the court's business, any documents which they produce need careful scrutiny.

Application granted. Order of certiorari quashing applicants convictions. Order for payment of applicants' costs out of central funds

Solicitors for the applicants: J A Backhouse & Sons, Blackburn.
Solicitors for the Crown Prosecution Service: Crown Prosecution Service, Newport.
Reported by Miss Clare Noon, Barrister.

A2–07 The duty of the magistrate or clerk accepting the information to consider the application of section 1(2)(b) is of particular importance because, of course, there should be a contemporaneous note on the court file confirming that the point was considered. A court should always be warned that the jurisdictional point is to be taken and the absence of such a note is strong evidence that the requirements of the section were not complied with.

A2–08 Jurisdictional issues are also important in the increasing number of cases which follow checks on commercial vehicles which have been, or will be, operating in Europe. A court in England or Wales can have no jurisdiction where the offence is both started and completed outside England and Wales. However, where the offence is committed partly here and partly in Europe, the English and Welsh courts will have jurisdiction subject to the *"Abergavenny"* decision.

A2–09 By way of example, the court would not have jurisdiction if the offence was that of driving for more than $4^{1}/_{2}$ hours without taking 45 minutes break in the course of a working day that both started and finished in Europe. When, however, that same working day finished in Dover at the end of a ferry crossing, the court in Dover or, subject to *"Abergavenny"*, elsewhere would have jurisdiction as the offence would have continued into the jurisdiction.

A2–10 It should be remembered that, for these purposes, Scotland is a "foreign" country and offences that do not cross the border may not be prosecuted here.

A2–11 The jurisdiction point is often missed by both defence advocates and the courts, even though it can be relevant in many cases. Whenever the defendant faces allegations in relation to offences that clearly occurred, if they occurred elsewhere the jurisdictional point should always be considered.

DEPARTMENT OF TRANSPORT CODE OF PRACTICE – SAFETY OF LOADS ON VEHICLES

CONTENTS

General Requirements		Page **A3–01**
Section 1	Introduction	109
Section 2	Principles of Load Safety	111
Section 3	Choice of Vehicle and Arrangement of Loads	114
Section 4	Anchorage Points, Headboards and Internal Partitions	117
Section 5	Load Securing Equipment	121
Section 6	General Requirements for Securing Loads	124

Additional Requirements for Specific Types of Loads		
Section 7	General Freight	131
Section 8	Metal Loads	137
Section 9	Timber Loads	146
Section 10	Loose Bulk Loads	149
Section 11	Pallets	151
Section 12	Containers	154
Section 13	Engineering Plant	157
Section 14	Carriage of Vehicles by "Piggy back"	178

APPENDICES		
Appendix A	Regulations concerning the safety of loads on vehicles	180
Appendix B	Regulations concerning "Dangerous Goods" carried road vehicles.	181
Appendix C	Regulations concerning the transit of animals by road vehicles	183

Acknowledgements

The following organisations and departments collaborated in the production of this revised Code of Practice.

Association of Webbing Load Restraint Equipment Manufacturers

Cordage Manufacturers Institute

Freight Transport Association

Health and Safety Executive

Metropolitan Police

Metropolitan Police Forensic Science Laboratory

Road Haulage Association

Road Transport Industry Training Board

Society of Motor Manufacturers and Traders

Department of Transport

Section 1. Introduction

1.1 Not only is it a legal requirement but it is commonsense to make sure that all loads carried on vehicles are adequately secured so that there is no likelihood of them moving or falling off with the very real possibility of danger to the driver and other road users. This applies to all vehicles and to all types of load. Loose objects or materials etc. falling or blowing off open vehicles may not always be a danger but are likely to be at least a nuisance and at worst fatal. Remember, if a load either causes or is likely to cause danger or nuisance to people in the vicinity of the vehicle an offence might be committed — see Regulation 97 of the Motor Vehicles (Construction and Use) Regulations 1978 the text of which is given in Appendix A.

1.2 Sections 1–6 of this Code outline the general requirements and basic principles of load safety. Sections 7–14 provide advice, based on proven good practice, about satisfactory methods for securing the more common types of load.

1.3 Because of the extreme variety of loads, vehicles and operating conditions it is not possible to cover all the circumstances likely to be encountered by drivers and operators so the contents of this Code must not be regarded as exhaustive or exclusive. Satisfactory securing methods not mentioned in this Code are in existence and others will be developed in the future. However, the basic principles described in this Code must be complied with irrespective of the actual method used to secure the load.

1.4 In addition to the load safety methods described in this Code extra precautions are necessary when dangerous goods, eg toxic and corrosive chemicals and flammable substances, are carried on road vehicles. A list of the main regulations and approved Codes of Practice currently applicable to the carriage of these substances is given at Appendix B.

1.5 High Loads

Particular attention should be paid to the dangers of high loads that might have to pass under bridges or other structures across roads. Every year several hundred bridges are hit by lorries loaded too high or which are themselves too high to pass underneath, resulting in some cases in both drivers and other people being killed or injured. Even a slight impact on a railway bridge can dislodge the rails which could result in a derailed train and many casualties.

It is already a requirement in Regulation 80A of the Motor Vehicles (Construction and Use) Regulations 1978, as amended by Amendment No. 5 of 1978: S.I. 1978 No. 1317, that skip carriers, engineering plant, and vehicles carrying containers, demountable bodies and engineering equipment display the total travelling height of the vehicle in the cab if this height is over 12 feet (3.66 metres). Any driver of a high vehicle should watch for bridges and advance warning signs indicating the safe clearance height, and exercise extreme caution.

1.6 Ro-Ro Ferry Operations

The guidance given in this Code is intended to ensure the safety of loads on vehicles on the road taking into account acceleration, braking and cornering. However, when a vehicle is carried on a ship, as in roll-on, roll-off ferry operations, the vehicle and its load will be subject to different forces due to the rolling and pitching motions of the vessel, and hence a restraint system that is suitable for road use will often not be adequate at sea.

The Department of Trade Merchant Shipping Notice M849 (or any subsequent revision) gives some guidance on the securing of vehicles on ships and an indication of the forces likely to be encountered at sea. Vehicle operators intending to use ro-ro ferries should ensure that their load restraint systems are capable of withstanding such forces.

The securing of the vehicle to the ship is also important and the vehicles should therefore be fitted with lashing points that are, again, of adequate strength to withstand the forces likely to be encountered at sea and easily accessible to deck crews – not obstructed by fuel tanks, batteries etc. If necessary advice on this latter point should be sought from the ferry operators.

1.7 Suggestions for Improvements

Inevitably, as a result of further experience and a continual development of load securing systems, this Code of Practice will need to be periodically reviewed and amended. Suggestions for improving or adding to its content are welcomed and should be sent to:

The Department of Transport
Vehicle Standards and Engineering Division
2 Marsham Street
LONDON SW1P 3EB

Section 2. Principles of Load Safety

2.1 Forces are generated on the load when a vehicle brakes, accelerates, changes direction or crosses road undulations (see Figs 1 & 2).
These forces are frequently greater than the frictional restraint between the load and platform, therefore a load that is not secured by some form of restraining device may not be secure.

2.2 The forces acting on the load during braking increase with the rate of deceleration and the weight of the load. Therefore as braking efficiencies and payloads increase it becomes increasingly important that loads are adequately secured.

2.3 It requires much more force to stop a load which has started moving than it does to prevent movement in the first place. This 'battering ram' effect increases rapidly with the increase in distance through which the load moves relative to the vehicle. It is essential therefore that the load is restrained in such a way that movement relative to the vehicle is prevented.

2.4 The basic principle upon which this Code of Practice is based is that the combined strength of the load restraint system must be sufficient to withstand a force not less than the total weight of the load forward and half of the weight of the load backwards and sideways (see Fig. 3). Vertical movements may occur but these should be overcome if the conditions above are met. These principles are based on the maximum forces likely to be experienced during normal road use but will not be sufficient to restrain the load when a vehicle is involved in an accident. The recommendations in this Code are therefore not intended to cover an accident situation where greatly increased forces are likely to be encountered.

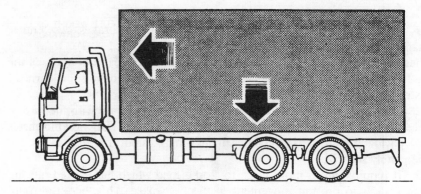

Figure 1

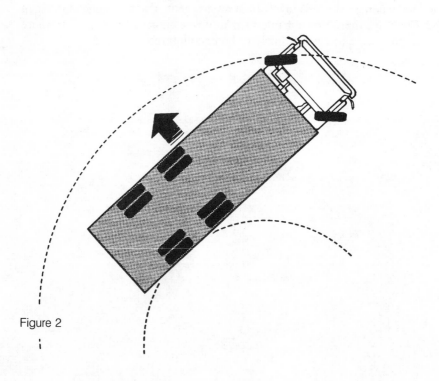

Figure 2

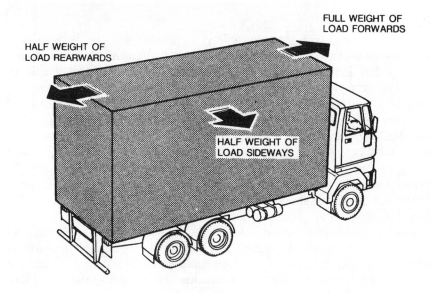

Figure 3

SECTION 3. CHOICE OF VEHICLE AND ARRANGEMENT OF LOADS

Choice of Vehicle

3.1 It is management's responsibility to provide suitable vehicles and securing equipment for each load carried and to ensure that drivers and loading staff are competent and have received sufficient instruction in its use. It is the driver's duty to check and ensure that the load is adequately secured at all times.

3.2 The design and construction of the vehicle and its bodywork should be suitable for the loads which it is likely to carry, particularly in terms of the characteristics and strengths of the materials used. Rotproofing and anti corrosion treatments of load bearing components are highly desirable. When a vehicle is to be carried on a ship, as in roll-on, roll-off, ferry operations provision should be made for the extra load restraint needed and chassis anchorage points to secure the vehicle to the deck.

3.3 The maximum expected load on the floor should be ascertained so that the floor itself and the section and spacing of supporting crossbeams is sufficient. In any calculation account should be taken not only of the load itself but also any extra forces due to the loading method eg the use of fork lift trucks on the floor during loading/unloading.

3.4 The relationship between the vehicle's wheelbase, body length and body overhang should be carefully considered in relation to the composition of the loads to be carried especially if full use is to be made of permitted maximum axle loads.

3.5 The overall height of a loaded vehicle must be checked to ensure that it is less than that of any overhead obstruction likely to be encountered en route. The regulations (see Section 1 paragraph 5) require certain types of vehicle, and others carrying certain loads, to have the maximum height of the vehicle displayed inside the cab so that it is clearly visible to the driver.

3.6 To prevent vehicles grounding on level crossings etc regulations require that a certain minimum ground clearance for trailers must be maintained (see Regulation 74A of the Motor Vehicles (Construction and Use) Regulations 1978, as amended by Amendment No. 2 of 1983: S.I. 1983 No. 471). This is particularly important for low loading trailers.

Arrangement of Loads

3.7 Before a vehicle is loaded it should be checked to ensure that its load platform, bodywork, anchorage points or twist locks, as appropriate to the load, are in sound and serviceable condition.

3.8 It is imperative that the maximum permitted axle and gross weight limits are not exceeded. Where part of the load is to be picked up or removed in the course of a journey the effect on axle and gross weights must not be overlooked. Although removal of part of the load will reduce the gross weight the change in weight distribution may cause individual axles to become overloaded.

3.9 Normally the load should be arranged so that it does not obstruct the driver's field of vision including rear view through the driving mirrors. In

114

the case of wide or long projecting loads or where the load obscures obligatory lights, reflectors, rear markings or registration plates care must be taken to comply with the requirements of the Road Vehicles Lighting Regulations 1984 S.I. 1984 No. 812.

3.10 If practicable, the load should be placed in contact with a headboard. Where this is not practicable then additional means of securing must be used. Possible methods include:

(a) an obstacle fitted transversely across the vehicle platform and firmly attached to the chassis frame;

(b) blocks, scotches or wedges to prevent individual items of a load moving in any direction. Care must be taken to ensure that these are adequately secured to the vehicle platform;

(c) additional lashing.

3.11 In order to achieve maximum vehicle stability the load should be placed so that the centre of gravity is kept as low as practicable and near to the vehicle's longitudinal centre line.

This means that where practicable:

(a) the load should be spread to give an even weight distribution over the floor area;

(b) when a load is stacked the larger and heavier items should be placed at the bottom (see Fig. 4);

(c) the heavier items should be placed nearer to the longitudinal centre line of the vehicle and the lighter ones towards the sides.

3.12 The weight of heavy loads of small dimensions should be distributed across the vehicle platform by the use of load spreading devices.

3.13 Great care must be taken when loading semi-trailers which have no means of support other than the retractable legs. If the front of the trailer is loaded first it is possible for it to "nose dive". Trestles or similar supports should be used beneath the fifth wheel coupling plate if it is necessary to work underneath a laden or part laden semi-trailer.

3.14 Before setting off on a journey all tensioners and turn buckles must be adequately tightened and properly stowed. However they must not be over tightened by using levers etc which are longer than those recommended by the manufacturer because this leads to over stressing and possible failure of the lashing or damage to the load.

3.15 The load should be checked frequently for security and the lashings tested for adequate tension after the vehicle has travelled a few miles and again at intervals during the journey. Weather conditions affect the tension of rope lashings and this may lead to damage of the load or loss of security if these are not correctly re-tensioned.

3.16 All loose chains, for example those used for loading skip containers, loose ropes, and other means of lashing, must be properly stowed.

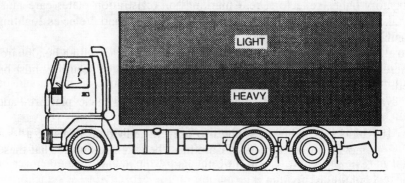

Figure 4

SECTION 4. ANCHORAGE POINTS, HEADBOARDS AND INTERNAL
PARTITIONS

Anchorage Points

4.1 Traditional rope hooks cannot restrain other than light loads. For this reason it may be necessary to equip some vehicles, particularly those with platform bodies, with additional load anchorage points. These should be designed and integrated into the structure so that the forces imposed on them are transmitted to the main chassis frame of the vehicle.

4.2 *Capacity*: Load anchorage points should be rated at capacities of 0.5 tonne, 1.0 tonne or 2.0 tonne and upwards. The capacity of each anchorage point may not be indicated on the vehicle but the vehicle manufacturer or bodybuilder should provide information on the capacity of each anchorage point. The design and construction must allow a safety factor of twice the specified capacity acting in any direction through which the lashing can be attached.

4.3 *Design*: No specific recommendations are made about the design of anchorage points but they must be compatible with the type of securing equipment used.

4.4 *Fitting*: Anchorage points should be firmly attached either directly to the chassis or to a metal crosspiece or outrigger. Anchorage points which are secured only to wooden members are unlikely to provide the restraint required. The fitting of additional anchorage points to existing vehicles must in no way weaken the chassis or body structure. In particular, holes must not be drilled in the top or lower flanges of the chassis side members and welding to the chassis without the approval of the original manufacturer is not recommended. Fig. 5 illustrates a suggested anchorage point of 2.0 tonne load capacity.

4.5 *Number to be fitted*: Sufficient load anchorage points should be provided in relation to platform length with at least three each side or such greater number as is necessary to ensure that the sum of the capacity of the anchorage points is not less than the maximum rated load of the vehicle. Thus a 3.0 tonne rated load would require at least three per side each of 0.5 tonne capacity. In the case of higher rated loads the number of anchorage points and their capacity will also depend on whether the vehicle is purpose built for a particular type of traffic or is to be engaged in general haulage operations where the size and weight of individual items may vary considerably. Thus an operator of a 20 tonne rated load vehicle used exclusively for a particular commodity might need to choose between specifying 40 x 0.5 tonne points, 20 x 1.0 tonne points, or 10 x 2.0 tonne points depending on the character of the load. On the other hand, the general haulier with a similar vehicle used for miscellaneous loads would in all probability need six or more 2.0 tonne points plus enough 1.0 tonne or 0.5 tonne points to make up at least the required 20 tonne of restraint. Here again the precise pattern would depend upon foreknowledge of the types of load to be carried.

4.6 *Number to be used*: The number of anchorage points actually used on a particular journey will depend on the weight and dimensions of the load

117

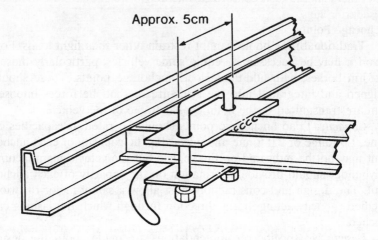

Approx. 5cm

Figure 5

being carried and its location on the platform in relation to the headboard or other additional means of restraint.

The table below gives some suggested values *but* in some cases additional restraint by the headboard or other means would be required.

1.2 Axle Vehicles(Flats/Pickups/Drop Sided)

BODY LENGTH		NUMBER OF ANCHORAGE POINTS				
		Minimum 0.5 tonne anchorages				
	PAYLOAD (tonnes)	UP TO 2	2–4	4–6	6–8	8+
MINIMUM	TO 12FT (3.65m)	6	8	10	12	—
12FT	TO 16FT (4.87m)	8	10	12	16	18
16FT	TO 2OFT (6.09m)	10	12	14	18	20
20FT	T0 24FT (7.31m)	12	14	16	20	24

2.3 To 4 Axle Vehicles		Minimum 0.5 tonne anchorages			
	PAYLOAD (tonnes)	UP TO 10	10–12	12–16	16+
MINIMUM	TO 18FT (5.48m)	14	16	18	20
18 FT	TO 24FT	18	20	22	24
24FT	ABOVE	20	22	24	28

FOR VEHICLES CARRYING HEAVY CONCENTRATED LOADS ON A REGULAR BASIS IT IS PREFERABLE TO HAVE WELDED ØEYE BOLTS/SHACKLES LET INTO DECKING/SIDE RAVES AT A JOINED CROSS MEMBER.

118

3. TRAILERS

Trailers should also conform to the above weight/length dimensions for securing lugs.

∅ EYE BOLTS TO BS 4278
∅ SHACKLES TO BS 3032 and BS 3551
∅ STEEL HOOKS TO BS 2903

Headboards and Front Bulkheads

4.7 A headboard, when fitted, should be treated as part of the load restraint system since a headboard meeting this Code should be able to restrain half the rated payload of the vehicle in the forward direction. [Some exceptions are listed at the end of this section.]

4.8 *Strength*: A headboard should be capable of withstanding a horizontal force uniformly distributed over its vertical area equal to half the rated payload of the vehicle. IMPORTANT see Section 7 paragraph 1 for factors which reduce effectiveness. The design must be such that the whole body and vehicle structure will withstand the forces imposed on it when the headboard is loaded as described above.

4.9 *Width*: The headboard width should be equal to the width of the loading platform unless the type of load permits a narrower headboard. It should however not be less than the width of the cab.

4.10 *Height*: The headboard height should be sufficient to obstruct forward movement of the type of load which the vehicle is designed to carry unless adequate load restraint is provided by other means.

4.11 The headboard should not have apertures large enough to allow penetration by any part of the load. Large apertures should be covered with a steel mesh or similar material.

4.12 When loads such as metal bars, beams, girders, sheet metal etc are liable to penetrate the cab in the event of failure of the securing devices the headboard must be adequately reinforced to resist damage from individual elements of the load.

4.13 *In Use*

(i) *Loading*

For the maximum benefit to be derived from a headboard it is essential that the load is in contact with it. If a space is left so that the load can move forwards before reaching the headboard then its restraining capacity will be greatly reduced.

(ii) *Damage*

Headboards should be examined frequently for damage. Particular attention should be given to timber panels or boards and to the headboard to chassis mounting points. Damaged headboards should not be used for restraint purposes.

119

4.14 Bulkheads on small closed vans
In the case of closed vans of 3.5 tonne gross vehicle weight (G.V.W.) or more, where the cab is an integral part of the body, a bulkhead must be fitted, between the load compartment and the cab. Such a bulkhead should afford adequate protection to cab personnel and should be designed to resist a uniformly distributed horizontal force of at least 0.5 x the weight of the load.

INTERNAL PARTITIONS
4.15 Vehicles are sometimes divided by internal partitions into a number of compartments each of which is self-sufficient in terms of load restraint. The headboard or internal partition should be designed to resist a uniformly distributed horizontal force of 0.5 x rated load for that compartment.

EXCEPTIONS (see paragraph 4.7)
4.16 Bodies designed specifically for loads which are to be restrained by means other than the headboard. *e.g.* refrigerated vans (load should not bear against the reefer unit). These vehicles should carry a manufacturer's plate clearly stating the types of load for which they are intended and the method of load restraint to be used.
4.17 Trestle type headboards or bolsters for supporting long loads. These should carry a manufacturer's plate clearly stating the rated load capacity both vertically and horizontally because the forces will be determined by the type of load carried. *e.g.,* a bolster to support a crane jib will not require the same horizontal strength as a bolster to support one end of a steel girder.
4.18 Vehicles used for the carriage of carcass meat. These should be equipped with rails and sliding hooks and be adequately lit. The rails should be fitted with fixed hinged "stops" at 4–5ft intervals to prevent the surging or sliding of carcases due to motion of the vehicle or brake application.
   When loading the vehicle the carcasses should be distributed evenly on all rails and the stops applied. If part off-loading takes place the remaining load should be re-distributed evenly and the "stops" re-applied.
4.19 At all times the floor of the vehicle should be kept clear of blood and other slippery matter.
   In addition to the load safety methods described in this Code extra provisions are necessary when animals are carried on road vehicles. A list of the main regulations and approved Codes of Practice currently applicable to the carriage of animals is given at Appendix C.

SECTION 5. LOAD SECURING EQUIPMENT

5.1 The selection of the best means of securing a load to a vehicle will depend on the type and composition of the load to be carried. Operators should equip themselves with the correct securing equipment for the types of load carried and where general cargoes are carried various types should be available. Clamps, special bolts, steel wire ropes, chains, webbing harnesses, nets, ropes and shoring bars are all suitable devices for use in load restraint but it is essential to ensure that they are strong enough for the weight of loads carried.

5.2 All equipment used for securing loads should be regularly inspected for wear or damage. Special attention should be paid to webbing and rope to ensure that there is no visible deterioration due to constant use, such as fraying of the strands, and that they have not been cut or damaged in any other way through misuse. If there is any doubt as to whether repairs are required, reference should be made to the manufacturer or suppliers of the lashing.

5.3 Steel wire rope made up into special straps or slings is suitable for securing a load when used in conjunction with other devices such as shackles and thimbles. The strength of steel wire rope will depend on the quality of the steel used, the number of strands, the number of wires in each strand, the diameter of the rope and the method of construction. Wire ropes must have a safe working load compatible with the requirements of the load being carried. Recommendations for the minimum breaking load of various sizes and types of wire rope are contained in BS 302, BS 1290 gives safe working loads for wire rope slings, and BS 6210 is a Code of Practice for wire rope slings. Wire ropes having a diameter of less than 8mm will not be suitable for load restraint purposes. Wire ropes should be free from rust and must not be used if they show evidence of weakening such as broken wires or strands. Other coupling equipment used with wire rope must be of corresponding quality and strength. Sharp bends will reduce the effective strength of wire rope.

5.4 Chains are suitable for lashing loads when used in a similar manner to steel wire ropes. Three properties determine the strength of a chain: the length of its links, the quality of metal used and thickness of the links. A chain with a given link diameter and material will possess varied strengths depending upon the length of the link. The longer the link the more susceptible is the chain to damage — long links can easily be deformed if they are tensioned over a corner. The chain used should be compatible with the requirements of the load carried.

Recommendations for the safe working of various sizes of steel chain are contained in BS 6405, BS 1663, BS 4942 and BS 6304. The use of iron or split link chain is not recommended. Chains will be used in conjunction with tensioners and turn buckles which must have a safe working load compatible with that of the chain

5.5 Webbing assemblies are suitable for securing many types of load. They usually consist of a webbing strap with some form of end fittings and incorporate a tensioning device. It is recommended that webbing assemblies manufactured to comply with BS 5759 are used. These will be marked with a Rated Assembly Strength which should never be exceeded. Sleeves and corner protectors should be used to avoid damage to either the load or the webbing where the harness crosses the sharp corners of a load. Care should be taken to ensure that the metal components of the harness do not become corroded or damaged, that the webbing is not cut and that all stitching is sound. Advice should be sought from the manufacturers before repairs are carried out.

5.6 Nets securing or retaining some types of load may be constructed from webbing straps or ropes of either natural or man-made fibres or steel wire. Webbing nets are generally used as barriers to divide the load space into compartments. Rope or cord nets may be used to secure loads either to pallets or direct to the vehicle as the primary restraint system. Lighter nets can be used to cover open bodied vehicles and skips when the type of load makes it unnecessary to use a sheet. It is recommended that nets which comply with BS 6451 should be used. Care should be taken to ensure that the metal components of nets do not become corroded or damaged, that the webbing is not cut and that all stitching is sound. Rope and cord nets should be checked for cuts or other damage to the fibres. If necessary repairs should be carried out by a competent person before the net is used again.

5.7 Rope used for lashings should preferably be manufactured from polypropylene, polyester, sisal or manilla. Polyamide (nylon) ropes are not so suitable as they tend to stretch under load. Ropes should be of 3 strand construction and must have a minimum nominal diameter of at least 10mm. The ends of the rope should be spliced or otherwise treated to prevent fraying. Rope should be selected having regard to the maximum loading to be imposed in each lashing and it is recommended that ropes manufactured to BS 2052 or 4928 should be used. The maximum rated load for these ropes should be indicated by the manufacturer on an attached label or sleeve. Knots and sharp bends will reduce the effective strength of rope and the strength of sisal or manilla rope is also likely to be reduced by water saturation. Wet ropes should always be allowed to dry naturally. When a rope passes over sharp edges of a load some form of corner protector or sleeve should be used to prevent the rope being cut or otherwise damaged.

5.8 Purpose made clamps are suitable for securing loads which are fitted with lifting pockets, brackets or other specially designed attachments. In most cases it will be necessary to reinforce the deck of the vehicle in the vicinity of the clamp position. The design of the clamp and reinforcement should be carried out in accordance with the recommendation of the vehicle manufacturer. A minimum of four clamps should be used and three of these must be strong enough to restrain the load if one clamp fails to function correctly.

5.9 ISO freight containers may be secured to the vehicle by means of special container locks commonly known as twist locks. In most cases twist locks will be fitted to the vehicle during manufacture but where they are fitted at a later date then modifications to the chassis/structure should be carried out in accordance with the recommendations of the vehicle manufacturer. Twist locks should be inspected regularly for wear, damage and correct operation. Locking devices, which are intended to prevent the operating levers from moving during transit, should be given special attention. A minimum of four twist locks should be provided for each container carried.

5.10 For use of sheets see Section 6 paragraphs 11–13 and Section 7 paragraphs 8 and 11.

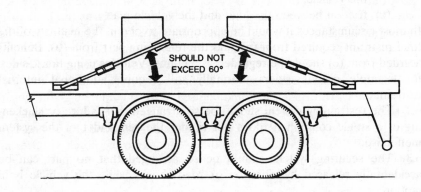

SHOULD NOT EXCEED 60°

Figure 6

SECTION 6. GENERAL REQUIREMENTS FOR SECURING LOADS

6.1 The total load restraint system will generally consist of a combination of:

(a) lashings secured to anchorage points attached to the vehicle chassis which includes cross bearers, outriggers etc;

(b) baulking arrangements including headboards, bulkheads, spigots, transverse beams, shoring bars etc which are securely attached to the vehicle;

(c) friction between the load and the vehicle platform.

In most circumstances it would be appropriate to obtain the majority of the total restraint required from (a), and the remaining part from (b). Benefits accrued from (c) should be regarded as a bonus. Vehicles using fabric sides, for example curtain siders, normally still require additional internal restraints.

6.2 The restraining system should be so arranged that failure or slackening of a single component does not render the remainder of the system ineffective.

6.3 The securing system should be so arranged that no part can be accidentally released by vibration or road shocks while the vehicle is in motion.

6.4 Headboards, sideboards and tailboards fitted to vehicles, if adequately constructed, may provide some restraint to movement of the load. Light loads may be carried on this type of vehicle without additional restraint provided that the height of the load is less than the height of the boards, and that there is no risk of the load moving and breaking through any of the boards. In any instance where the load exceeds the height of any of the boards some form of lashing must be used.

6.5 On platform vehicles some form of load restraining device will always be required.

6.6 All items of loose equipment not in use (sheets, ropes, dunnage etc) and loose surplus equipment in service (rope ends etc) must be securely restrained at all times and wherever they are placed.

6.7 In order to obtain the maximum efficiency from every part of the restraint system it is essential that the requirements described in the following paragraphs are met.

A. Lashings

6.8 The lashings and fastening devices (ropes, webbings, chains, cables, clamps etc) should be in sound condition and must be capable of withstanding all normal forces. To avoid movement of the load, lashings must be properly tensioned at all times using a tensioning device specified by the manufacturer of the lashing. Never overtension lashings by the use of levers.

6.9 It is most important that lashings which provide forward restraint are as near to the horizontal as possible and never at an angle of more than 60°, because the loading increases sharply as the lashings approach the vertical position (see Fig. 6).

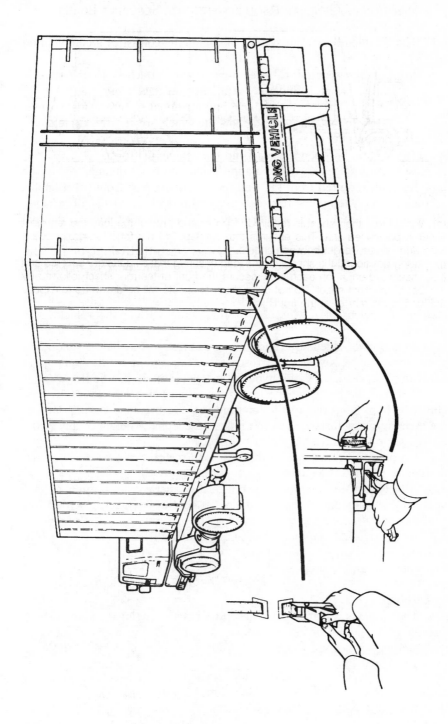

Figure 7

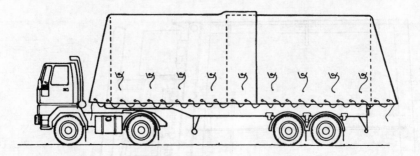

Figure 8

(a) Where more than sheet is required to cover and protect the load the rearmost sheet is positioned first. This ensures that overlaps do not face forward allowing wind and rain etc to get between sheets.

(b) Having positioned the sheets on the load ensuring that all parts are covered and that sheets are equal on each side, secure the front of the rear sheet followed by the rear of the front sheet. Do not overtighten or sheets will be drawn up to expose the load at the rear or at the front.

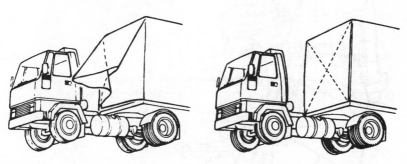

Figure 9

(c) The next stage is to secure the front of the sheet.
1. Step 1. Draw in surplus sheet from sides, cross over front and secure.
   Step 2. Draw down over cross-overs the remaining surplus sheet to form a full width flat front flap.

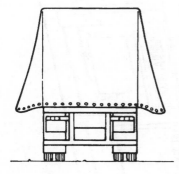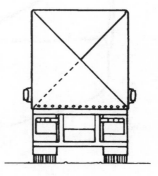

Figure 10

(d) Having secured front sheet, secure the sides of the rear sheet to the rearmost corners.
(e) Rear of the load should be sheeted and folded as illustrated above (right).

Figure 11

6.10 Lashings should be protected against abrasion and/or cutting by the use of corner protectors or protective sleeves.

B. Sheets

6.11 Except in the case of very light bulk loads conventional sheets (tarpaulins) should be regarded as providing no more than weather protection and the load must be independently secured. However, purpose made load sheets embodying webbing straps are available (see Fig. 7) and are satisfactory up to their rated load capacity provided the straps are secured to body attachments of equivalent strength.

6.12 Where more than one sheet is needed to cover a load the rearmost one should be put on first and then the following ones put on working progressively towards the front of the vehicle (see Figs. 8–10). This will ensure that the overlapping part of the sheets faces rearwards so preventing the penetration of wind, driving rain, snow and sleet. The same principle should be applied to folds at the front or on the sides of the vehicle so that wind pressure will tend to close any gaps or folds in the sheet. There should be no loose flaps or tears in the sheet which might cause danger to other road users when the vehicle is moving (see Fig. 11). Care should be taken to avoid striking passers-by when throwing lashings over loads during the securing operation.

6.13 After the sheeting and roping is completed ensure that all loose rope ends have been tied up and that the lights, reflectors, number plates and rear markings etc have not been obscured by any part of the sheet.

C. Nets

6.14 Nets and their attachments (lashing ropes, border ropes, hooks etc) should be in sound condition.

6.15 The maximum rated loading of the net should never be exceeded.

6.16 Nets must be properly tensioned using a tensioning device specified by the net manufacturer. Never overtension a net by the use of a lever or other unauthorised device.

6.17 The mesh size should always be less than the smallest item the net is expected to retain; except that this will not always apply to nets used to retain loose bulkloads because these are not subject to the same loading conditions.

6.18 Protection against abrasion and/or cutting should be provided by the use of corner protectors or corner sleeves.

D. Baulking

6.19 Chocks, wedges and scotches may be used to prevent individual items of a load from moving in any horizontal direction. Care must be taken to ensure that these are stout enough and are adequately secured to the vehicle platform.

E. Dunnage

6.20 It is preferable for all the individual units or packages comprising a load to be packed closely together before any restraint lashings are applied.

If this is not possible then some form of packing, commonly known as dunnage, must be used to fill any gaps which exist between parts of the load or between the load and the vehicle sides.

6.21 The use of loose dunnage between the load and the platform should be avoided wherever possible but where it must be used to support an awkwardly shaped load it should be secured so as to prevent movement during the journey.

6.22 Care must be taken not to damage the load by using unsuitable dunnage and therefore the choice of material will be governed to some extent by the type of load being carried. A number of materials are suitable for use as dunnage, the most common being timber, folded cardboard, hardboard, high density foam, and air bags. Timber dunnage should be of uniform thickness and maximum possible width. The minimum width should, where practicable, be twice the thickness and it is always preferable to use only a single layer.

F. Friction

6.23 A slippery platform surface is always dangerous and the aim should be to obtain the maximum advantage from the frictional restraint by keeping both the base of the load and the platform surface as clean, dry and free from grease as possible.

G. Load Anchorage Points

6.24 Lashings used to restrain the load must always be attached to anchorage points which have sufficient strength to absorb the expected loading. Always remember that any restraint system is only as strong as its weakest component.

6.25 Anchorage points should themselves be firmly attached either directly to the chassis or to a metal crosspiece or outrigger.

6.26 Anchorage points which are secured to wooden members only are not likely to be strong enough to provide the restraint required.

6.27 Rope hooks should only be used for roping, and then only for relatively light loads. They should not be used in place of the proper anchorage points.

6.28 The rated load capacity of the anchorage point must never be exceeded.

Section 7. General Freight

7.1 The loading and securing of general freight loads on goods vehicles is difficult due to the wide diversity of shape, size and nature of this type of load. Vehicles equipped with headboards, tailboards or sideboards, or van bodies, will provide some restraint to movement of the load. However, additional load restraining devices will be required under the following conditions:

(a) If there is a risk that the load may break through the walls, sideboards or tailboard of the vehicle;

(b) When the load is higher than the headboard, sideboard or tailboard of the vehicle;

(c) If the load is liable to be damaged should it move during transit.

7.2 When general freight loads are carried on platform vehicles some form of load restraining device will always be required.

Loading Arrangement on Vehicle

7.3 Two essential requirements must be satisfied when loading vehicles. These are that the load must be so distributed that

(a) the maximum permitted gross vehicle weight and axle weights are not exceeded, and

(b) maximum stability is ensured when the vehicle is braked, or accelerated or changes direction.

7.4 For maximum stability the items comprising the total load are required to be evenly spread to achieve minimum height and to be so arranged as to form a unified whole so that no excessive stress is applied to whatever restraining devices are used. Where a part of the load is to be picked up or removed in the course of a journey the effect on gross vehicle weight, individual axle weights and on the securing and stability of the load then being carried must not be overlooked. Although removal of part of the load will reduce the gross vehicle weight, it may so change the weight distribution as to cause individual axles to exceed their plated weight and this possibility must be borne in mind during the initial loading operation.

7.5 In addition to the general principles outlined above the following procedures should be followed whenever applicable:

(a) Where mixed loads involve heavy solid articles and light crushable boxes etc, the former should provide the base and rear part ("A" in Fig. 12) and the light portion to be loaded on top and to the front ("B" in Fig. 12).

(b) Throughout the journey, the load should frequently be checked for security and the lashings tested for adequate tension after the vehicle has travelled a few miles and again at intervals during the journey. Weather conditions can effect the tension of ropes and this may lead to damage of the load or loss of security if these are not correctly re-tensioned.

(c) Where mixed goods involve different sizes of container, small items should be central, with the larger items forming the outer walls of the load. Avoid as far as possible obstructions or projections beyond the vehicle sides (see Fig. 13).

(d) Keep irregular shaped items for the upper part of the load where it is not possible to place them centrally within the load.

(e) The load must be packed tightly before applying restraint.

(f) Special precautions may have to be taken when dangerous substances are included in a load, *e.g.* segregation of substances which may interact together; protection from rain; careful handling and stowage to reduce the risk of damage to vulnerable containers (see Section 1 paragraph 4).

Restraint Devices

7.6 A variety of materials may be used for restraining general freight loads. These include rope chains, steel wire rope, webbing, strapping or net. For the securing of loads inside van bodies and similar load containers, specially designed shoring poles used in conjunction with the appropriate securing fixtures on the vehicle deck and sides are suitable. Purpose built restraining devices should only be used for application and in the manner approved by their respective manufacturers.

7.7 The selection and use of restraining devices should be based on the principles contained in Section 5 of this Code. However, there are some special points which need to be considered when dealing with general freight and these are outlined in the following paragraphs.

7.8 Sheets may be used subject to the conditions outlined in Section 6 paragraphs 11–13 of this Code. Where several sheets are required to cover one load they should be put on at the rear of the load first (see Figs. 8–10). This ensures the overlapping portions of the sheets face rearwards so preventing wind, driving rain, snow and sleet penetrating between them. The same principle must be applied to folds in the sheets at the front or on the sides of the vehicle – so that wind pressure will tend to close any gaps or folds in the sheet. After being sheeted and roped a vehicle should present a neat, compact and safe picture – not only when the vehicle is stationary but also on the move. The following points should always be checked:

(a) The lights, reflectors, number plates and rear markings etc should not be obscured;

(b) All loose rope ends should be tied up;

(c) There should be no loose flaps or tears in the sheet liable to cause danger to other road users when the vehicle is moving (see Fig. 11).

Loading Methods

7.9 In view of the wide diversity of general loads it is not possible to suggest loading methods for all the types of loads likely to be encountered. However the basic precautions outlined in Section 6 of this Code will always be applicable. Loading methods for certain general categories of loads are outlined in the following paragraphs.

7.10 *Rolls, Drums or Cylindrical Loads*

(a) Rolls or cylindrical items should ideally be placed with their axis across the vehicle in order that the rolling tendency will be to the front or rear. Use chocks and lashings liberally to secure them. Fig. 14 illustrates a load consisting of paper or cardboard rolls. When the bottom layer of rolls has been positioned and secured on the platform and the first roll of the second layer ("A" in Fig. 14) loaded, the overlashings are laid over "A" and across the top of the remaining bottom layer rolls. No tension is applied to the lashings at this stage. The remaining rolls in the second layer are now loaded and at the conclusion the "between-layers" lashings are secured to the rear of the vehicle and "top-over" lashings applied if required. A tarpaulin sheet is normally added to assist with lateral restraint and to give weather protecton (see Fig. 15). "Between-layers" lashings, as illustrated, may be omitted when metal or concrete pipes are carried, since the weight and abrasive nature of the load would excessively damage the lashings.

Only the top lashings are retained but liberal use of chocks is essential. The use of fore and aft lashings between layers provides extra security on acceleration and braking whilst also providing some side-thrust-resistance from lashings "biting" into rolls. NB. these particular lashings may have to be omitted if the customer so dictates or if the "biting" damages the load. The omission should be made good by extra top lashings and chocks and cradles.

(b) If the length of the cylinders is less than twice their diameter they should be placed on end unless instructions are given to the contrary by the consignor. If the length is greater than twice the diameter, but less than the width of the vehicle, they must be positioned so as to roll forwards. Each row must contact the one in front, and rear ones must be chocked to prevent rolling backwards or forwards.

(c) If the drums, rolls etc are standing on end, lashings must be used to prevent lateral movement and further cross lashings must be applied. If on their sides, they should have at least one cross lashing for each item. If there is more than one layer the rearmost roll must be restrained by lashing or blocking against rearward motion.

7.11 *Boxes.* Boxes must be loaded so that they are prevented from moving in any direction. They must interlock if possible, and be loaded to a uniform height. Heavier boxes should be at the bottom of the load. There must be at least one lashing for each row of boxes across the vehicle and any sheeting employed must be considered supplementary to the primary load restraint system. Any box which is above the general height of the load must have at least one cross lashing, and more depending on weight and size.

7.12 *Sacks.*

(a) When possible sacks should be laid on their sides with alternate layers in opposite directions. In any event no more than two successive layers should be in the same direction. The load should be of uniform height when possible.

(b) There must be at least one cross lashing for each sack length. Loads of sacks should be sheeted if possible.

(c) With certain loads the use of tensioners may be desirable. This is particularly true of loads which tend to settle around the lashings.

(d) Empty sacks, which can fall from a vehicle when in motion, can be extremely hazardous and these must therefore be securely restrained to the vehicle's platform.

7.13 *Sheet Glass.* This type of load should normally be carried on purpose built vehicles embodying specially designed glass clamps and supports. However, when sheet or plate glass is carried in crates or on timber pallets load restraint precautions as for general freight apply.

7.14 *Loose Bricks.* Loose brick restraining systems must restrain both the bulk mass of the load and individual bricks. These requirements can be met by load-surrounding sides, bulkhead and tailboard all of which satisfy requirements given in Section 4. The load height should not exceed the height of the surrounding body. Purpose-made restraint systems may also be used for securing this type of load providing the strength of both these and the load securing points used is equal to the load being restrained. Sheeting should only be used subject to the conditions given in Section 6.

7.15 *Mixed Loads.* When a load is composed of different items each part of the load must be secured in a manner suitable to a load of its type. This applies mainly to cross lashings. The longitudinal lashings must be adequate for the total weight of the load, and separators must be used so that no part of the load can move forward independently.

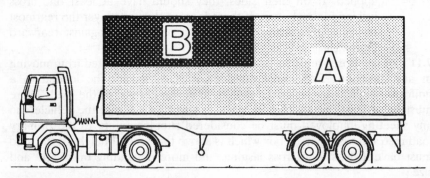

Figure 12

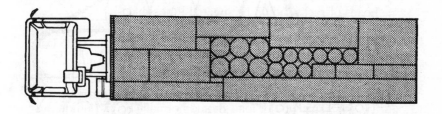

Figure 13

Figure 14

A tarpaulin sheet is normally added to assist with lateral restraint and give weather protection: see Figure 15.

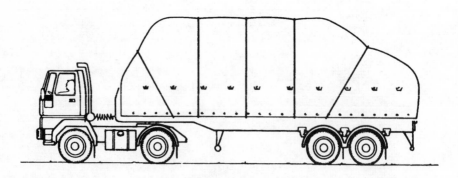

Figure 15

Section 8. Metal Loads

General

8.1 Small relatively heavy items, such as small castings, if not palletised, should be carried on sided vehicles. The headboard, sideboards, and tailboard must be higher than the load and must be strong enough to withstand the forces generated by the vehicle's motion.

8.2 Careful attention should be paid to points where lashings pass over corners of the load to ensure that the load is not damaged by chain links etc nor that the lashings are damaged by sharp edges. Corner protectors should be used whenever necessary.

8.3 The friction between individual items in a load will generally be low, particularly if the metal is oiled, and should therefore be disregarded when assessing the total load restraint required. The friction between load and vehicle platform will also be considerably reduced if either is wet or greasy.

8.4 A large mass is less likely to move about on a vehicle platform than a number of small items and therefore whenever possible loads should be aggregated into the largest or heaviest unit feasible. This will be controlled to some extent by the facilities available at the point of unloading.

8.5 Banding (steel or plastic), commonly used for binding loads together, is not an adequate method for securing loads to vehicles. The wide range of banding available makes it difficult to ensure that the type to be used has sufficient strength for the task and there is a real risk that it will work loose during the journey. If this happens the driver has no means of re-tightening it.

8.6 Metal loads can take various forms but they can be broadly divided into 6 categories:

    (a) flat sheet
    (b) long sections
    (c) coils
    (d) large units and castings
    (e) scrap metal
    (f) scrap vehicles.

Flat Sheet

8.7 When mixed sizes of sheet or plate are being carried the smallest should normally be loaded on top and at the front of the vehicle so that they cannot slide forward.

8.8 Oiled flat sheet should be bundled and packed in steel sheets which form a box around the bundle, commonly known as trumpeting.

8.9 It is essential that the lashings are always in firm contact with the top surface of the load. If the load is level with, or lower than, the side raves of the vehicle then the lashings are likely to be ineffective. In these instances the load should be raised off the floor by the use of timber packing.

8.10 Flat sheet is sometimes loaded onto pallets in which case the advice given in Section 11 should also be followed.

Long Sections

8.11 This type of load will generally be carried along the length of the vehicle and can pose particular problems since one item can easily penetrate a headboard or driver's cab if it is allowed to move. It is essential therefore that the vehicle is loaded in such a way that the complete load forms a unit and no single item can move independently.

8.12 The load will always need to be restrained by lashings, preferably chains or webbings. If possible these should be attached to the vehicle by means of load anchorage points as described in Section 5. When the vehicle is not fitted with such anchorage points it is common practice to pass the lashings around the vehicle to form a continuous loop which is not physically attached to the vehicle in any way. If this method is used the utmost care should be taken to avoid damage to the chassis frame or other vehicle components. A minimum of 4 lashings must be used. It is essential to realise that, although this form of lashing might provide reasonable sideways restraint, forward restraint is provided only by friction and this may be inadequate to restrain the load during heavy braking and some additional means of forward restraint may be necessary. Because there is no "give" in metal products it will often be an advantage to place a piece of timber at a convenient point between the lashings and the load. This will allow a greater tension to be applied to the lashing.

8.13 If the load is stacked it should be kept as low as possible with the heavier items at the bottom and the lighter ones on top. No layer should be bigger than the one underneath it.

8.14 To prevent forward movement the load should be placed in contact with a headboard or otherwise be securely restrained. To achieve an even weight distribution long loads are sometimes carried on a bolster type headboard so that the load projects forward over the driver's cab. In this case individual items should be aggregated into the largest or heaviest unit feasible and forward restraint provided by lashing the entire load securely to the bolster. Additional restraints will need to be provided at the rear.

8.15 If stanchions, either attached to the vehicle or to specially made bolsters, are used to prevent sideways movement they should extend to the height of the load. Sideboards should not be relied upon to provide more than a minimum of sideways restraint.

Coils

8.16 To avoid confusion over terminology, in the following paragraphs a coil with its hollow centre or bore horizontal is referred to as "bore horizontal" and a coilwith its hollow centre or bore vertical as "bore vertical". A coil may be either asingle coil or a number of coils bound together with the bores in line so as to form a cylindrical unit.

8.17 Before loading, the coil banding and packaging should be examined to ensure that it is intact and not likely to break apart whilst e.g. in transit. When banding is used to strap coils and pallets together it is important to appreciate that the banding is intended only to secure the pallet to the coil. Therefore it will usually be necessary to secure the entire unit to the vehicle. Securing the pallet alone is unlikely to be sufficient.

Coils of Wide Sheet – Bore Horizontal

8.18 These coils, when loaded bore horizontal, will preferably be carried on vehicles having a coil well built into the load platform. If there is a likelihood of the coils moving in the well then lashings should be used as necessary. Alternatively coils may, when specialised vehicles are not available for instance, be carried packed on cradles similar in construction to that shown in Fig. 16 subject to the conditions laid down in the following paragraphs.

8.19 The coils must be securely attached to the cradle by at least two webbing lashings or by an approved steel strapping. The lashings must be in contact with the surface of the coil and the softwood wedges.

8.20 Coil and cradle units may be carried in rows on the vehicle platform but all coils in a row should be of approximately equal height and contact the row in front or a timber spacer.

8.21 If a coil well is not used, coils or coil and cradle units should be secured to the vehicle by chain or webbing lashings which incorporate tensioning devices. For securing purposes each line of coils across the vehicle is considered separately and each one must be lashed.

8.22 Cradles should not be loaded over coil wells unless a well cover is used having adequate strength to support the weight of the coil.

Coils of Wide Sheet – Bore Vertical

8.23 Coils carried bore vertical are usually loaded onto platform vehicles and are one of the most difficult loads to secure. Figure 17 shows a suitable restraint system employing a cruciform which can be used with chains or webbing to secure the larger diameter coils loaded bore vertical. The coil is placed on the centre line of the vehicle and the cruciform placed on top of the coil with the spigots located inside the bore. The cruciform should be positioned with the open through channel across the line of the vehicle to accommodate a conventional securing chain lashing. Lashings should be attached to the vehicle anchorage points and tensioned in the usual way.

8.24 It is possible to secure such coils without using the clamp described, but great care must be exercised in positioning the webbing or chains to ensure they are fully capable of preventing movement (see Fig. 18). Normally it will be necessary to provide heavy duty floor anchorages and to ensure that adequate tensioning methods are available.

8.25 Lighter coils are sometimes packed onto pal lets. These should be treated in a similar way to coils packed on cradles and the advice given in paragraphs1 7–21 of this Section should be followed.

Coiled Rod and Bar

8.26 These products should be carried bore horizontal in a single layer loaded either transversely or longitudinally on the vehicle platform. Unless the vehicle is fitted with special loading frames or cradles designed to contain the coils all the sideways restraint will have to be provided by the lashings, preferably chain or webbings fitted with tensioning devices. One method of carrying these coils longitudinally between parallel rows of timber is described at the end of this Section – paragraphs 35–37.

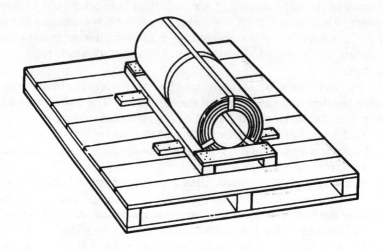

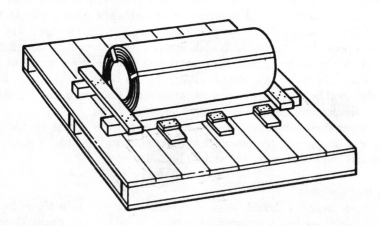

Figure 16

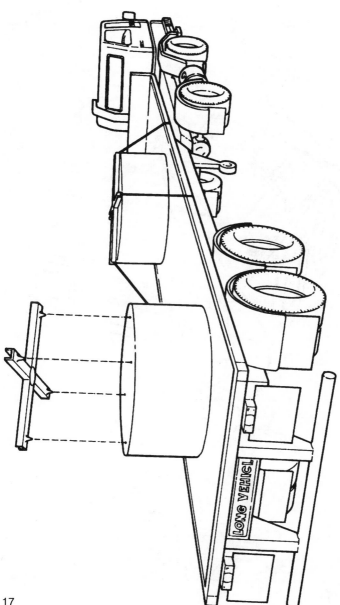

Figure 17

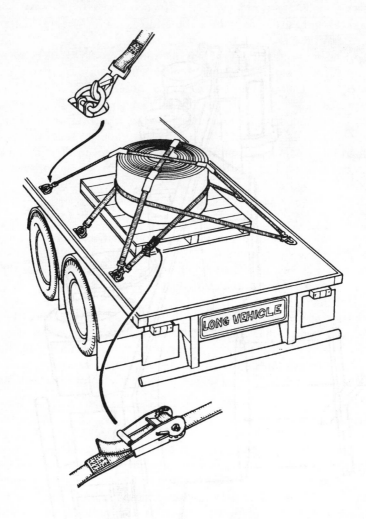

Figure 18

Large Units and Castings

8.27 These loads are normally carried in a purpose built cradle which must be sufficiently strong to withstand the forces likely to be imposed on it during transportation.

8.28 To achieve a satisfactory weight distribution it will often be impossible to place this type of load against the headboard and therefore it will be necessary to use securely fixed baulking in addition to the lashing.

8.29 Because these loads are usually fairly high the lashings must be arranged to prevent the load toppling as well as to prevent movement on the load platform. Therefore it will be necessary either to lash over the top of the load or to points high on the cradle or load, even though baulking and lashings are used at platform level to provide the majority of the restraint.

Scrap Metal

8.30 Scrap metal can take many forms from machine swarf to motor vehicles. Some loads may come into one of the categories already covered in this Section in which case the loading and securing arrangements should follow the guidance given in that particular sub-section.

8.31 Loose items of scrap may be carried in sided vehicles with no additional means of restraint, provided that the headboard, sideboards, and tailboard are higher than the load. It may be an offence under the Construction and Use Regulations to allow any part of a load to fall or be blown from a vehicle. Therefore it will usually be necessary to cover the load with a sheet or net. Further advice on the carriage of loose bulk loads is given in Section 10.

Scrap Vehicles

8.32 Scrap vehicles are likely to be difficult to transport safely on platform vehicles because the tyres and suspension will permit the load to move making it inherently unstable. Chain or webbing lashings which incorporate tensioning devices should be used to secure these loads.

8.33 Scrap vehicles should not be stacked on each other because it will be almost impossible to position and adequately secure the upper layers in such a way that movement is prevented whilst braking or cornering.

8.34 The practice of securing derelict motor vehicles by means of a lorry mounted crane exerting pressure on the roof of the uppermost vehicle is not considered to provide adequate load security because this method relies upon friction for most of the restraint and failure of a single part of the restraint system, eg the crane, will immediately lead to the load becoming insecure. Further advice on the satisfactory methods of securing motor vehicles to platform bodies is given in Section 14.

One Method of Securing Coiled Rod and Bar

8.35 A recommended method of carrying coiled rod and bar is shown in Fig. 19. The principle of this system is to form the coils into a tube parallel to the length of the vehicle, retention equipment being applied to the rear end to hold the front end firmly against a stack of coils bore vertical that are against the vehicle headboard.

8.36 Either one or more rows of coils may be carried depending upon the size and weight of each coil. All of the coils in each row must be of approximately equal diameter.

8.37 The loading is commenced by placing a stack of coils bore vertical onto the double rows of timber at the front of the load platform and in contact with the headboard. The remaining coils are then stacked bore horizontal between the rows of timber leaning against the vertical stack at the front. The coils should be inclined at an angle of approximately 70 degrees to the horizontal. The coils are restrained by placing one end of a short length of stout timber into the bore of the rearmost coils with the other end in contact with the load platform. This piece of timber is then held rigidly against the coil and load platform by a tensionable webbing or chain lashing which is attached to anchorage points slightly forward of the point where the lashing crosses the piece of timber.

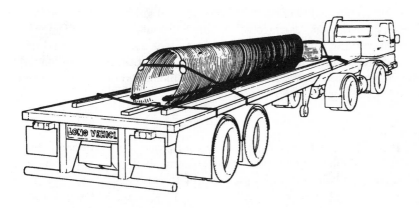

Figure 19   A tarpaulin sheet may be added to give
             weather protection – see Figure 20.

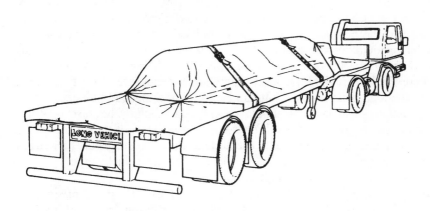

Figure 20

Section 9. Timber Loads

9.1 This section is intended to provide general guidance on the measures necessary for the safe carriage of timber, both bulk and sawn. Timber is a "live" commodity which can lead to independent movement of parts of the load if the restraint is inadequate. It is essential that timber is not loaded to a height, or in such a way, as to result in the likelihood of either the vehicle or load becoming unstable.

Sawn Timber

9.2 It is important to ensure that, wherever practicable, the load is placed against the headboard or similar fixed restraint. If this is not possible then all the restraint will have to be provided by the lashings.

9.3 Bulk packaged sheets of timber such as plywood, chipboard etc are generally strapped or wired at each end and before loading the straps should be checked for security. If the straps are damaged or insecure extra care must be taken to ensure that the complete load is adequately secured to the vehicle.

9.4 Loose timber is generally made up into standard sets which should be loaded to a uniform height on the vehicle. The uneven ends should where possible be at the rear of the vehicle and packed out to prevent whip. Generally the use of dunnage should be as outlined in Section 6 paragraphs 20–22.

9.5 Light loads of timber, eg for retail deliveries, can be carried on sided vehicles where the height of the load does not exceed the height of the headboard, sides or tailboard, thus avoiding the need for constant lashing and relashing of the load. Where the height of the load exceeds the height of either the headboard, sides or tailboard, lashings must be used.

Restraining Devices

9.6 In general the use of chain or webbing lashings is recommended. The number of lashings required should be in accordance with the weight of the load and the number of anchorage points used. At least one intermediate lashing should be passed around the lower half of the load only. Care must be taken to ensure that restraining chains or webbing are placed at points where the load is rigid, *i.e.* where there are no uneven ends of timber, and that the load is protected from damage by toggles or load binders.

9.7 All types of lashings should be checked regularly because they may need to be retightened several times during the course of the journey as the timber settles on the vehicle, particularly in the early stages of the journey.

9.8 Any loose ends of timber at the rear of the vehicle should also be secured with rope or webbing to minimise whip.

9.9 Certain types of timber loads present a particular problem since the outside lifts and tends to spread sideways, causing the load to belly outwards. To avoid this the vehicle should be fitted with side stanchions that reach the height of the load (see Fig. 21). It is essential that the stanchions are capable of resisting any outward movement of the load.

Round Timber

9.10 In general the principles of load distribution outlined in Section 3 should be adhered to and again it is important to ensure that, whenever possible, the load is placed against the headboard or similar fixed restraint. The use of chain or webbing lashings is recommended and all lashing should be capable of being tightened by use of a toggle or load binder. The lashings should be attached to suitable anchorage points and should be regularly checked during the journey and retightened if necessary.

Stacks on the Longitudinal Axis

9.11 Each outer log or piece of timber shall be supported by at least two uprights Pieces shorter than the distance between two uprights should be placed in the interior of the load. The uprights should be fitted with top chains, so as to be capable of resisting the load's outward movement. Where a pile is supported by only two pairs of uprights, the ends of the outer logs should extend at least 300mm (12 inches) beyond the uprights where practicable. Logs should preferably be laid top to tail alternatively so as to ensure an even balance of the load. Each pile should be lashed together and the lashing secured by a suitable device. Where necessary, staples may be used in conjunction with chains. A single chain stretched between uprights, even if well secured, is not enough. For barked round-wood at least two lashings are required.

Whole Trees

9.12 The carriage of whole trees is a highly specialised field of timber haulage that is generally accomplished using pole vehicles or vehicles where the timber load is secured to a trailing dolly at one end. Vehicles should be fitted with bolsters and stanchions of sufficient strength to restrain the load. Chains or webbing lashings are necessary for securing the load and generally a minimum of 3 chains or webbing lashings should be used, one of which should bind together any overhanging tails or the middle of an awkwardly shaped load. The lashings should be capable of being tightened using a toggle or load binder.

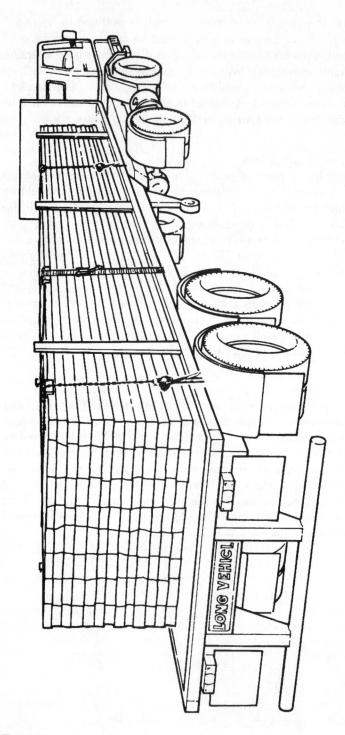

Figure 21

SECTION 10. LOOSE BULK LOADS

10.1 Loose bulk loads can be described generally as those which do not readily lend themselves to any form of packaging such as sand, ballast, aggregate etc and for ease of loading they are usually carried in open bodied vehicles. Removable open topped containers, commonly known as skips and which are normally used for transporting waste materials, also come into this load category.

10.2 Clearly the loading and securing of such loads do not pose some of the problems associated with other types of load but nevertheless they do present problems peculiar to themselves. Particular attention should be paid to granular or flaked materials which may settle in transit.

10.3 Shedding of loose bulk loads is more likely to take the form of small quantities of material either falling through gaps in the bodywork or being blown from the top of the load compartment.

10.4 The load compartment should be kept in good condition to minimise the risk of leakage. Special attention should be given to drop sides and tailboards where damage or distortion can easily lead to loss of part of the load through any small gaps which are created.

10.5 All the body to chassis attachment points and body fittings such as hinge pins and brackets, tailboard locking mechanisms, drop side fasteners, etc should be secure and in sound condition.

10.6 The body sides should be of sufficient height not only to completely contain the material when it is loaded but also to reduce the likelihood of any part of the load, which might have moved during the journey, from falling or being blown over the edge.

10.7 Body height extensions should only be used where conditions and type of load permit. Where these are used their supports must be adequately fixed to the existing body. It is not considered adequate to rely upon the load within the parent body of the vehicle for support. Where necessary tie chains should be used transversely at the top of body extensions to prevent sideways spread.

10.8 To reduce the risk of part of the load falling or being blown off the top of the load compartment it will usually be necessary to use some form of cover. The necessity for a cover and the type to be used will depend on the nature of the load being carried. Materials such as dry sand and ash, metal turning swarf etc should be covered by a sheet to prevent them from being blown off by wind action. Loads which consist of large items such as scrap metal and builders' waste etc can sometimes be adequately retained by covering with a net.

10.9 Skip containers, when loaded onto the carrying vehicle, must be adequately secured against movement when subjected to braking and cornering forces (see Section 2). Loading chains must be properly stowed.

10.10 Special problems are likely to be encountered with skip containers because the driver does not usually have any control over the packing. However, when the skip container is accepted for loading onto the vehicle the driver must assume responsibility for the safe carriage of the skip and its contents. Therefore the general guidance given in this Section on loads carried in open bodied load compartments should be followed. A sheet or net will usually be needed to prevent the contents from spilling onto the road.

SECTION 11. PALLETS

11.1 The safe carriage of pallets often represents a two fold problem. First there has to be considered the stability of the items stacked on the pallet and secondly the restraint of the pallet and its cargo on the vehicle platform. In the case of small containers and cased machinery, usually only the second factor need be considered. When banding or other similar means are used to unitise a pallet and its cargo it is most important to appreciate that the banding etc is intended only to secure the pallet to its cargo and not the cargo to the pallet. Therefore it will usually be necessary to secure the entire unit to the vehicle. Securing the pallet alone is unlikely to be sufficient.

11.2 There are two basic types of pallet; those which have a number of horizontal bottom members in contact with the vehicle platform and those supported by corner legs and feet. Pallets themselves serve a double purpose in that they enable goods of similar nature and size to be made up into unit loads and also palletised loads can be more easily handled mechanically which reduces the effort required to handle and transport them. Because of the wide variation in the weight and sizes of pallets, situations will arise when the vehicle load space cannot be fully utilised without either exceeding the permitted gross weight or the axle weights. This free load space will increase the likelihood of pallets, which are not property restrained, moving when the vehicle is braking or cornering.

11.3 Before loading, the pallets should be examined for damage or other obvious signs of weakness. If there is reason to suspect that the pallets are not of sufficient strength to withstand the load carried on them they should not be accepted for loading.

11.4 Where pallets are carried on vehicles with van bodies, lashings will be required to restrain the pallets if there are spaces between them or between the pallets and the vehicle sides or headboard. This is because, if there is space for the pallet to move, they could develop sufficient momentum to break through the sides or headboard when the vehicle is braking or cornering. Where, for practical reasons, lashings cannot be used then the spaces must be filled with suitable dunnage to prevent movement of the pallets.

11.5 In order to utilise the full payload capacity of the vehicle it may be feasible to stack palletised loads. However the upper layers of pallets must be positioned so that they are stable and adequately secured to prevent them from falling from the vehicle. Unless the upper pallet is directly supported by the lower one, the cargo on the lower pallets must be of sufficient structural strength to withstand the weight of the upper pallet without becoming distorted.

11.6 Individual items in the load must be firmly secured to the pallet if they are not to be dislodged when the vehicle is in motion. Movement of the cargo on the pallet may lead to a failure of the restraint system attached to that pallet and those adjacent to it. Bagged items tend to settle under vibration to fill air spaces between the bags, thus loosening any strapping.

11.7 The following provisions apply to the movement of all types of palletised loads:

   (i) The arrangement of the pallets on the vehicle must be such that the maximum permitted gross vehicle weight and axle weights are not exceeded.

  (ii) Unless the pallets are adequately constrained by the body or sideboards and headboard of the vehicle, additional means of restraining the horizontal and vertical movement of the pallet should be provided.

 (iii) The pallets should be positioned so that the load is balanced across the vehicle.

 (iv) Where the load space is not fully utilised and where weight distribution is a problem, pallets should if possible be placed along the longitudinal centre line of the vehicle and 'Closed Up' to one another.

  (v) Where pallets are stacked on open platform vehicles restraining lashings or nets must be used to prevent movement of each layer of pallets carried. Tarpaulin sheets and covers are not by themselves adequate for this purpose.

 (vi) Where pallets are loaded onto vehicles which have been equipped with a roller loading system extra care should be taken to ensure that the pallets are adequately restrained.

(vii) When part of the load is removed from the vehicle care must be taken that the remaining pallets do not cause the vehicles maximum axle weight to be exceeded or its lateral stability to be impaired.

Restraint Equipment

11.8 A variety of materials are suitable for restraining palletised loads. These include chains, steelwire or fibre rope, webbing lashings and webbing or rope nets. Although the metal restraining devices may be stronger they are less convenient and require to be used with end attachments such as shackles, thimbles etc and unless the load is adequately protected it might be damaged, which could result in permanent distortion of the load and slackening of the restraint system.

11.9 Webbing lashing assemblies which incorporate special end fittings and tensioning devices are suitable for securing palletised loads to vehicles. The webbing is usually made from man-made fibres and has the property of being slightly elastic in use which helps to prevent the load from working loose. It is preferable to use webbing assemblies which are manufactured to the requirements of BS 5759.

11.10 Rope or webbing nets are suitable both for securing the cargo to the pallet and for securing the palletised load to the vehicle.

Restraining Methods

11.11 The restraining method adopted will depend on the type and size of the vehicle, the position and number of anchorage points and the size, weight and number of pallets in the load. However, the following principles should be followed for whatever scheme is chosen:

(i) Vertical and tipping motions should be prevented by a lashing placed across the top of the pallet load.

(ii) Lashings should be positioned to prevent movement of the pallets in any direction.

(iii) The pallet lashings should not be attached to or pass under, the strapping or binding used to secure the pallet to the cargo.

(iv) Where pallets are stacked, cross lashings must be such that each pallet of the top layer has at least one cross lashing. Any pallet which is above the general height of the load should have at least two cross lashings.

11.12 Dunnage may be used in some cases to assist in restraining the load. If the sideboards, headboard and tailboard are sufficiently strong and the pallets occupy all the vehicle platform space then dunnage alone may be sufficient to restrain the load horizontally, but some vertical restraint may be necessary. If pallets are stacked, however, additional lashings will be needed for the upper pallets.

SECTION 12. CONTAINERS

12.1 In this section the term "container" is used to describe both a box type construction and an open frame structure enclosing the load or tank and which may in either case be lifted off the vehicle as a single unit comprising container and load. In many instances the advice on loading box type containers can be applied equally to vehicles with box van bodies.

ISO/BS CONTAINERS

12.2 The majority of containers in use are constructed to International (ISO 1496) or British (BS 3951) standards. A common feature in the construction of these containers is that specially designed corner castings are incorporated which can be used, in conjunction with twist locks fitted on the vehicle, to provide a simple and positive means of restraint (see Fig. 22).

12.3 This type of container should normally be carried on vehicles fitted with twist locks. Twist locks must be maintained in serviceable condition and a minimum of four used for each container carried (see Section 5.9). Provided that the twist locks are fully engaged and locked in position, the container will be adequately secured and no further restraint will be necessary.

12.4 If carried on a vehicle not fitted with twist locks, a retention system must be used that fulfils the requirements set out in Sections 3–7.

Other Types of Container

12.5 Containers which do not have the ISO type corner castings may be fitted with special attachment brackets or lashing rings. Safe methods for securing these containers will therefore vary according to the type being transported but the restraint system used must fulfil the requirements set out in Sections 3–7.

12.6 Containers should not project beyond the rear or sides of the vehicle loading platform because permanent distortion of the container may take place if part of its base is left unsupported.

12.7 Lashings or other securing devices should only be attached to those points on the container intended for the purpose, or for lifting or mechanical handling when laden, such as lashing rings or special brackets. All attachment points on the container should be examined to ensure that they are in sound condition and all the available attachment points should be used to secure it to the vehicle platform.

Stowage of Goods in Containers

12.8 Incorrect loading of a container may result in dangerous situations occurring when the container is handled or transported; in addition serious damage may be caused to the goods carried. In many instances the driver will have no control over the packing of a container nor be able to inspect its contents when he accepts it for carriage. If it is apparent that the container has not been safely stowed then it should not be accepted.

12.9 Inadequate stowing arrangements within the container might result in the load shifting which could adversely affect the stability of the vehicle.

12.10 The following general stowage rules which affect road safety should always be observed:

(a) The load should not exceed the permitted payload of the container;

(b) The load should be evenly distributed across the floor area of the container. In no case should more than 60% of the load be in less than half the length of the container;

(c) Heavy goods should not be stowed on top of lighter goods and wherever possible the centre of gravity of the loaded container should be below the mid-point of its height;

(d) The load should be secured in the container against any reasonable forces which might be expected to occur during the journey. A tightly packed load will be less likely to move than one which has spaces between parts of the load;

(e) After the packing of the container is completed, steps should be taken to ensure that the load and dunnage will not fall out when the doors are opened. Webbing lashings or nets are often suitable for this purpose, alternatively a timber or metal gate can be constructed.

12.11 More detailed information on the stowage of goods in containers can be found in British Standard BS 5073.

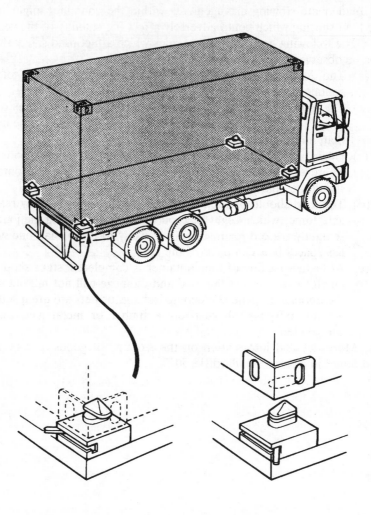

Figure 22

SECTION 13. ENGINEERING PLANT

13.1 This section provides guidance on the measures necessary for the safe carriage of tracked and wheeled engineering plant by vehicles constructed to comply fully with the Motor Vehicles (Construction and Use) Regulations 1978 and thereby permitted unrestricted use of the roads. It does not deal with the carriage of large machines etc on special purpose vehicles whose use on the roads is restricted by current regulations. However, the general advice contained in this section will apply in many cases.

13.2 Heavy engineering plant is normally transported on purpose built vehicles which are specifically designed to provide easy loading and unloading facilities and are usually provided with adequate anchorage points for attaching the lashings. Lighter engineering plant may in some circumstances be carried on general purpose vehicles. However, in these cases the method used to secure the load should provide equal security to that obtained by using purpose built vehicles.

13.3 High loads may endanger bridges etc over roads, so when these are carried it is essential that the driver knows the exact height of the load above the ground. Since loads with a high centre of gravity might seriously affect the vehicle's stability such items of engineering plant should only be transported on vehicles with a low platform height.

13.4 A wheeled or tracked vehicle must be lashed down in position on the carrying vehicle, with the parking brake applied. The effectiveness of the parking brake on its own will be limited by the frictional resistance between the vehicle and the deck of the carrying vehicle, and even in normal driving conditions this will be inadequate and the vehicle will therefore require additional restraint. This additional restraint should take the form of a lashing system and some arrangement whereby the load is prevented from moving either forward or to the rear by an obstacle (or obstacles) securely fixed to the vehicle which butt against the wheels or tracks or some other part of the equipment carried.

13.5 Engineering plant should be dismantled as far as is necessary to keep its overall dimensions within the length and width limits of the carrying vehicle. Where this is not possible then care should be taken that the conditions and restrictions contained in Regulation 140 of the Motor Vehicles (Construction and Use) Regulations 1978: S.I. 1978 No. 1017, and the relevant provision of the Motor Vehicles (Authorisation of Special Types) General Order 1979: SI 1979 No. 1198, concerning the carriage of wide or long loads are also complied with.

13.6 All moveable assemblies such as jibs, brackets, booms, slewing super structures and cabs etc must be left in the position recommended for transportation by their manufacturers and must be secured to prevent movement relative to the main body of the machine.

13.7 All hydraulic booms, arms etc, must be lashed down to prevent rising or slewing during transit.

13.8 When the machine has been stowed and the engine stopped, the pressure in the hydraulic system should be relieved by moving all of the control levers through all their positions. This operation should be done at least twice. Controls should be set so as to prevent movement of ancillary items during transit.

13.9 Bags, tool kits, or other heavy objects should not be left loose in the operator's cab of the plant being carried.

13.10 The positioning of the engineering plant and any of its detached assemblies must be so arranged that the legal axle weight limits are not exceeded and the safe handling of the vehicle is not impaired. The clearance between the undersides of low loading vehicles and the road surface should be checked before moving off (see Section 3 paragraph 6).

13.11 The machine should be positioned on the carrying vehicle's platform so that forward movement is prevented either by part of the main body of the vehicle, eg swan neck, step or headboard, or by an attached transverse member securely attached through the platform to the vehicle's chassis frame.

13.12 All items removed from the machine such as buckets, grabs, blades, shovels and lifting appliances should be lashed to the deck of the vehicle.

13.13 Wheeled and light tracked machines should be restrained so that the effect of bouncing caused by road shocks transmitted from the carrying vehicle and amplified by the machine's tyres or suspension units is minimised. Where possible the suspension unit of the machine should be locked and vertical movement limited by lashings or other means of restraint. Otherwise the machine's frame or chassis should be supported on blocks.

13.14 Unless the machine is supported, the full contact area of its tyres, tracks, or rolls should rest on the deck of the carrying vehicle. If the tracks extend outside the frame of the carrying vehicle then the machine's frame or chassis should be supported.

13.15 The machine should be restrained against forward, backward and sideways movement by chain or webbing lashings attached to anchorage points on the vehicle. All lashings should incorporate some form of tensioning device.

13.16 In deciding the number of anchorage points to be used when arranging a restraint system, the following factors should be considered:

    (i) The need to position the machine to achieve the correct load distribution to meet the legal axle load requirements and to ensure that the vehicle's handling is not impaired;

    (ii) The extent to which other load restraint features are incorporated in the design of the vehicle;

    (iii) Whether the machine has wheels, tracks or rolls;

    (iv) The weight of the machine to be carried.

However, there should never be less than four anchorage points used.

Restraining Devices

13.17 Apart from specialised fixing devices, the selection of materials for use in tie down schemes for engineering plant will be limited to chains, steel wire rope, webbing and their associated tensioning and coupling devices.

13.18   Where a transverse beam is used as a baulk it should be securely fixed so that all loads imposed on it are transmitted to the carrying vehicle's chassis frame. Where individual wheels or rolls are chocked with blocks or scotches these must be robust enough to resist crushing and be securely attached to the vehicle's platform where possible.

13.19   The lashings or securing devices should only be attached to those parts of the engineering plant which are of sufficient strength to withstand the stresses likely to be imposed on them.

13.20   The loaded machine should be inspected after the vehicle has been driven for a short distance in order to check that no movement has taken place and that restraining devices are fully secure. Periodic inspections should be made during the course of the journey.

Suggested Tie Down Schemes

13.21   The tie down schemes described in the following figures 23–31 and related schedules are typical systems which might be adopted for the securing of the various types of engineering plant. Variations to any of these schemes would be acceptable provided that all the basic safety precautions outlined earlier have been complied with. For simplicity the figures show mainly chains used for lashings but in practice other lashing materials may be substituted — see Section 5.

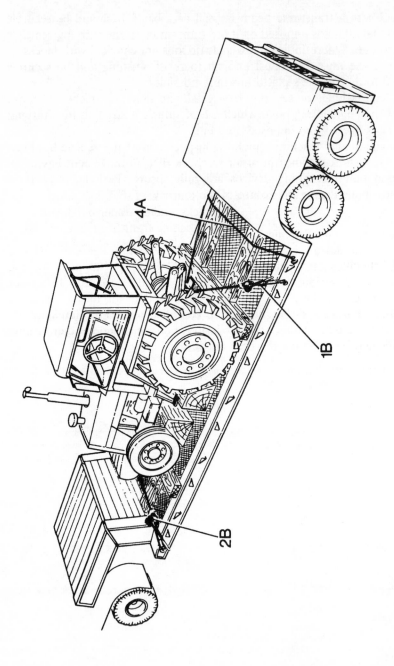

Figure 23

Agricultural Type Tractors   (See Figure 23)

POSSIBLE HAZARD	PRECAUTION
1. Forward movement of machine	**A.** Front wheels butted against chocks against trailer bulkhead. **B.** Lashing chains from rear towing hook to anchorage points on trailer side members. **C.** Rear wheels butted against chocks.
2. Rearward movement of machine	**A.** Rear wheels butted against chocks against trailer bulkhead. **B.** Lashing from front axle or towing hook to anchorage points on trailer side members. **C.** Front wheels butted against chocks.
3. Sideways movement of machine	**A.** Restraint provided by lashings used for forward and rearward restraint.
4. Movement of ancillaries	**A.** Lashings across baulking to anchorage points on trailer side members.

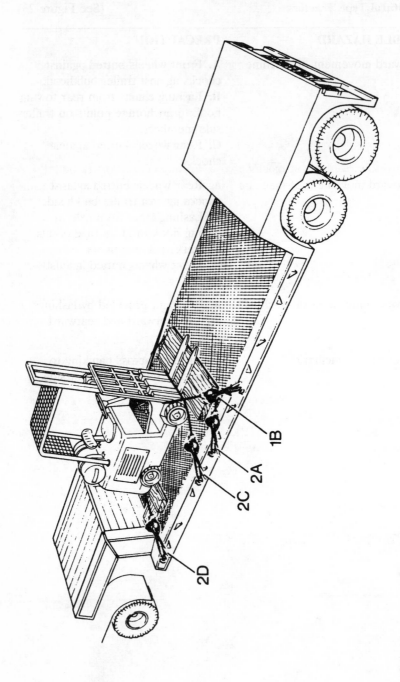

Figure 24

Industrial Fork Lift Trucks   (See Figure 24)

POSSIBLE HAZARD	PRECAUTION
1. Forward movement of machine	**A.** Rear wheels or counterweight of truck butted against chocks against trailer bulkhead.
	B. Lashing arounds the rear of the mast to anchorage points on trailer side members.
2. Rearward movement of machine	**A.** Front wheels of truck butted against chocks which are lashed to anchorage points on trailer side members.
	B. Forks lowered on to chocks and hydraulic pressure relieved by operation of controls twice with engine switched off.
	C. Lashings across the rear of the fork to the anchorage points forwards.
	D. Lashing from truck towing point to anchorage points on trailer side members.
3. Sideways movement of machine	**A.** Restraint produced by lashings used for forward and rearward restraint.

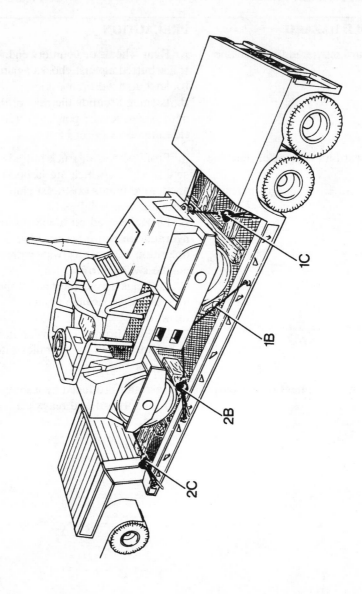

Figure 25

Road Roller   (See Figure 25)

POSSIBLE HAZARD	PRECAUTION
1. Forward movement of machine	**A.** Front roll butted against chocks against trailer bulkhead. **B.** Lashing from frame and/or across member to anchorage points on trailer side members. **C.** Lashing from rear frame or towing hook to anchorage points on trailer side members.
2. Rearward movement of machine	**A.** Rear roll butted against chocks against trailer bulkhead. **B.** Lashing from frame and/or cross member to anchorage points on trailer side members. **C.** Lashing from front frame or towing hook to anchorage points on trailer side members.
3. Sideways movement of machine	**A.** Restraint provided by lashings used to prevent forward and rearward movement.

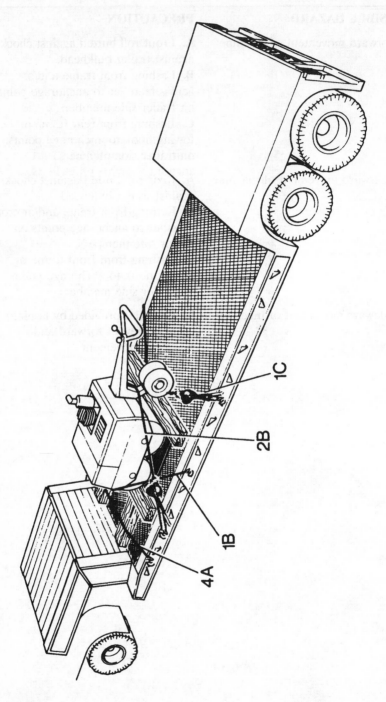

Figure 26

Pedestrian Roller (See Figure 26)

POSSIBLE HAZARD	PRECAUTION
1. Forward movement of machine	**A.** Front roll butted against chocks against trailer bulkhead. **B.** Lashing from and across the front of the machine body to anchorage points on trailer side members. **C.** Lashing around and across the rear of the rear wheel strut to anchorage points on trailer side members.
2. Rearward movement of machine	**A.** Rear roll butted against chocks. **B.** Lashing from and across the rear of the machine body to anchorage points on trailer side members.
3. Sideways movement of machine	**A.** Restraint provided by restraints to prevent forward and rearward restraint.
4. Movement of ancillaries	**A.** Lashing across baulking.

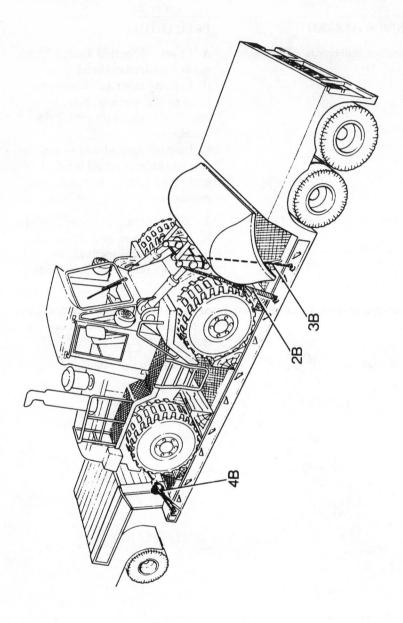

Figure 27

Wheeled Tractor Shovel (See Figure 27)

POSSIBLE HAZARD	PRECAUTION
1. Articulation of front plant of machine relative to rear part	**A.** Privot locking bar bolted in position, in the case of privot steer machines.
2. Movement of bucket assembly	**A.** Relieve hydraulic pressure in system by operating all controls twice, with the engine switched off. **B.** Lashings to secure bucket to the anchorage points on the trailer side members.
3. Forward movement of machine	**A.** Rear wheels butted against chocks against trailer bulkhead. **B.** Lashing from front axle or towing hook to anchorage points on trailer side members.
4. Rearward movement of machine	**A.** Front wheels butted against chocks. **B.** Lashing from rear axle or towing hook to anchorage points on trailer side members.
5. Sideways movement of machine	**A.** Restraint provided by lashings used to prevent forward and rear movement.

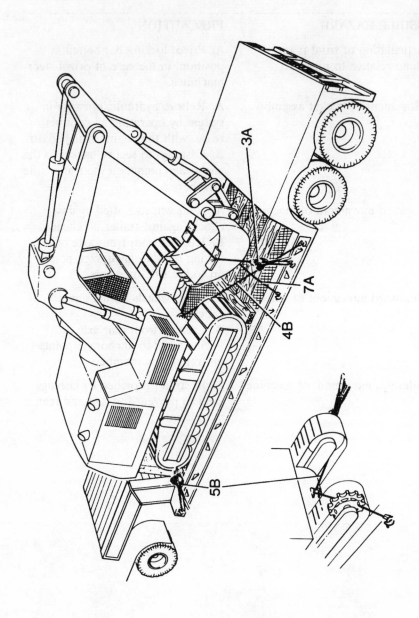

Figure 28

Hydraulic Excavator (Tracked)   (See Figure 28)

POSSIBLE HAZARD	PRECAUTION
1. Machine striking overhead obstruction	**A.** Stow equipment in position to give lowest overall height.
2. Movement of cab and superstructure relative to chassis of machine	**A.** Relieve hydraulic pressure by operating all controls twice, with engine switched off. **B.** Apply slew lock or slewing ring.
3. Movement of dipper arm away from stowed position	**A.** Lashing securing the bucket to anchorage points on the trailer side members.
4. Forward movement of machine	**A.** Tracks butted against the trailer bulkhead. **B.** Lashing chains from excavator front towing point or chassis cross member to anchorage points on trailer side members.
5. Rearward movement of machine	**A.** Tracks butted against chocks. **B.** Lashing chains from excavator rear towing point or chassis cross member through the idler sprocket to anchorage points on trailer side members.
6. Sideways movement of machine	**A.** Restraint provided by lashing chains used to prevent forward and rearward movement. Do not wedge heavy objects between the bucket and the machine chassis.
7. Movement of ancillaries	**A.** Lashings over baulkings.

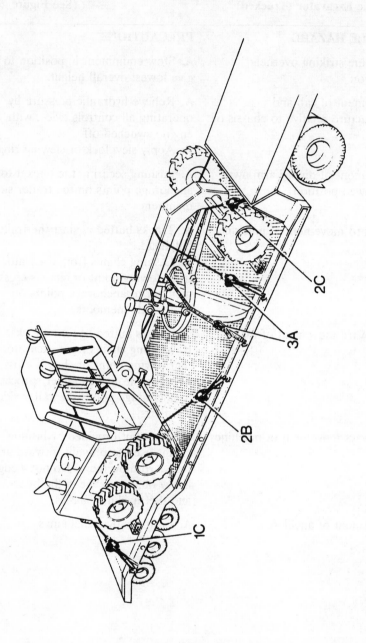

Figure 29

Motor Grader (See Figure 29)

POSSIBLE HAZARD	PRECAUTION
1. Forward movement of machine	**A.** Blade and scarifier lowered to trailer deck. **B.** Front wheels butted against trailer bulkhead. **C.** Lashing from towing hook to anchorage points on trailer side members. **D.** Front wheels of tractor butted against chocks.
2. Rearward movement of machine	**A.** Rear wheels of tractor and front wheels of grader butted against chocks. **B.** Lashing from cross frame member to anchorage points on trailer side members. **C.** Lashing from front of mainframe to anchorage points on the trailer bulkhead.
3. Vertical movement of machine	**A.** Restraint provided by lashings over the mainframe and blade and those providing forward and rearward restraint.
4. Sideways movement of machine	**A.** Restraint provided by lashings used for other restraints.

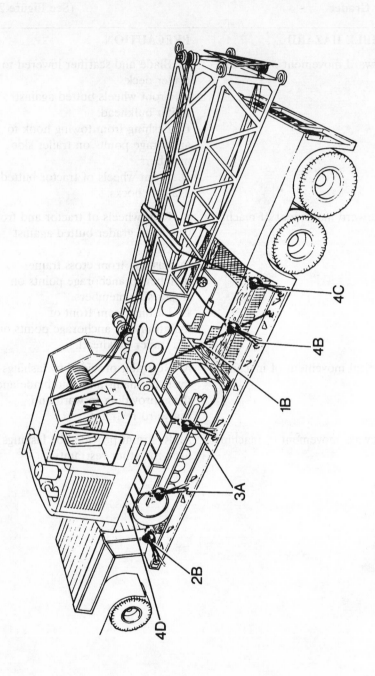

Figure 30

Roped Excavator (Tracked)   (See Figure 30)

POSSIBLE HAZARD	PRECAUTION
1. Forward movement of machine	**A.** Tracks butted against chocks against trailer bulkhead. **B.** Lashing from chassis cross member or front towing hook to anchorage points on trailer side members.
2. Rearward movement of machine	**A.** Tracks butted against chocks against trailer bulkhead. **B.** Lashing from chassis cross member or rear towing hook to anchorage points on trailer side members.
3. Sideways movement of machine	**A.** Lashings over tracks to anchorage points on trailer side members. **B.** Restraint also provided by restraints for forward and rearward movement.
4. Movement of ancillaries	**A.** Break down boom and slew boom to rear and apply slew lock on slewing ring. **B.** Position bucket centrally on trailer and lash to anchor points on trailer side members. **C.** Lower the jib onto the rear deck and lash to trailer side members. **D.** Support under counter-balance weights.

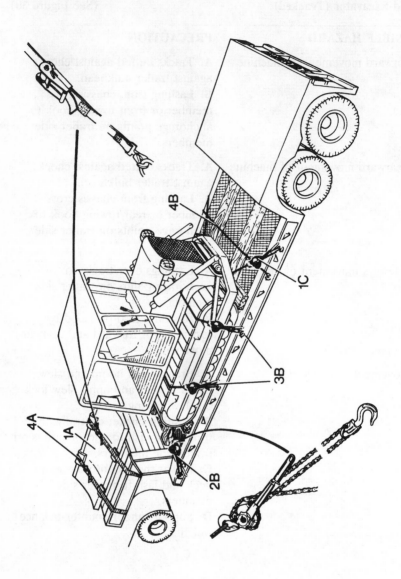

Figure 31

Tracked Dozer   (See Figure 31)

POSSIBLE HAZARD	PRECAUTION
1. Forward movement of machine	**A.** Dozer blade removed placed on front deck of trailer. **B.** Tracks butted against chocks against trailer bulkhead. **C.** Lashing from dozer blade U-frame trunnions to anchorage points on trailer side members.
2. Rearward movement of machine	**A.** Tracks butted against chocks against trailer bulkhead. **B.** Lashing from towing point to trailer side members.
3. Sideways movement of machine	**A.** Restraint provided by restraints to prevent forward and rearward movement. **B.** Lashings across tracks to anchorage points on trailer side members.
4. Movement of ancillaries	**A.** Dozer blade stowed on front deck. Lashing across blade to trailer side members. **B.** Lashing across baulking.

SECTION 14. CARRIAGE OF VEHICLES BY "PIGGYBACK"

14.1 Vehicles and trailers should be carried on other vehicles that are suitable for that purpose with appropriate lashing points fitted and appropriate lashing equipment supplied. In general the securing arrangements should follow the same basic principles as suggested for the carriage of engineering plant in Section 13, but the additional points that follow should be noted.

14.2 The vehicle or trailer should be carried with the parking brake in the "on" position, preferably with the wheels chocked, and (where applicable) the transmission in neutral. If possible the chocks should be securely attached to the carrying vehicle's deck.

14.3 The vehicle or trailer being carried should be positioned so that its weight is fully supported by the carrying vehicle, so it is important to ensure that the carrying vehicle's deck is long enough to take the vehicle or trailer without excessive overhang. If necessary spreader plates should be used to avoid high localised loading – *e.g.* by the landing legs of a semi-trailer.

14.4 The restraint provided by the friction between the tyres and the deck with the parking brake on will not be sufficient to prevent movement so the vehicle or trailer being carried should be lashed to the carrying vehicle using appropriate lashing equipment as detailed in Section 5. A tensioning device should be used in each lashing and the lashings used to restrain the fore and aft movement should be set at an angle of less than 60° from the horizontal to obtain the maximum effect. The lashings should be tested for adequate tension after the vehicle has travelled a few miles and again at intervals during the journey and be retensioned if necessary.

14.5 Lashing should be made onto parts of the vehicle's or trailer's axles or chassis that are adequate for the purpose. Care should be taken to avoid straining or damaging other vehicle components such as brake pipes, hoses, electrical cables etc, through lashing over or near them.

14.6 The carriage of laden vehicles is not recommended but if this is necessary then extra attention should be paid to the resultant higher centre of gravity of the carrying vehicle and the possible consequential loss of stability when cornering or braking. It may also be necessary to put extra lashings onto the chassis of the vehicle or trailer being carried to pull it down on its springs and hence help to avoid an unstable load.

14.7 If more than one vehicle or trailer is carried in "piggyback" fashion then each vehicle carried should be lashed to the one on which it rests and then all those carried should be lashed to the carrying vehicle.

14.8 All loose equipment on the vehicles or trailers being carried, and on the carrying vehicle, should be securely stowed.

14.9 An example of a recommended lashing arrangement is shown in Fig. 32.

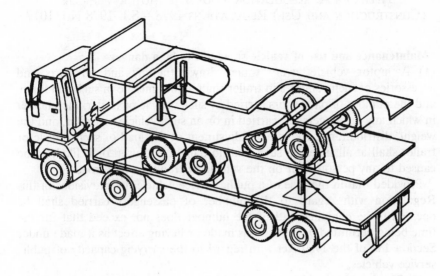

Figure 32

179

APPENDIX A: REGULATION 97 OF THE MOTOR VEHICLES
(CONSTRUCTION AND USE) REGULATIONS 1978 – S.I. 1978 No. 1017

"Maintenance and use of vehicle so as not to be a danger
(1) A motor vehicle, every trailer drawn thereby and all parts and accessories of such vehicle and trailer shall at all times be in such condition, and the number of passengers carried by such vehicle or trailer, the manner in which any passengers are carried in or on such vehicle or trailer, and the weight, distribution, packing and adjustment of the load of such vehicle or trailer shall at all times be such that no danger is caused or is likely to be caused to any person in or on the vehicle or trailer or on a road.

Provided that in the case of a public service vehicle the provisions of this Regulation with regard to the number of passengers carried shall be deemed to be complied with if the number does not exceed that for the time being permitted by regulations made or having effect as if made under Section 148 of the 1960 Act with regard to the carrying capacity of public service vehicles.

(2) The load carried by a motor vehicle or trailer shall at all times be so secured, if necessary by physical restraint other than its own weight, and be in such a position, that neither danger nor nuisance is likely to be caused to any person or property by reason of the load or any part thereof falling or being blown from the vehicle or by reason of any other movement of the load or any part thereof in relation to the vehicle.

(3) No motor vehicle or trailer shall be used for any purpose for which it is so unsuitable as to cause or be likely to cause danger or nuisance to any person in or on the vehicle or trailer or on a road."

Appendix B: Regulations Concerning "Dangerous Goods" Carried by Road Vehicles

Order of Secretary of State (No. 11) dated September 20, 1924, byelaws as to the conveyance of explosives on roads and in certain special cases – SRO 1924 No. 1129.

The Conveyance of Explosives Byelaws 1951 – S.I. 1951 No. 869

The Conveyance of Explosives Byelaws 1958 – S.I. 1958 No. 230.

The Conveyance by Road of Military Explosives Regulations 1977 – S.I. 1977 No 888.

Poisons Rules 1970 – S.I. 1970 No. 798.

The Gas Cylinders (Conveyance) Regulations 1931 – SRO 1931 No. 679.

The Compressed Gas Cylinders (Fuel for Motor Vehicles) Conveyance Regulations 1940 – SRO 1940 No. 2009.

The Gas Cylinders (Conveyance) Regulations 1959 – S.I. 1959 No. 1919.

The Petroleum (Inflammable Liquids and other Dangerous Substances) Order 1947 – S.I. 1947 No. 1443.

The Petroleum Spirit (Conveyance by Road) Regulations 1957 – S.I. 1957 No. 191.

The Petroleum (Carbon Disulphide) Order 1958 – S.I. 1958 No. 257.

The Carbon Disulphide (Conveyance by Road) Regulations 1958 – S.I. 1958 No. 313.

The Petroleum Spirit (Conveyance by Road) Regulations 1958 – S.I. 1958 No. 962.

The Carbon Disulphide (Conveyance by Road) Regulations 1962 – SI. 1962 No. 2527.

The Petroleum Spirit (Conveyance by Road) (Amendment) Regulations 1966 – S.I. 1966 No. 1190.

The Petroleum (Carbon Disulphide) Order 1968 – S.I. 1968 No. 571.

The Petroleum (Corrosive Substances) Order 1 970 – S.l. 1970 No. 1945.

The Corrosive Substances (Conveyance by Road) Regulations 1971 – S.I. 1971 No. 618.

The Petroleum (Inflammable Liquids) Order 1 971 – S.l. 1971 No. 1040.

The Inflammable Liquids (Conveyance by Road) Regulations 1971 – S.I. 1971 No. 106l.

The Inflammable Substances (Conveyance by Road) (Labelling) Regulations 1971 – S.I. 1971 No. 1062.

The Petroleum (Organic Peroxides) Order 1973 – S.I. 1973 No. 1897.

The Organic Peroxides (Conveyance by Road) Regulations 1973 – S.I. 1973 No. 2221.

The Dangerous Substances (Conveyance by Road in Road Tankers and Tank Containers) Regulations 1981 – S.I. 1981 No. 1059.

Health and Safety at Work etc. Act 1974 – ISBN 0 105 437 743.

The Radioactive Substances (Carriage by Road) (Great Britain) Regulations 1974 – S.I. 1974 No. 1735.

The Radioactive Substances (Road Transport Workers) (Great Britain) Regulations 1970 – S.I. 1970 No. 1827.

The Radioactive Substances (Road Transport Workers) (Great Britain) (Amendment) Regulations 1975 – S.I. 1975 No. 1522.

Code of Practice for the Carriage of Radioactive Materials by Road (1982 Impression).

Northern Ireland only. The Radioactive Substances (Carriage by Road) Regulations (Northern Ireland) 1983 – SR 1983 No. 344.

European Agreement concerning the International Carriage of Dangerous Goods by Road (ADR).

Note: New comprehensive controls of all aspects of the conveyance by road of dangerous substances are being prepared by the Health and Safety Commission and the Department of Transport. Regulations dealing with road tankers and tank containers conveying dangerous substances were introduced in 1981. The Classification, Packaging and Labelling of Dangerous Substances Regulations should be introduced in 1984 and be fully in force by 1986. These regulations will require all dangerous substances to be properly packaged and labelled both for supply and for conveyance by road. Proposals for Dangerous Substances (Conveyance by Road in Packages etc) Regulations were published as a Consultative Document in March 1984. These draft regulations are planned to replace the outdated existing legislation with more comprehensive controls. The Consultative Document included a draft approved Code of Practice which gives practical guidance on operational aspects of the conveyance by road of dangerous substances in packages etc.

APPENDIX C

Appendix C: Regulations Concerning The Transit of Animals by Road Vehicles

Conveyance of Live Poultry Order 1919 — S.I. 1919 No. 933.
The Transit of Animals (General) Order 1973 – S.I. 1973 No. 1377.
The Transit of Animals (Road and Rail) Order 1975 – S.I. 1975 No. 1024.
The Transit of Animals (Road and Rail) (Amendment) Order 1979 – S.I. 1979 No. 1013.
The Code of Practice on the care of farm animals and horses during their transport on roll-on/roll-off ferries (Ministry of Agriculture and Fisheries and Food 1983).

DEPARTMENT OF TRANSPORT CODE OF PRACTICE FOR WEIGHING OF GOODS VEHICLES ON DYNAMIC AXLE WEIGHERS

INTRODUCTION

A4–01 1. The object of the Code is to provide operators, drivers and road traffic enforcement officers with information on the correct setting-up and operational use of dynamic axle weighing systems. This Code supplements The Weighing of Motor Vehicles (Use of Dynamic Axle Weighing Machines) Regulations 1978. S.I. 1978 No. 1180.

DESCRIPTION OF DYNAMIC AXLE WEIGHING SYSTEM

2. The basic concept of this equipment is that it will weigh vehicles (individual axles and gross weight by summation) whilst moving at a slow speed over the weighbeam. This new technique, known as "dynamic" weighing, has the advantage both of speeding up the rate of weighing and of representing more accurately the axle load transmitted to the road when the vehicle is in motion, which varies slightly from the static weight recorded by a vehicle at rest.

3. The weighing equipment comprises two units – the weighbeam recessed into the ground on a prepared site and the recording console remotely mounted and connected to the beam by a low voltage electrical cable. The recording console shows on a digital display the weight of axles of a vehicle passing over the weighbeam in tonnes to two decimal places, and also prints the axles weights on a paper "tally" roll together with the vehicle gross weight.

VERIFICATION PROCEDURE

4. Each Dynamic Axle Weigher shall be the subject of the following test procedure to establish initial acceptability and continuing accuracy.

    (a) Each machine should be the subject of an initial test at the manufacturers premises. The test shall be conducted in the static mode to the full capacity of the equipment. The digital readout and tally roll printout shall be checked at 1 tonne intervals and should be accurate within a tolerance of + or − 10 kg.

(b) The machine shall thereafter be installed at the proposed weigh site observing the procedure set down at Paragraph 5 hereafter.

(c) A dynamic weigh test shall then be conducted by a qualified Inspector of Weights and Measures in the following manner using three fully loaded vehicles being a 2 axle rigid, a 4 axle rigid and a 4/5 axle artic.

> (i) Vehicles shall be first weighed on a conventional weighbridge of known accuracy in a single weighing to ascertain the Gross/Train weight.

> (ii) There should follow 9 test runs on the dynamic axle weigher varying the vehicle speed within the capability of the machine (*i.e.* a black printout should be achieved). The weighing position on the plate should also be varied *e.g.* 5 test runs on the centre of the weighplate, a further 2 to the offside of the plate and 2 to the nearside.

> (iii) This test should be repeated with each vehicle and the machine shall be deemed to be accurate provided that the Gross/Train weight of each vehicle is within a tolerance calculated at the rate of + or − 100 kg per axle when compared with the initial weight established on the conventional weighbridge. Further, the individual axle weights shall not vary by more than ± 100 kg when all the results for each individual axle recorded to the machine under test are averaged. Compensating axles should be taken into account as indicated in para. 7(j).

> (iv) A 10th run should then be made at a speed in excess of the machine's speed specification to ensure that the overspeed device functions in accordance with the manufacturer's specification.

(d) The dynamic weight test set out at (c) above shall be carried out at not greater than 6 monthly intervals when the machine is in use.

(e) The certificate of test (Appendix 1) shall be signed by the testing officer being a qualified Inspector of Weights and Measures on completion of the test. The certificate should be retained together with the printroll for each test as an indication of the machine's accuracy valid for the ensuring period of no more than 6 months.

INSTALLATION OF THE WEIGHBEAM

5. The following procedure should be carried out in installing the weighbeam:—

(a) Remove all foreign matter from the weighbeam pit;

(b) Manoeuvre the weighbeam into position above the recess;

(c) Lower weighbeam into the recess taking care not to trap the cable;

(d) Check that the surface of the weighbeam does not deviate from straight by more than 3 mm under a 3 metre straight edge with the adjacent concrete apron. If it is too low the weighbeam should be raised and metal plates placed between the references plates and the load cells. If it is too high then remedial work to the site will be necessary.

PREPARATION FOR DYNAMIC WEIGHING

6. The following step-by-step procedure should be carried out before weighing of vehicles commences:—
   (a) Inspect concrete apron, weighbeam and side plates for any sign of damage and mis-alignment; also ensure that the concrete apron is clear of debris (stones etc.) which could affect the weighing.
   (b) Check that cable connector to the console is clean and dry;
   (c) Position console on a stable level surface and connect to main power source or battery (or similar).
   (d) Switch on equipment and check Low (zero) and High (16.00 tonnes) readings using instrumentation switch or button. Leave equipment switched on for a minimum period of 10 minutes until figures remain constant.
   (e) Re-check Low (zero) and High (16.00 tonnes) indications and make printout. Weighing of vehicles should not commence until these indications remain constant.
   (f) Instruct the police to commence stopping of vehicles for weighing. The site and approaches should be marked by signs in accordance with Police advice.
   (g) Officers called upon to operate the equipment should familiarise themselves fully with instruction in the manufactures' handbook.

WEIGHING OF VEHICLES

7. The following procedure should be adopted for weighing of vehicles:—
   (a) Vehicle to be weighed is to be stopped a minimum distance of 6 metres from the weighbeam on level approach; avoid stopping on uneven ground; e.g. with one or more wheels on the curb.
   (b) Possible errors caused by surges in the liquid load or single compartment unbaffled tanker should be taken into account.
   (c) The enforcement officer operating the console is to re-check and reprint the Low and High indication, set the equipment in the dynamic mode and, where appropriate, set the direction selector switch to suit the vehicle approach. He must also press the totalisor button to ensure that any residual information in the totalisor has been cleared.
   (d) Where vehicles under 3 tonnes unladen weight are to be checked, and the equipment has a Low Weight mode, this button should be depressed before weighing commences.

(e) An enforcement officer should then instruct the driver of the vehicle to drive across the weighbeam at a steady speed not exceeding 2.5 miles per hour; during this run the driver must neither accelerate nor use his brake. This can normally be achieved by engaging lowest forward gear and driving at a tick-over speed over the weighbridge.

(f) The vehicle is to be observed at all times during the weighing procedure to ensure that a consistent speed is maintained. In the case of a foreign driver who cannot speak English it is desirable for him to be guided by an enforcement officer walking alongside the vehicle.

(g) If at any time during the weighing a driver accelerates above the permitted speed, thus causing a red printout, or no printout, to be registered, or if he uses his brakes to cause a sharp deceleration, the weighing should be disregarded and the vehicle weighed again until a satisfactory weighing and an all-black printout is achieved.

(h) At the conclusion of a satisfactory weighing, with an all-black printout showing axle weights, the operator should press the appropriate button to give a summation of the axle weights. The registration number of the vehicle should then be written on the print-roll adjacent to the read-out.

(i) Each weighing is to be followed by a zero and high indication check which will be shown on the print-roll.

(j) Following weighing of the vehicle, normal Road Traffic Act procedures are to be followed in the light of the Weighing of Motor Vehicles (Use of Dynamic Axle Weighing Machines) Regulations 1978 (S.I. 1978 No. 1180). The prescribed Certificate of Weight should be issued to the driver. The recorded weights should be assessed in the light of the presumed accuracy limits, laid down in the Regulations, of ± 150 kg per axle, with the consequent accuracy limit on gross vehicle weight of ± 150 kg, multiplied by the number of axles; compensating axles as usual, should continue to be assessed as a combined weight against the combined plated weights.

(k) The print-roll should be left intact for the complete day's weighings, then removed, dated and retained by the enforcement staff.

SITE REQUIREMENTS

8. In order to minimise the effects of changing forces or loads being presented to the weigher, the standard level of the approach and exit to the concrete apron should be constructed and maintained as follows:—

(a) For 8 metres either side of the weighbeam the levels should be within a tolerance of ± 3 mm. Additionally the finished surface should not deviate from straight by more than 3 mm under a 3 metre straight edge.

Department of Transport   APPENDIX 1

CERTIFICATE OF ACCURACY – DYNAMIC AXLE WEIGHER

Date	Inspector	Serial No.	Result

Vehicle Reg. No. ....   Tractor Make/Type ....

Axle Layout Diagram

Trailer Make/Type ....

Compensating Axle Specify ....

General Condition and Description of Vehicle and Load ....
....

Location and Description of Conventional Weighbridge ....
....

Static Recorded Weight .... Tonnes Gross/Train

General Weather Conditions ....

TEST	Digital Readout/Printout (Tonnes)						Train Error (Kgs)	Speed MPH	Position on Plate	Remarks
	AX1	AX2	AX3	AX4	AX5	Gross/ Train				
Static									*i.e.* centre offside nearside	
Dynamic 1st Run										
2nd Run										
3rd Run										
4th Run										
5th Run										
6th Run										
7th Run										
8th Run										
9th Run										
10th Run										

General observations ....Signature ....
....(Inspector of Weights and Measures)
....Date ....

DEPARTMENT OF TRANSPORT CODE OF PRACTICE FOR THE WEIGHING OF GOODS VEHICLES TO CHECK WHETHER THEY ARE OVERLOADED USING CONVENTIONAL WEIGHBRIDGES OR AXLE WEIGHING DEVICES DESIGNED TO WEIGH STATIONARY VEHICLES

INTRODUCTION

1. This Code of Practice provides drivers and operators of goods vehicles **A5–01** with information on the procedure for road traffic enforcement weighing of vehicles on conventional static weighbridges and other non-dynamic weighing equipment. It does not apply to checks on the weights of vehicles by the use of dynamic axle weighbridges for which there is a separate Code of Practice, (GV230) or to the use of "pad" weighing vehicles on which the wheels of stationary vehicles have to be located to determine the weight of the vehicle or its individual axles.

2. The main aim of check weighing is to enforce U.K. law regarding weight limits. These exist to reduce damage to roads and bridges, to protect the environment, and to improve road safety.

TYPES OF WEIGHBRIDGES USED

3. There are two types of weighing equipment used for static weighings.
   - (i) Weighbridges stamped as fit for weighing for trade purposes by a Trading Standards Officer.
   - (ii) Weighbridges and other weighing equipment such as axle weighing devices capable of weighing the axles of stationary vehicles which for various reasons are not used for trade purposes or tested as above but have been examined and certified by a Trading Standards Officer as being suitable for road traffic enforcement purposes.

Weighbridges and weighing equipment may be of either mechanical or electronic operation: may give the weight indications by means of a steelyard, manual or digital readout and may incorporate a ticket printing mechanism.

OPERATION OF WEIGHING EQUIPMENT

4. Weighbridges etc. will be operated only by or under supervision of a duly Authorised Officer fully conversant with the operation of the weighing

equipment and with approved methods of weighing. Weighing by the method known as "double-weighing" will only be carried out by a Trading Standards Officer whose professional qualifications and experience will enable him to give expert evidence as to the accuracy of this weighing procedure; or by a duly Authorised Officer at sites which have been examined and approved as suitable for double weighing by the local Trading Standards Officer, and who will if necessary be available to give expert evidence in Court. NOTE: double weighing occurs when the results of two or more individual weighings of a vehicle's axles are summated to produce the total gross weight of the vehicle.

WHO CAN DO THE WEIGHING

5. Your vehicle may be weighed by either a Traffic Examiner of the Department of Transport, and authorised officer of a highway authority or a constable authorised by his Chief Constable. These officers will have a written authority to check and weigh your vehicle. Authorised officers may require your vehicle to be weighed at any time.

WHERE WILL CHECKS BE HELD?

6. Checkpoints for enforcement weighing are chosen in consultation with the police and may be at a variety of locations including for example lay-bys, little used roads, private premises and testing stations.

WHO WILL STOP YOUR VEHICLE?

7. Your vehicle will only be stopped or directed on a road by a uniformed officer following which the police officer or other authorised officer, on production of his authority, may direct you to the weigh site. Authorised enforcement officers will then undertake the task of carrying out the weight check and matters arising from it. An authorised officer may however direct you to a weighbridge at any time when you are stationary without the need for a police officer in uniform to be involved.

WHAT INSTRUCTIONS WILL THE DRIVER RECEIVE?

8. If you are directed to a weighbridge or weigh site clear instructions will be given and a simple direction form may be used. You must drive directly to the weighbridge without detour. A watch may be made for any attempt to evade being check weighed or to offload or redistribute the vehicle's load. Most check points will be reasonably close to a weighbridge. However, an authorised officer has the power to direct you to a weighbridge at any distance from the point where you have been stopped. If a vehicle is

directed more than 5 miles to a weigh site and is found to be within the permitted weight limits, certain provisions for payment of expenses may apply. It is an offence for the person in charge of the motor vehicle to refuse or neglect to comply with a request to weigh made by an authorised officer. Maximum penalty £1,000.

AT THE WEIGHBRIDGE

9. The procedure will be as follows:
    (a) Normally only one authorised officer will check weigh your vehicle.
    (b) You and any passengers should remain in the vehicle during weighing as you are part of the weight transmitted to the road.
    (c) When requested you should move your vehicle smoothly onto the weighbridge plate.
    (d) The engine should be switched off but left in gear during weighing. When a vehicle's individual axles are being check weighed both the hand and footbrakes should be released.
    (e) If your vehicle is too long to go on the weighing plate or is over the weight capacity of the machine it may require 2 or more weighings to get a total weight for your vehicle. (See also paragraph 4).
    (f) You may be required to have your axle weights checked and in positioning your vehicle you should carefully follow instructions given by the authorised officer.
    (g) A certificate of weight will be issued for each vehicle weighed and will be handed to you. In some cases, where circumstances permit, you may be invited to see the weight recorded on the indicator. The certificate of weight exempts a vehicle from being weighed again on the same journey *with the same load* if stopped at another weight check. You should pass the certificate of weight to your employer as soon as you reach your base.
    (h) You should also note that previous overloading offences may be detected by checks on weighbridge records.

WHAT IF MY VEHICLE IS ABOVE THE PERMITTED WEIGHT LIMIT?

10. If the weight recorded is above the permitted limit, the driver or any other person who uses, causes or permits the use of the vehicle which may include the consignor, may be liable to be prosecuted. The vehicle's movement may be prohibited until the weight is reduced to within the permitted limit. Maximum penalty on conviction, for each overload, is £1,000. In any case where an offence is disclosed an authorised officer is entitled to such information as is necessary to enable him to complete his report of the offence.

WHAT HAPPENS IF I AM ISSUED WITH A PROHIBITION?

11. Under the Road Traffic Act 1972 an authorised officer may prohibit all movement of your overweight vehicle either absolutely or subject to a

specific purpose such as safe unloading. You will be issued with a prohibition notice which will come into effect immediately.

12. While a prohibition notice is in force it is an offence for your vehicle to be moved on a road. All prohibition notices must have been cancelled in writing by an authorised officer before the vehicle can proceed. This may entail the re-weighing of your vehicle to establish that it is within the legal weight limits. An authorised officer has discretion to direct in writing that a vehicle must be moved to a place where parking or offloading of the excess weight can be carried out safely. Certain conditions may be imposed on this movement.

13. Where an articulated vehicle or draw-bar combination is prohibited, the prohibition remains in force until the authorised officer is satisfied that the weight of *that particular combination* has been reduced.

14. If, for practical reasons you wish to drive away your towing unit only, and provided it is safe to leave the trailer, the towing unit may be issued with a clearance notice. Where this happens the clearance notice will be endorsed specifically "for Towing Unit only".

15. Where a prohibition is issued, it is the responsibility of you or your employer to make satisfactory arrangements for the excess weight to be offloaded. This is normally done by providing an additional vehicle. The authorised officer will advise you how to obtain a removal notice. You are responsible for the security of any offloaded goods and you must make arrangements for their safe-keeping. Authorised officers will ensure that prohibitions are removed as soon as reasonably practicable, having regard to all of the circumstances.

16. A copy of any prohibition notice issued to a driver will be sent to the owner or the operator of the vehicle or a driver's employer and if relevant the licensing authority who issued the operator's licence.

LOADS MERITING SPECIAL CONSIDERATION

17. The law relating to the weighing of vehicles applies equally to all vehicles irrespective of the kind of load they are carrying. Driver and operators cannot claim exemption from weight checks and the risk of subsequent prohibition through overloading because of the special or unusual nature of the load.

18. Authorised officers carrying out checks are fully aware of the problems associated with special loads, and the following information should reassure drivers that care will be taken to safeguard vehicles and loads.

19. Loads accepted as requiring special consideration include, for example:

— Vehicle carrying livestock
— Vehicles carrying perishables or loads which rapidly deteriorate
— Vehicles carrying high value loads
— Vehicles carrying dangerous loads
— Vehicles carrying abnormal indivisible loads
— Customs sealed loads.

Vehicles Carrying Livestock

20. At the weigh site the authorised officer will ensure that any vehicle carrying livestock has priority, providing conditions permit, since enforcement authorities recognise that it is essential that livestock are conveyed to their destination with the minimum of delay. If you are the driver of a vehicle containing livestock you must bring this fact to the attention of the authorised officer immediately when you arrive at the weigh site.

21. Drivers of vehicles containing livestock and authorised officers should be aware of the main hazards to animal welfare and the precautions to which particular attention should be paid at a weight check. These are:

   (a) Ventilation — this is one of the most important factors affecting the welfare of animals in transit. This should be adjusted to provide adequate ventilation when the vehicle is stationary, even for short periods, and re-adjusted as necessary before the journey is resumed;

   (b) exhaust fumes — to avoid causing the animals distress, you should ask for your vehicle to be moved away from other vehicles at the earliest opportunity;

   (c) exposure to extremes of temperature — during hot weather you should if possible park your vehicle in the shade and where there is a current of fesh air. In very cold weather your vehicle should again if possible be parked in a sheltered place;

   (d) feeding and watering — animals in transit should be fed and watered according to their needs. If any unexpected and prolonged delay could cause difficulty in complying with this condition, *you will be responsible* for bringing it to the attention of the authorised officer.

22. If after check weighing you are found to be overloaded it will be necessary to keep the animals on board until a further vehicle has been obtained. The transhipment of animals must always be in accordance with the relevant legal requirements. Local movement of the overloaded vehicle will be permitted by the authorised officer where this is necessary to avoid unnecessary hardship to the animals.

Perishable Loads

23. Authorised officers will endeavour to ensure that special consideration is given to any vehicle carrying a load which is perishable or is subject to rapid deterioration. Such loads would include, for example, perishable foods, ready mixed concrete etc.

High Value Loads

24. Carriers of high value loads normally give their drivers special instructions to be followed whenever they are stopped by a police officer. If your

employer has issued special instructions, ensure that you comply with them. If your employer has not given you any special instructions, inform the police officer who has stopped the vehicle and he will deal with the matter.

DANGEROUS LOADS

25. Drivers of vehicles carrying inflammable, corrosive and other dangerous loads should be fully aware of the legislation relating to that load and should bring them to the attention of the authorised officer carrying out the weight check.

ABNORMAL INDIVISIBLE LOADS

26. Abnormal indivisible loads are subject to special requirements but are liable to be check weighed. At the weigh site the driver of a vehicle conveying an abnormal indivisible load should inform the authorised officer of the nature of his load and any special conditions attached to its movement. He should also produce to the authorised officer any documents relating to that load, its weight or routing, which he may carry with him.

CUSTOMS SEALED LOAD

27. If a customs sealed load has to have the seal broken to allow excessive weight to be removed, a Customs Officer will have to attend to supervise the breaking open and re-sealing of the load. It is the responsibility of the driver, vehicle operator or his agent to arrange for this to be done.

DRIVER'S RESPONSIBILITY

28. It is the responsibility of the driver to inform the authorised officers requiring the vehicle to be weighed of any unusual characteristics of his vehicle or load.

OPERATOR'S RESPONSIBILITY

29. It is the responsibility of vehicle operators to ensure that their drivers are fully briefed on the nature of the load they are carrying and any action they would need to take, should that vehicle be required to be weighed. Operators should also ensure that their drivers know the position of the Ministry "plate" on the vehicle including the trailer and that they are aware of the vehicle's maximum permitted axle loadings and gross weight.

DEPARTMENT OF TRANSPORT SUPPLEMENT TO THE CODE OF PRACTICE FOR THE WEIGHING OF GOODS VEHICLES ON CONVENTIONAL WEIGHBRIDGES ETC.

[For The Use of Enforcement Staff Only]

1. THE SELECTION AND ORGANISATION OF SITES

(a) Department of Transport Examiners, Trading Standards Officers and Police should agree a programme of weight checks to ensure maximum utilisation of manpower. The programme should be circulated on a confidential basis in order to obtain as even a spread of activity as possible.

(b) Sites to be used for directing/stopping vehicles should be agreed with Senior Police Officers.

(c) The need for warning signs and other devices to ensure the safety of participating personnel and other road users should be agreed by the Senior Police Officer.

(d) When selecting sites, consideration should be given to the possibility that vehicles will be prohibited from further driving on the road, and the need for some place to park them safely, without interfering with the check.

(e) Where the stopping point is not adjacent to the weighbridge to be used, ensure adequate communication between stop points and weighbridge by radio or car escort.

(f) Ensure that there is available adequate information at the checkpoint to assist any prohibited driver to obtain the means of off-loading any excess weight, thereby clearing the offending vehicle from the check area.

(g) Ensure that the person who operates the weighbridge is competent to do so.

(h) Police officers at checkpoint to stop vehicles should be instructed before the check starts what traffic should be stopped for checking, and the instruction to be given to the driver when stopped.

2. DESCRIPTION OF THE CATEGORIES AND TYPES OF STATIC WEIGHING EQUIPMENT

There are two categories of static weighing equipment:

(a) Weighbridges, which because of their form of construction and location, are stamped as fit for weighing for trade purposes by a Trading Standards Officer.

(b) Weighbridges and other weighing machines which are not suitable for stamping as trade machines or whose owners do not wish them to be used for trade, but are certified as being suitable for road traffic enforcement work by a Trading Standards Officer.

The above categories of weighing equipment can be either mechanical or electronic types, as indicated below:

(c) Weighbridges or weighing machines whose weight indication is arrived at by means of a steelyard on which is a moveable carriage and numbered graduations with or without loose poises. These can be sub-divided into:

    (i) Those machines which indicate the correct balance and the correct weight when the steelyard moves slowly from the bottom (horizontal) of its limit of travel up to the top limit and just stays there. This type is called an *accelerating steelyard.*

    (ii) Those machines which indicate the correct balance and the correct weight when the steelyard vibrates slowly in the horizontal position equidistant between the top and bottom of its limits of travel. This type is called a *vibrating steelyard.*

(d) Dial indicating machines with or without a ticket printing facility.

(e) Electronic digital indicating machine with or without a ticket printing facility.

3. Particular Categories of Weighbridges

(a) *Public Weighbridges* — These are machines which are stamped and regularly tested by an Inspector of Weights and Measures and are designated "Public Weighbridges" by their owners who may charge a fee for weighing vehicles on request. Public weighings may only be done by persons who after examination hold a Certificate of Competence issued by a Chief Trading Standards Officer. The operation of the weighbridge must be in accordance with Weights and Measures law. This means that records of every public weighing must be kept for two years and be produced if demanded by a Trading Standards Officer.

(b) *Trade Weighbridges* — These machines are stamped by Trading Standards Officers as fit for use for trade purposes and are regularly tested as required by the Weights and Measures law.

(c) *Other Weighing Machines* — Other non-trade weighbridges and weighing machines for weighing the axles of stationary vehicles may be used for weighing vehicles for the purposes of enforcing the Road Traffic Act but only if they have been examined and certified by a Trading Stndards Officer as being suitable for road traffic enforcement purposes.

4. The use of Weighbridges by Authorised Officers and Weighing Procedure

A duly authorised officer may use any of the above equipment only with the consent of its owner but if at all possible the authorised officer should carry out the weighing operation.

Machines described in Paragraphs 3a and 3b are regularly tested by Trading Standards Officers as required by weights and measures law but machines described in 3c are only tested at the request of the owners or enforcement agency, for which a fee may be charged.

In any proceedings it may be necessary for the authorised officer to prove the accuracy and suitability of the weighbridge or the axle weighing machine used for enforcement purposes. One method of establishing and subsequently proving the accuracy and suitability of weighbridges and other weighing machines regularly used for enforcement purposes is to arrange for the equipment to be tested at regular six monthly intervals. To prove the accuracy of a weighbridge or other weighing machine only used occasionally for enforcement purposes it may be necessary to arrange for the particular machine used to be tested after any enforcement use from which legal proceedings flow. These tests must be conducted by a Trading Standards Officer who should be asked to provide a statement of accuracy for the equipment and a certificate of its suitability for enforcement use by means of a statement in evidential form.

Before commencing an enforcement weight check, the following procedure must be adhered to by the authorised officer:

(a) Ensure that the weighbridge plate has adequate clearance all round and is not binding.

(b) Ensure the weighbridge is in balance when no weigh is imposed. If not, the owner should be asked to balance it.

(c) For steelyard machines the steelyard should indicate balance (see Paragraph 2c) and dial and electronic machines should indicate zero when there is no load on the plate.

(d) In the case of steelyard machines with loose removable poises which must be added to a hanger at the end of the steelyard to balance major increments of increase in the weight of the load, ensure that there are enough of these poises.

(e) For all machines ensure that the load to be weighed does not exceed the maximum capacity of the weighbridge.

(f) Digital machines should have had the electricity supply switched on long enough for them to warm up before they are used. A minimum period of ten minutes is recommended.

(g) Note any possible influence of the wind on the recording mechanism.

(h) With a steelyard machine of the accelerating type NEVER back weigh. *[Back weighing occurs when, after the first estimate of the weight made by location of the carriage and the movement of the steelyard to the top of its travel, the carriage is again moved until the steelyard drops. The steelyard MUST always travel from the bottom stop towards the top stop, never from the top down]* With steelyard machines make sure the major carriage (that giving the larger weight increments) is firmly located in its notch.

(j) Always use the locking gear whenever a vehicle is driven onto or off the weighbridge so that no shock load is transmitted to the mechanism.

(k) Before deciding to use a weighbridge for double weighing an authorised officer should confirm that a Trading Standards Officer has approved the use of the weighbridge for that purpose and the authorised officer should also ensure that he is aware of any particular requirements relating to its use. [NOTE: double weighing occurs when the results of two or more individual weighings of the axles of a vehicle are summated to produce the total gross weight of the vehicle].

NB. *In the case of weighbridges used for double weighing the method of weighing for that site will be specified in writing by the Trading Standards Officer and must be adhered to at all times.*

When weighing a vehicle the authorised officer should ensure that:

  (i) The driven is given clear instructions.
 (ii) The driver and passengers remain in the vehicle during the weighing unless the officer considers it practicable for the driver to be shown the indicated weights.
(iii) The vehicle moves smoothly onto the weighbridge and the driver does not accelerate or brake violently.
 (iv) The vehicle is wholly on the plate and that no tyre is partly on the surround to the weighbridge plate.
  (v) When weighing vehicles fitted with compensating axles care is taken to weigh the compensating axles together as one unit.
 (vi) Where a conventional weighbridge is used to determine the weight of one axle, regard is had to the general suitability of the weighbridge for that purpose, and particularly that the weighbridge approaches are reasonably level.
(vii) The engine is stopped and the vehicle is in gear or the brakes applied according to the circumstances of weighing.
(viii) The weights are accurately recorded and if possible a ticket printed.

A Certificate is to be issued to the driver who should be advised to forward it to the operator of the vehicle.

5. Procedure Subsequent to Weighing

(a) If the vehicle is overloaded the driver should be interviewed and reported in line with the previously stated instructions.
(b) The vehicle's movement may be prohibited until the weight is reduced.
(c) Both the driver and operator and any other person causing or permitting use should be reported, by the authorised officer, for all offences revealed. Where an authorised officer has reason to believe that overloading is the result of the action of other persons, either at the point of loading or elsewhere then the officer should report this fact in order that further enquiries can be made and ultimate responsibility established.
(d) Where an articulated combination is prohibited, the prohibition remains in force until the authorised officer is satisfied that the weight of *that particular combination* has been reduced.

(e) When completing the overload check report, ensure that the situation is illustrated clearly, *i.e.* the position of the vehicle when weighed, the position of any slope while the vehicle was weighed, both in relation to the weighbridge plate, any striking feature about the load or its position on the vehicle, all of which will assist any person not present at the check to have a clear picture of the situation.

(f) When weighing vehicles which claim to be "Special Types" it must be remembered that they revert to C & U limit if they do not comply with the condition of "Authorisation of Special Types General Order".

(g) When vehicles which are classified as "Security Category" become involved in the check expect a cautious attitude from the driver or crew, arrange for them to be escorted to the nearest Police Station in the first instance to assure them that you are genuine. Once at the Police Station arrangements can be made to carry out your statutory enforcement.

SPECIFIC REQUIREMENTS RELATING TO THE TRANSFER OF OFF-LOADING OF ANIMALS FROM VEHICLES WHICH ARE FOUND TO BE OVERLOADED

1. Authorised officers should be aware that there exists specific legislation (The Animal Health Act 1981) which is designed to prevent the spread of animal diseases and they should ensure that their enforcement procedures do not conflict with its requirements relating to the movement and transhipment of animals. Before commencing any enforcement activity likely to involve the check-weighing of vehicles conveying livestock authorised officers should be fully aware of any outbreak of animal disease and any current restrictions on the movement of transhipment of animals.

2. In normal circumstances and in the absence of an outbreak of animal disease or controls on the movement of animals, cattle and sheep can be offloaded or transferred from one vehicle to another without restriction. However, special controls are permanently in force in relation to the movement and transhipment of swine.

3. When any vehicle carrying livestock is found to be overloaded and is prohibited from further movement until the load is reduced it is the responsibility of the person in charge of the animals to ensure that the requirements of the Animal Health Act are complied with in relation to any offloading or transfer of animals. The offloading of excess animals or their transfer to another vehicle may have to take place at a nearby cattle market or farm where suitable facilities exist, but where safe to do so a transfer could take place directly from one vehicle to another. Loads of mixed livestock or aggressive animals such as bulls or boars may need special attention and facilities.

4. In circumstances where there is an outbreak of animal disease, where there are controls on the movement of animals (as during the period for the compulsory dipping of sheep) or where swine are being carried then the

transfer of offloading of the excess animals carried on a vehicle found to be overloaded is subject to special arrangements. In such circumstances the transfer to another vehicle or offloading of the excess animals may only be done under a specific authority from the Divisional Veterinary Officer of the Ministry of Agriculture, Fisheries and Food (DVO-MAFF). This authority must be obtained by the person in charge of the animals before any transfer or offloading takes place; it may be given verbally and confirmed in writing later. Failure to comply with these requirements may result in the prosecution of the offender.

5. Local and restricted movement of a vehicle carrying livestock, which is found to be overloaded, should be permitted by authorised officers to avoid unnecessary or offloading of the excess animals.

6. The transfer of animals between vehicles is likely to fall into one of the following circumstances.

6.1 Cattle or Sheep

In normal circumstances there are no restrictions on the movement of these animals and they may be transferred from one vehicle to another without specific authority.

In circumstances where movement controls or a disease situation exists an authority to transfer animals between one vehicle and another must be obtained from the DVO-MAFF.

6.2 Swine

The transfer of swine from one vehicle to another is prohibited at all times. An authority to transfer swine between vehicles must be obtained from the DVO-MAFF.

6.3 Additional Requirements

In any case where animals are transferred from one vehicle to another the vehicle into which the animals are transferred must be thoroughly cleaned out before any loading takes place, unless that vehicle had immediately prior to loading been carrying similar animals originating at the same farm and no other animals had been carried.

In any case where animals are transferred from one vehicle to another the person having charge of the animals on the first vehicle must give to the person taking charge of the animals on the second vehicle sufficient information to enable him to complete the animal movement records required by The Transit of Animals (Road and Rail) Order 1975.

7. It is the responsibility of the person in charge of the animals to comply with the requirements. Non compliance may result in the prosecution of offenders. Authorised officers' enforcement procedures should not conflict with the requirements of the Animal Health Act.

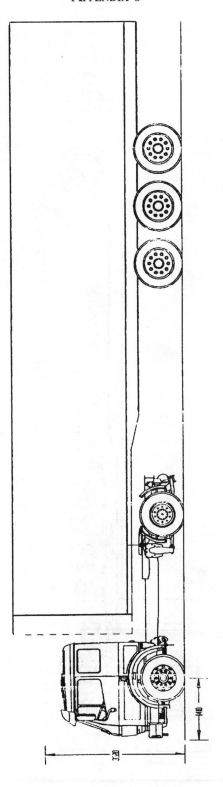

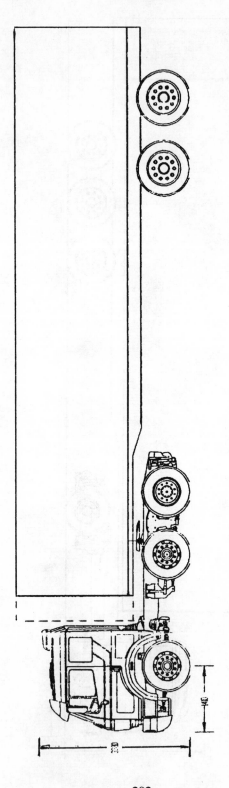

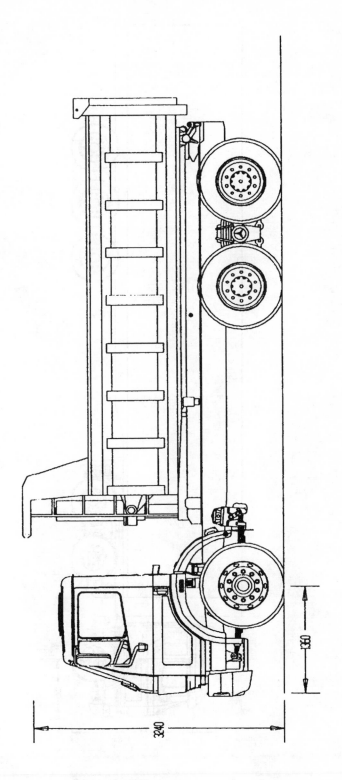

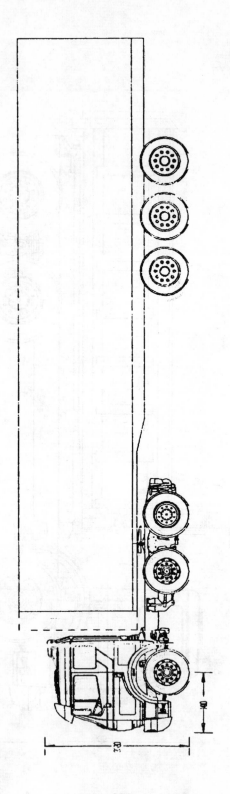

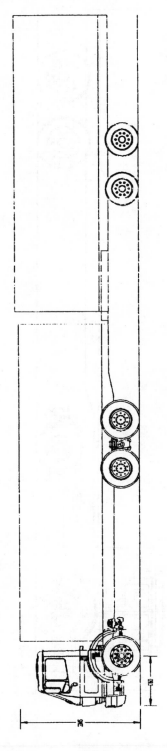

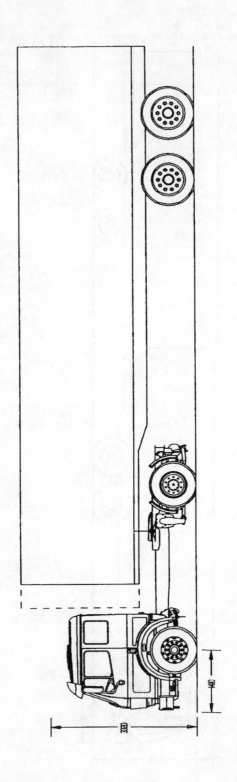

TACHOGRAPH CHART
CENTRE FIELD

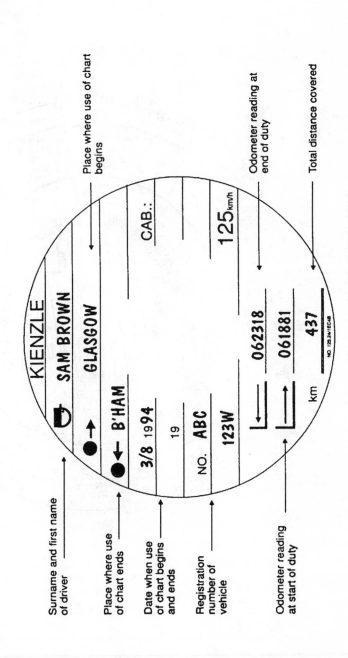

Surname and first name of driver

Place where use of chart ends

Date when use of chart begins and ends

Registration number of vehicle

Odometer reading at start of duty

Place where use of chart begins

Odometer reading at end of duty

Total distance covered

TACHOGRAPH CHART

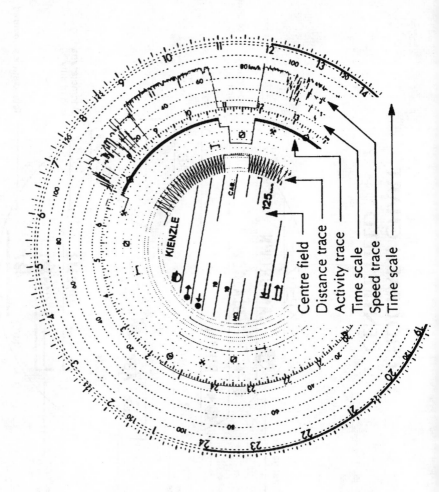

Centre field
Distance trace
Activity trace
Time scale
Speed trace
Time scale

WEEKLY SHEET

1. DRIVER'S NAME

2. PERIOD COVERED BY SHEET

WEEK COMMENCING (DATE) _____

TO WEEK ENDING (DATE) _____

DAY ON WHICH DUTY COMMENCED	REGISTRATION NO OF VEHICLE(S) 3	PLACE WHERE VEHICLE(S) BASED 4	TIME OF GOING ON DUTY 5	TIME OF GOING OFF DUTY 6	TIME SPENT DRIVING 7	TIME SPENT ON DUTY 8	SIGNATURE OF DRIVER 9
MONDAY							
TUESDAY							
WEDNESDAY							
THURSDAY							
FRIDAY							
SATURDAY							
SUNDAY							

10. CERTIFICATION BY EMPLOYER

I HAVE EXAMINED THE ENTRIES IN THIS SHEET

SIGNATURE _____

POSITION HELD _____

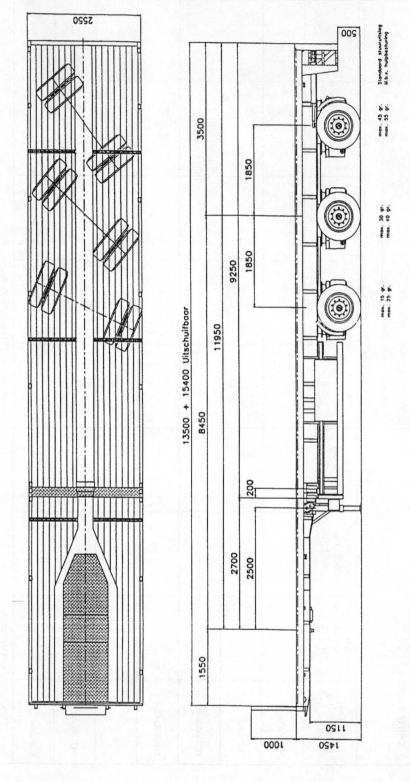

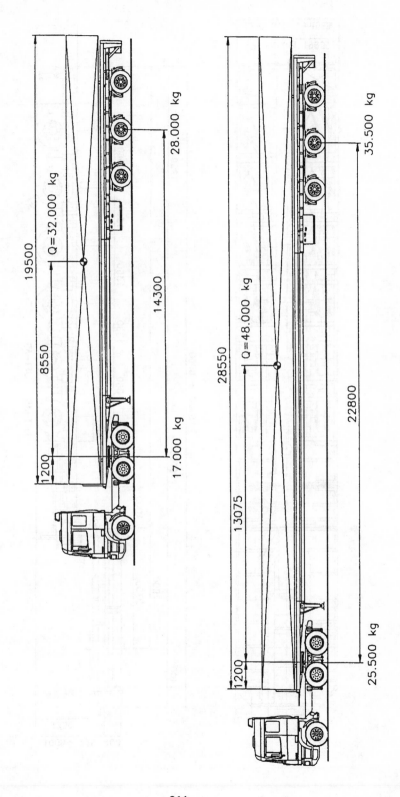

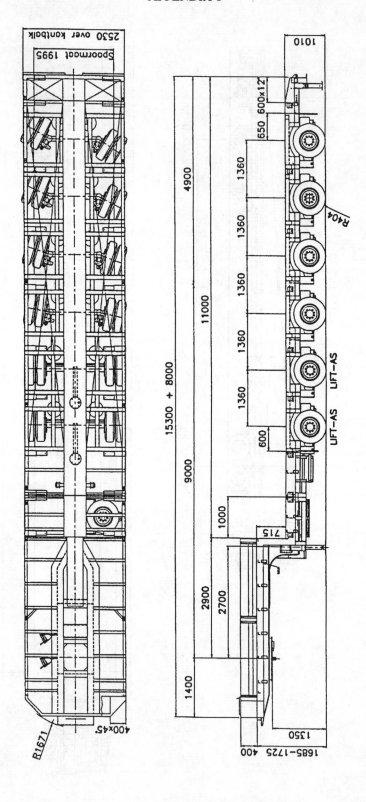

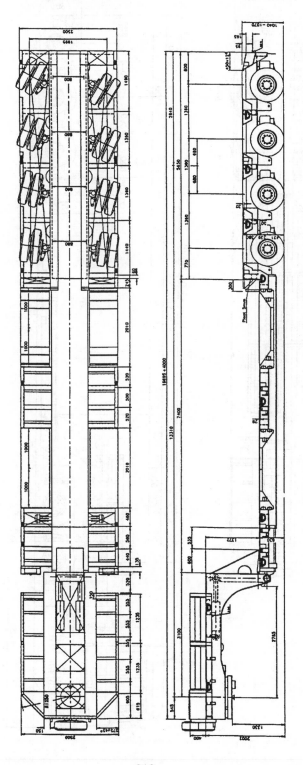

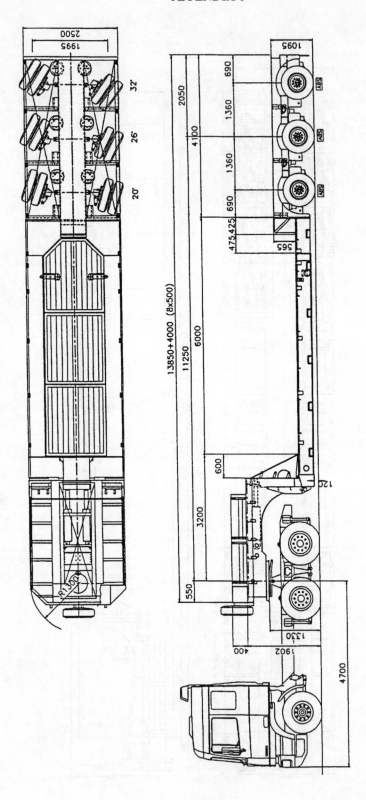

214

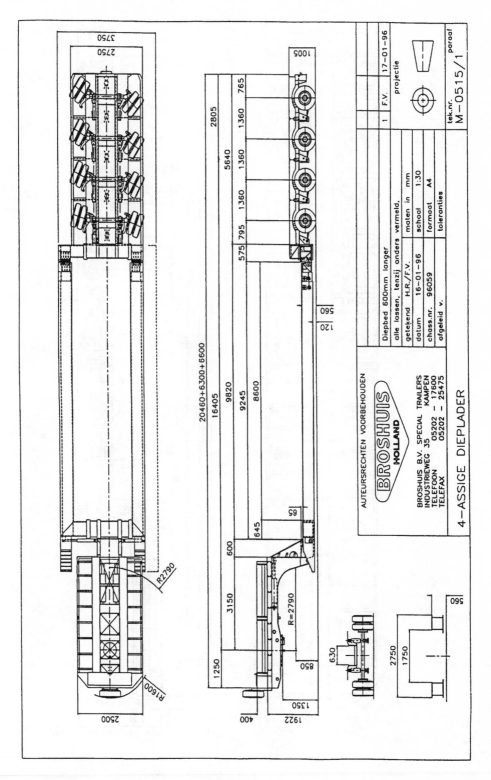

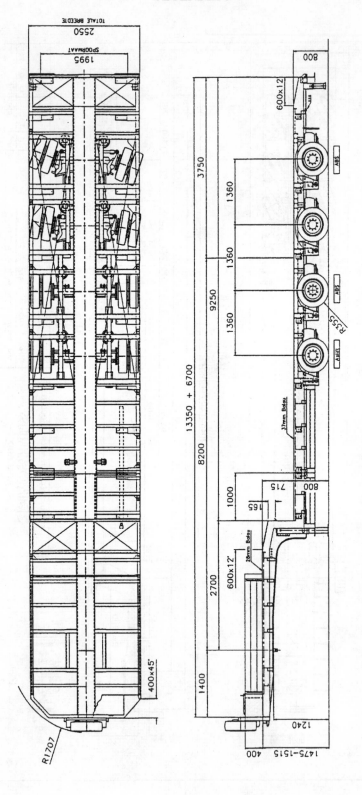

APPENDIX 6

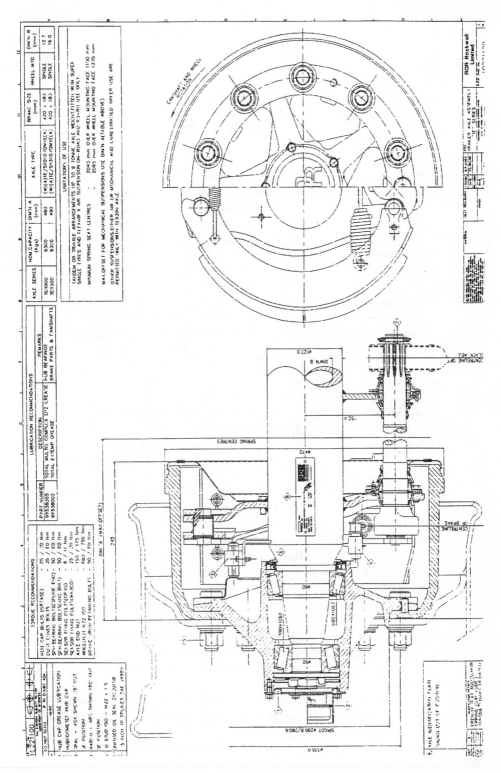

217

GLOSSARY

A7–01 Artic — Articulated vehicle.

Compensating Axles — Adjacent axles with a compensating mechanism designed to equalise the weight transmitted to the road surface by each axle, the weight being aggregated together when a vehicle is weighed.

Curtainsider. [See *Tautliner*.]

Draw-bar Trailer — A trailer that will stand on its own and is pulled by a rigid vehicle.

Fifth wheel coupling — The plate on the rear of an articulated tractor unit by means of which, with the locking device, the pin on the semi-trailer is attached to the tractor unit.

Gross Weight — Maximum permitted weight of rigid vehicle or tractor unit of articulated outfit.

Groupage — A load consisting of multiple consignments collected together to form one load.

Magic button — A concealed switch or wire enabling the driver to disconnect the tachograph.

Pallet — A wood or metal frame on which loads, usually of no more weight than 1,000 kg, are secured to facilitate handling by fork-lift truck.

Plated Weight — Maximum permitted weights shown on the Ministry and Manufacturer's "plates" affixed to the vehicle.

Pulling a fuse — The removal of a fuse to prevent either the tachograph or speed limiter from working.

Reefer (also **Fridge**) — A refrigerated vehicle.

Semi-trailer — A trailer that is only capable of being towed by an articulated tractor unit, being attached to the tractor unit by a fifth wheel coupling.

Suzie — Coiled plastic pipe, usually red, yellow or blue, used to connect the airlines on the braking system of the articulated tractor and trailer.

Tautliner — An articulated trailer the sides of which are formed by curtains of strong plastic material which can be drawn back to facilitate loading and unloading.

Tractor — The drawing unit of an articulated vehicle.

Train Weight — Maximum permitted weight of vehicle and trailer combination, either articulated outfit or rigid vehicle and drawbar trailer combination.

Tremcard — Traffic emergency card carried by vehicles transporting hazardous chemicals designed to give the emergency services immediate advice about the product.

Wagon and Drag — A draw-bar combination.

x

INDEX

Abnormal loads, 4–01—4–22
  assistants, 4–18
  axles, 4–12, 4–15
  defence, 4–13—4–18
  definition, 4–02
  dimensions, 4–16
  enforcement authorities, 4–16
  evidence, 4–10—4–12
  indemnity, 4–17
  indivisible loads, A5
  information, 4–20—4–21
  legislation, 4–01—4–11, 4–16
  mitigation, 4–19—4–22
  notice, 4–04—4–05, 4–10—4–11, 4–17
  permits, 4–03
  police, 4–04, 4–11, 4–18
  prosecution, 4–06—4–12
  Trading Standards Officer, 4–10, 4–11
  vehicle excise duty, 14–30—14–31
  Vehicle Inspectors, 4–10, 4–11
  weight, 4–14—4–14, 4–21, A5
  weighbridges, 4–22
Absolute discharges, 15–08, 15–09
Accidents
  brakes, 2–13, 2–26
  fatal, 3–12, 10–01
  Scotland, 16–02
  tyres, 11–29
Accord Dangerous Routiers, 7–02, 7–04—7–06
Accord Transports Perishables, 5–02—5–03, 5–15
Agricultural vehicles, 14–43
Anchorage points, A3–4.1—4.6, A3–6.24–6.28
Animals, A3–C, A5, A6
Appeals
  Goods and Passenger Carrying Vehicle Operators Licensing System, 12–14, 12–29
  Transport Tribunal, 12–29

Articulated vehicles
  brakes, 2–18
  dangerous or insecure loads, 3–17
  slow roll phenomenon, 3–17
  vehicle excise duty, 14–22
  weighbridges, 6–14
Assistants, 4–18
Attendants, 9–16
Axles
  abnormal loads, 4–12, 4–15
  Code of Practice for Weighing of Goods Vehicles on Dynamic Axle Weighers, A4
  overloading, 6–01, 6–04—6–07, 6–09—6–10, 6–22—6–23, 6–26—6–27, 6–34, A5
  wheels, 10–08

Baulking, A3–6.19
Blow-outs, 11–08, 11–32
Boxes, A3–7.11
Brakes, 2–01—2–43
  accidents, 2–13
  adjustment, 2–16, 2–30
  articulated vehicles, 2–18
  "braking efficiency", 2–09
  contamination, 2–27
  condition, 2–06
  dangerous vehicles, 8–03
  Defect Notices, 2–41
  defects, 2–04, 2–05, 2–30, 2–36, 2–41, A1–13
  defence, 2–17—2–29
  employers, 2–35—2–37
  enforcement authorities, 2042
  engineers, 2–38—2–43
  evidence, 2–10—2–16
  hire, 2–20
  inspections, 2–10—2–12
  leaks, 21–4—2–15, 2–20—2–30
  legislation, 2–05—2–09, 2–17, 2–19

Brakes—*cont.*
  maintenance, 2–16, 2–39
  mitigation, 2–30—2–38
  police, 2–13
  prosecution, 2–05—2–16, 2–34
  rolling road test, 2–23
  safety checks, 2–31, 2–33
  service, 2–12
  standards, 2–7, 2–21—2–22
  stroke, 2–25, 2–31
  summons, 2–17—2–19
  systems, 2–01—2–04
  Testers Manual, A1–13
  Testing Station, 2–10
  vehicle inspectors, 2–10—2–12
  warning devices, 2–03
  wear and tear, 2–40
  wheels, 10–08
Bricks, A3–7.14
Bulk loads, A3–10.1—10.10
Bulkheads, A3–4.14
Buses, 14–09

Carriage of vehicles piggyback style,
    A3–14.1—14.9
Cement carriers, 14–42
Certificates
  Code of Practice for Weighing of
      Goods Vehicles on Dynamic
      Axle Weighers, A4
  dangerous substances, 7–05,
      7–08, 7–20
  forgeries, 5–25
  perishable food, 5–05,
      5–09—5–10, 5–15
  overloading, 6–18, 6–24
  vehicle excise duty, 14–04
  weight, 6–18
CHIP, 7–04
Coaches, 15–02
Code of Practice on Safety of Loads
    on Vehicles, 3–02, 3–05, 3–21,
    3–22, A3–01—A3–01—14.9
  anchorage points, A3–4.1—4.6,
      A3–6.24–6.28
  arrangement of loads,
      A3–3.7—3.16

Code of Practice on Safety of Loads
    on Vehicles—cont.
  boxes, A3–7.11
  baulking, A3–6.19
  bricks, A3–7.14
  bulk loads, A3–10.1—10.10
  bulkheads, A3–4.14
  carriage of vehicles by piggyback,
      A3–14.1—14.9
  choice of vehicle, A3–3.1—3.6
  coils, A3–8.11–8.26, A3–8.35–8.37
  containers, A3–3.16, A3–5.9,
      A3–12.1—12.11
  dangerous substances, A3–1.4
  drivers, A3–3.1
  dunnage, A3–6.20–6.22, A3–11.12
  engineering plant,
      A3–13.1—13.21
  exceptions, A3–4.16–4.19
  ferries, A3–1.6, A3–3.2
  freight, A3–7.1—7.15
  friction, A3–6.23
  glass, A3–7.13
  headboards, A3–4.7—4.13
  instructions, A3–3.1
  internal partitions, A3–4.15
  large units, A3–8.27–8.29
  lashings, A3–6.8—6.10
  level crossings, A3–3.6
  loading methods, A3–7.9—7.15
  long sheets, A3–8.11–8.15
  loose bulk loads, A3–10.1—10.10
  metal loads, A3–8.1—8.37,
      A3–8.30–8.31
  mixed loads, A3–7.15
  nets, A3–6.14–6.18
  pallets, A3–11.1—11.12
  piggyback, A3–14.1—14.9
  principals of safety, A3–2.4
  restraint devices, A3–7.6—7.8,
      A3–9.6—9.9,
      A3–11.8—11.12,
      A3–13.17–13.20
  rolls, drums or cylindrical loads,
      A3–7.10
  sacks, A3–7.12
  scrap, A3–8.30–8.34
  securing equipment,
      A3–5.1—5.10, A3–6.1—6.9

Code of Practice on Safety of Loads on Vehicles—cont.
sheets, A3–6.11–6.13, A3–8.7—8.10, A3–8.18–8.25
stacks, A3–9.11
tie down schemes, A3–13.21
timber, A3–9.1—9.12
trailers, A3–3.9
weight, A3–3.8
Codes of practice. *See also Code of Practice Safety of Loads on Vehicles*
axles, A4
Code of Practice for Weighing of Goods Vehicles on Conventional Weighbridges, A6
Code of Practice for Weighing of Goods Vehicles on Dynamic Axle Weighers, A4
Code of Practice for Weighing of Goods Vehicles to Check Whether they are Overloaded, A5
dangerous or insecure loads, 3–02, 3–05, 3–21, 3–22
weight, 6–17, 6–23, 6–25, 6–28, A4, A5
Coils, A3–8.11–8.26, A3–8.35–8.37
Condition. *See also* Maintenance
brakes, 2–06
dangerous or insecure loads, 3–09
dangerous vehicles, 8–01—8–13
enforcement authorities, 1–01
penalties, 1–01
tyres, 11–29
vehicle excise duty, 14–14
Construction and Use, 3–09—3–35, A3–A
Containers
Code of Practice Safety of Loads on Vehicles, A3–3.16, A3–5.9, A3–12.1—12.11
ISO/BS, A3–5.9, A3–12.2—12.4
overloading, 6–35, 6–40
sealed, 6–35
securing, A3–12.1—12.11

Containers—*cont.*
stowage, A3–12.8—12.11
types, A3–12.2—12.7
Customs sealed loads, A5
Cylinders, A3–7.10

Dangerous or insecure loads, 3–01—3–36. *See also Code of Practice Safety of Loads on Vehicles,* Overloading
adjustment, 3–22
articulated vehicles, 3–17
condition, 3–09
defects, 3–16—3–17, 3–19
defence, 3–16—3–26, 3–31
drivers, 3–28
emergencies, 3–29
engineers, 3–36
evidence, 3–12—3–15, 3–21, 3–31
fastening, 3–04—3–05, 3–12—3–13, 3–17—3–18, 3–21, 3–24—3–27, 3–36, A3–5.1—A5.10
fatal accidents, 3–12
foreseeability, 3–10, 3–19, 3–29, 3–31, 3–32
friction, 3–22
legislation, 3–08—3–35
lost loads, 3–15, 3–17
mitigation, 3–27—3–29, 3–35
passengers, 3–09
personal injuries, 3–12
police, 3–23
packaging, 3–25
prosecutions, 3–01, 3–06, 3–08—3–15, 3–20—3–21, 3–31
shifting, 3–13, 3–20
summons, 3–05, 3–16
tachographs, 3–17
trailers, 3–09, 3–31—3–32
Vehicle Inspectors, 3–18
Dangerous substances, 7–01—7–27
Accord Dangerous Routiers, 7–02, 7–04—7–06
certificates, 7–05, 7–08, 7–20
CHIP, 7–04

Dangeorus substances—*cont.*
Code of Practice Safety of Loads on Vehicles, A3–1.4
defences, 7–14—7–18
definition, 7–07
disasters, 7–08, 7–15
drivers, 7–20, 7–22
emergencies, 7–06
enforcement authorities, 7–08, 7–12
engineers, 7–24—7–27
European Union, 7–03
evidence, 7–11—7–13
experts, 7–15, 7–17
information, 7–04
inspection, 7–06
legislation, 7–02—7–05, 7–09—7–10, 7–15—7–18, App.3–B
markings, 7–06, 7–08, 7–19—7–20, 7–26
mitigation, 7–19—7–23
mixed loads, 7–26
prosecution, 7–07—7–13, 7–26
third parties, 7–18, 7–21
training, 7–24
warnings, 7–22
weight, A5
witnesses, 7–1207—13
Dangerous vehicles, 8–01—8–13
brakes, 8–03
defects, 8–13
defences, 8–04—8–08
design, 8–13
drivers, 8–10
engineers, 8–12—8–13
evidence, 8–09—8–10
experts, 8–10
inspection, 8–06—8–07
legislation, 8–02, 8–08
maintenance, 8–09, 8–12
mitigation, 8–09—8–11
overloading, 8–01, 8–03
prosecution, 8–01, 8–02—8–05, 8–08
Recall Notices, 8–13
summons, 8–08
trailers, 8–08

Dangerous vehicles—*cont.*
tyres, 8–01, 8–03, 8–04
Vehicle Inspectors, 8–13
weight, 8–06
Defects
brakes, 2–04, 2–05, 2–30, 2–36, 2–41, A1–13
categorisation, A1–08—A1–10
dangerous or insecure loads, 3–16—3–17
Defect Notices, 2–41
employers, 2–36
evidence, A1–01
information, A1–08
latent, 3–19
list, A1–03
notices, A1–02, A1–11
numbering, A1–04—A1–05
passengers, A1–09
P.G.9, A1–01—A1–14
prohibition notice, A1–02
prosecution, A1–01
reports, 2–36
Testers' Manuals, A1–01—A1–14
Testing Station, A1–07
tyres, 11–14, 11–26—11–28
Defences
abnormal loads, 4–13—4–18
brakes, 2–17—2–29
dangerous or insecure loads, 3–16—3–26, 3–32—3–33
dangerous substances, 7–14—7–18
dangerous vehicles, 8–04—8–08
drivers' hours, 13–39—13–40, 13–42—13–43, 13–69
length and width, 9–11—9–18
overloading, 6–20—6–32
perishable food, 5–14—5–20
tachographs, 13–38—13–45
tyres, 11–17—11–25
vehicle excise duty, 14–12—14–49
wheels, 10–09
Design
dangerous vehicles, 8–05, 8–13
overloading, 6–34
vehicle excise duty, 14–33

Information
  abnormal loads, 4–20—4–21
  dangerous substances, 7–04
  defects, A1–08
  length and width, 9–14, 9–19,
    9–22
  mitigation, 6–3
  overloading, 6–42
  Testers Manual, A1–08
Inspections. *See also* Safety checks,
    Vehicle Inspectors
  brakes, 2–10, 2–26
  dangerous substances, 7–06
  dangerous vehicles, 8–06—8–07
  tachographs, 13–05
  Testing Stations, 2–10
  wheels, 10–15
Institute of Road Transport
    Engineers, 10–16
Instructions
  *Code of Practice on Safety of
    Loads on Vehicles*, A3–3.1
  overloading, 6–19, 6–36
  perishable food, 5–23
  weight, A5

Jurisdiction, A2–01—A2–11
  drivers' hours, A2–01—A2–09
  legislation, A2–03—A2–08
  tachographs, A2–02
  Scotland, A2–10

Large units, A3–8,27–8.29
Lashings, A3–6.8—6.10
Leaks in brakes, 2–14—2–15,
    2–21—2–30
Length and width, 9–01—9–23
  attendants, 9–16
  defence, 9–11—9–18
  drivers, 9–20–9—22
  evidence, 9–08—9–10, 9–17
  information, 9–14, 9–19, 9–22
  legislation, 9–01—9–18
  measurement, 9–02, 9–08—9–09,
    9–13—9–14, 9–19
  mistakes, 9–01

Length and width—*cont.*
  mitigation, 9–19—9–23
  notice, 9–17
  prosecution, 9–03—9–10, 9–15,
    9–19
  trailers, 9–11
Level crossings, A3–3.6
Licences. *See also* Goods and
    Passenger Carrying Vehicle
    Operators Licensing System,
    Permits
  overloading, 6–03
  revocation, 1–02, 6–03
  Scotland, 16–07
  Traffic Commissioners, 1–02,
    6–03
Loads. *See* Abnormal loads,
    Dangerous substances,
    Dangerous or insecure loads,
    Length and width,
    Overloading, Perishable goods
Locomotives, 14–32—14–34

Maintenance. *See also* Condition
  brakes, 2–16, 2–39
  dangerous vehicles, 8–09, 8–13
  Scotland, 16–02
  systems, 2–39
  Traffic Commissioner, 1–02
  tyres, 11–26, 11–31
  wheels, 10–15
Markings, 7–06, 7–08, 7–19—7–20,
    7–26
Metal loads, A3–8.1—8.37,
    A3–8.30–8.31
Mitigation, 15–01—15–11
  abnormal loads, 4–19—4–22
  absolute discharge, 15–08—15–09
  brakes, 2–30—2–38
  coaches, 15–02
  dangerous or insecure loads,
    3–27—3–29, 3–35
  dangerous substances,
    7–19—7–23
  dangerous vehicles, 8–09—8–11
  drivers, 15–04

227

Mitigation—*cont.*
 drivers' hours, 13–46—13–48,
  13–70, 15–05
 engineers, 15–03
 experts, 15–06
 Goods and Passenger Carrying
  Vehicle Operators Licensing
  System, 12–12—12–31,
  12–32
 guilty pleas, 15–06
 length and width, 9–19—9–23
 overloading, 6–33—6–40, 15–09
 perishable food, 5–21—5–25
 repairs, 15–11
 Scotland, 16–02
 tachographs, 15–05
 technology, 15–05
 tyres, 11–26—11–28, 15–01
 vehicle excise duty, 14–50—14–52
 weight, 15–10
 wheels, 10–10—10–17, 15–07

Nets, A3–6.14–6.18
Notices
 abnormal loads, 4–04—4–05,
  4–10—4–11, 4–17
 dangerous vehicles, 8–13
 defects, A1–03, A1–11
 Goods and Passenger Carrying
  Vehicle Operators Licensing
  System, 12–11—12–12
 indemnity, 4–12
 length and width, 9–17
 prohibition, 12–11, A1–02, A5
 recall, 8–13
 Testers Manual, A1–02, A1–11
 Traffic Commissioner, 1–02
 tyres, 11–14
 vehicle excise duty, 14–06
 weight, A5

Overloading, 6–01—6–42
 animals, A6
 axles, 6–01, 6–04—6–07,
  6–09—6–10, 6–22—6–23,
  6–26—6–27, 6–34

Overloading—*cont.*
 certificates, 6–18, 6–24
 *Code of Practice for Weighing of
  Goods Vehicles to Check
  whether they are Overloaded*,
  A5
 containers, 6–35, 6–40
 dangerous vehicles, 8–01, 8–03
 defence, 6–20—6–32
 design, 6–34
 drivers, 6–35—6–37
 enforcement authorities,
  6–01—6–02, 6–42
 engineers, 6–40—6–42
 evidence, 6–11—6–19,
  6–36—6–37
 information, 6–33, 6–42
 instructions, 6–19, 6–36
 legislation, 6–08—6–12, 6–29
 licences, 6–03
 mitigation, 6–33—6–39, 15–09
 moving loads, 6–32, 6–40
 police, 6–11
 prosecution, 6–08—6–19
 traffic commissioners, 6–03
 weighbridges, 6–11—6–32,
  6–38—6–39
 weight, 6–01, 6–04—6–07,
  6–09—6–32, 6–38—6–42

Packaging, 3–25
Pallets, A3–11.1—11.12
Partitions, A3–4.15
Passengers
 dangerous or insecure loads,
  3–09
 defects, A1–09
 drivers' hours, 13–19, 13–68
 licensing, 12–01—12–32
 Testers Manual, A1–09
Performance
 enforcement authorities, 1–05
 tyres, 11–01
Permits, 4–03. *See also* Licences
Perishable food, 5–01—5–25
 Accord Transports Perishables,
  5–02—5–03, 5–15

Perishable food—*cont.*
  certificates, 5–05, 5–09—5–10,
    5–15
  defence, 5–14—5–20
  deterioration, 5–01
  enforcement authorities, 5–17
  evidence, 5–11—5–13
  falsification of documents, 5–13,
    5–20
  forgeries, 5–13, 5–20, 5–25
  instructions, 5–23
  legislation, 5–02—5–03, 5–07
  mitigation, 5–21—5–25
  prosecution, 5–08—5–13
  temperature, 5–04—5–07,
    5–16—5–17, 5–24—5–25
  Trading Standards Officers, 5–08
  weight, A5
Personal injuries
  dangerous or insecure loads,
    3–12
  wheels, 10–01
Piggyback, A3–14.1—14.9
Plant
  *Code of Practice Safety of Loads
    on Vehicles*, A3–13.1—13.21
  engineering, 14–46,
    A3–13.1—13.21
  securing, A3–13.1—13.21
  vehicle excise duty, 14–46
Pleas, 15–06
Police
  abnormal loads, 4–04, 4–18
  assistants, 4–18
  brakes, 2–13
  dangerous or insecure loads,
    3–23
  evidence, 11–15—11–16
  overloading, 6–11
  tyres, 11–15—11–16, 11–20
  vehicle excise duty, 14–05, 14–19
  weighbridges, 6–11
  wheels, 10–05—10–06
Prosecution
  abnormal loads, 4–10—4–12
  brakes, 2–05—2–16, 2–34
  dangerous or insecure loads,
    3–01, 3–06, 3–08—3–15,
    3–20—3–21, 3–31

Prosecution—*cont.*
  dangerous substances,
    7–07—7–08, 7–09—7–13,
    7–26
  dangerous vehicles, 8–01,
    8–02—8–05, 8–08
  drivers' hours, 13–25—13–37
  length and width, 9–03—9–10,
    9–15, 9–19
  overloading, 6–08—6–19
  perishable foods, 5–08—5–13
  tachographs, 13–25—13–26
  Testers Manual, A1–01
  tyres, 11–01, 11–11—11–23
  vehicle excise duty,
    14–02—14–11, 14–45
  wheels, 10–04—10–08
  witnesses, 7–12—7–13
Public enquiries
  Goods and Passenger Carrying
    Vehicle Operators Licensing
    System, 12–01—12–09,
    12–12—12–13
  evidence, 12–13
  Traffic Commissioners,
    12–01—12–09
Public roads
  Scotland, 16–05
  vehicle excise duty, 14–06, 14–12

Recovery vehicles, 14–27—14–29
Repairs, 15–11
Roads
  Scotland, 16–05
  vehicle excise duty, 14–06
Roadsweepers, 14–40
Rolling road test, 23
Rolls, A3–7.10

Sacks, A3–7.12
Safety checks, 2–31, 2–33
Scotland, 16–01—16–07
  accidents, 16–02
  causing or permitting offences,
    16–03
  enforcement authorities, 15–02

Scotland—*cont.*
evidence, 16–06
jurisdiction, A2–10
knowledge, 16–03
legislation, 16–01, 16–03
licence, 16–07
maintenance, 16–02
mitigation, 16–02
public roads, 16–05
Traffic Commissioners, 16–07
using offences, 16–03—16–04
Scrap, A3–8.30–8.34
Sentencing
absolute discharge, 15–08, 15–09
mitigation, 15–08, 15–09
Sheets, A3–6.11–6.13, A3–7.13,
A3–8.7—8.10, A3–8.18–8.25
Showmens' vehicles, 14–35
Special vehicles, 14–23, 14–36
Standards
brakes, 2–07, 2–21—2–22
Goods and Passenger Carrying
Vehicle Operators Licensing
System, 12–02
Stowage. *See* Abnormal leads,
Dangerous or Insecure loads,
Dangerous substances,
Overloading, Perishable goods
Summons
brakes, 2–17—2–18
dangerous or insecure loads,
3–05, 3–16
dangerous vehicles, 8–08
tyres, 11–17—11–18
vehicle excise duty, 14–29

Tachographs
dangerous or insecure loads, 3–17
defences, 13–38—13–45
definition, 13–04
either way offences,
13–30—13–36
employers, 13–36
European Union, 13–01,
13–06—13–07
false entries, 13–30—13–36
inspection, 13–05

Tachographs—*cont.*
jurisdiction, A2–02
legislation, 13–01, 13–06
mitigation, 15–05
operation, 13–04
prosecution, 13–25—13–26
warnings, 13–45
Taxation. *See* Vehicle excise duty
Technology
mitigation, 15–05
tyres, 11–01—11–10
Testers' Manual, 2–11,
A1–01—A1–14
Testing Stations
brakes, 2–10
defects, A1–07
Testers Manual, A1–07
Third parties, 7–18, 7–21
Tie down schemes, A3–13.21
Timber, A3–9.1—9.12
Tower vehicles, 14–44
Trading Standards Officers
abnormal loads, 4–10—4–11
perishable foods, 5–08
Traffic Commissioners
areas, 12094
disciplinary cases, 12–01,
12–10—12–14
drivers' hours, 13–48
Goods and Passenger Carrying
Vehicle Operators Licensing
System, 12–01—12–15,
12–27
licences, 1–02, 6–03
maintenance, 1–02
notification, 1–02
overloading, 6–03
powers, 12–06—12–08, 12–15
public inquiries, 12–01—12–09
Scotland, 16–07
Trailers
*Code of Practice Safety of Loads
on Vehicles*, A3–3.13,
A3–14.1—14.9
dangerous or insecure loads,
3–09, 3–32
dangerous vehicles, 8–08
length and width, 9–11

Trailers—*cont.*
  piggyback carriage,
    A3–14.1—14.9
  tyres, 11–05, 11–11, 11–13,
    11–22—11–23
  vehicle excise duty, 14–32
Training, 7–24
Trains, 13–20—13–21
Transport Tribunal, 12–28—12–29
Trucks, 14–36—14–49
Tyres, 10–20, 11–01—11–34
  accidents, 11–29
  blow-outs, 11–08, 11–32
  condition, 11–29
  damage, 11–06—11–07,
    11–26—11–28, 11–34
  dangerous vehicles, 8–01, 8–03,
    8–04
  defects, 11–11—11–14,
    11–26—11–28
  defence, 11–17—11–25
  drivers, 11–26
  engineers, 11–29—11–34
  evidence, 11–13—11–16, 11–21,
    11–26—11–28
  experts, 11–09
  flat spots, 11–29—11–30
  maintenance, 11–26, 11–31
  measurement, 11–19—11–22
  mitigation, 11–26—11–28, 15–01
  notice, 11–14
  performance, 11–01
  police, 11–15—11–16, 11–20
  prosecution, 11–01,
    11–11—11–23
  pressure, 11–32
  remoulds, 11–05
  scrub, 11–33
  summons, 11–17—11–18
  technology, 11–01—11–10
  trailers, 11–07, 11–11, 11–33
  tread, 11–05, 11–11, 11–13,
    11–22—11–23
  vehicle excise duty, 14–21
  Vehicle Inspectors, 11–13—11–14

Vans, A3–4.14

Vehicle Excise Duty, 14–01—14–52
  abnormal loads, 14–30—14–31
  agricultural vehicles, 14–43
  articulated vehicles, 14–22
  buses, 14–09
  cement-mixing vehicles, 14–42
  certificates, 14–04
  condition, 14–14
  defence, 14–12—14–49
  design, 14–33
  discs, 14–03, 14–16
  environmental protection, 14–41
  evidence, 14–04—14–11
  exemptions, 14–44
  forgery, 14–01, 14–11
  fraud, 14–01, 14–03, 14–11
  Gross Vehicle Weight,
    14–45—14–46
  legislation, 14–01—14–44
  locomotives, 14–32—14–34
  mitigation, 14–50—14–52
  notice, 14–06
  plant, 14–47
  plating, 14–47—14–48
  police, 14–05, 14–19
  prosecution, 14–02—14–11,
    14–45
  public roads, 14–06, 14–12
  recovery vehicles, 14–27—14–29
  revenue weight, 14–18, 14–21
  roadsweepers, 14–40
  roadworks, 14–13
  showmen's vehicles, 14–35
  special vehicles, 14–23, 14–36
  summons, 14–29
  tower wagons, 14–44
  trailers, 14–32
  tyres, 14–21
Vehicle Inspectors
  abnormal loads, 4–10—4–11
  brakes, 2–10—2–12
  dangerous or insecure loads,
    3–18
  dangerous vehicles, 8–13
  Testers' Manual, 2–11,
    A1–01—A1–14
  tyres, 11–13—11–14
  wheels, 10–05

Warnings
  brakes, 2–03
  prosecution, 13–45
Wear and tear, 2–40
Weight
  abnormal loads, 4–13—4–14,
    4–21, A5
  animals, A5, A6
  articulated vehicles, 6–14
  certificates, 6–18, A4
  Code of Practice for Weighing of
    Goods Vehicles on
    Conventional Weighbridges,
    A6
  Code of Practice for Weighing of
    Goods Vehicles to Check
    whether they are Overloaded,
    A5
    animals, A5
    drivers, A5
    enforcement, A5
    instructions, A5
    operation of equipment, A5
    operators, A5
    prohibition, A5
    special loads, A5
  Code of Practice for Weighing of
    Goods Vehicles on Dynamic
    Axle Weighers, A4
  description, A4
  preparation, A4
  site requirements, A4
  verification procedure, A4
  codes of practice, 6–17, 6–23,
    6–25, 6–29, A4, A5
  customs sealed loads, A5
  dangerous substances, A5
  drivers, A5
  equipment,
    description and types, A6
  high value loads, A5
  mitigation, 15–10
  overloading, 6–01, 6–04—6–07,
    6–09—6–32, 6–38—6–42,
    A5, A6

Weight—*cont.*
  perishable loads, A5
  police, 6–11
  records, 6–11, 6–14—6–15
  revenue, 14–18, 14–21
    site organisation, A6
  vehicle excise duty, 14–13
  weighbeam, A4
  weighbridges, 4–22, 6–11—6–32,
    6–38—6–39, A5, A6
    accuracy, 6–23
    authorised officers, A6
    procedure, A6
    types, 6–13—6–17, A5, A6
Wheels, 10–01—10–20. *See also*
  Tyres
  axles, 10–08
  brakes, 10–08
  defence, 10–09
  drivers, 10–11, 10–14, 10–19
  engineers, 10–16, 10–18—1–20
  evidence, 10–05—10–10
  fatal accidents, 10–01
  human error, 10–11
  inspections, 10–15
  Institute of Road Transport
    Engineers, 10–16
  legislation, 10–04
  loss, 10–01—10–17, 15–07
  maintenance, 10–15
  mitigation, 10–10—10–17, 15–07
  personal injuries, 10–01
  police, 10–5—10–06
  prosecution, 10–04—10–08
  summons, 10–09
  Vehicle Inspectors, 10–05
Width. *See* Length and width
Witnesses
  dangerous substances,
    7–12—7–13
  prosecution, 7–12—7–13
Works trucks, 14–36—14–49